COMBATING CORRUPTION, ENCOURAGING ETHICS
SECOND EDITION

COMBATING CORRUPTION, ENCOURAGING ETHICS

A Practical Guide to Management Ethics

SECOND EDITION

EDITED BY
WILLIAM L. RICHTER AND FRANCES BURKE

Published in cooperation with
THE AMERICAN SOCIETY FOR PUBLIC ADMINISTRATION

ROWMAN & LITTLEFIELD PUBLISHERS, INC.
Lanham • Boulder • New York • Toronto • Plymouth, UK

Published in cooperation with
THE AMERICAN SOCIETY FOR PUBLIC ADMINISTRATION

ROWMAN & LITTLEFIELD PUBLISHERS, INC.

Published in the United States of America
by Rowman & Littlefield Publishers, Inc.
A wholly owned subsidary of The Rowman & Littlefield Publishing Group, Inc.
4501 Forbes Boulevard, Suite 200, Lanham, Maryland 20706
www.rowmanlittlefield.com

Estover Road
Plymouth PL6 7PY
United Kingdom

British Library Cataloguing in Publication Information Available

Library of Congress Cataloging-in-Publication Data

Combating corruption, encouraging ethics : a practical guide to management ethics /
[edited by] William L. Richter & Frances Burke. — 2nd ed.
    p. cm.
 Includes bibliographical references and index.
 ISBN-10: 0-7425-4450-8
 ISBN-10: 0-7425-4451-6
 ISBN-13: 978-0-7425-4450-5
 ISBN-13: 978-0-7425-4451-2
1. Civil service ethics—United States. 2. Political ethics—United States. I. Richter, William L., 1939– II. Burke, Frances.
 JK468.E7C64 2007
  172'.2—dc22   2006026153

Printed in the United States of America

⊗™ The paper used in this publication meets the minimum requirements of American National Standard for Information Sciences—Permanence of Paper for Printed Library Materials, ANSI/NISO Z39.48-1992.

CONTENTS

PREFACE

Much has changed in the nearly two decades since the first edition of *Combating Corruption, Encouraging Ethics* was published in 1990. Management ethics—whether public, private, or nonprofit—has become a global dialogue, as exemplified by international conferences and active involvement by national and international organizations. Technology has changed, including the technology of government. Boundaries among public, private, and nonprofit management have been blurred, as represented in part by emphasis on New Public Management (NPM).

In this second edition, we have attempted to address these many changes, especially in a new chapter 3 on twenty-first–century challenges. Dynamic changes in management ethics are also considered throughout the book. New topics and themes include public oversight of private sector and nonprofit activities, Sarbanes-Oxley and privacy legislation, post-9/11 security issues, and "administrative evil."

Like the first edition, this volume seeks to address three audiences: (1) public servants at all levels of government and in nonprofit management who are frequently confronted with ethical issues and ethical choices; (2) students preparing for careers in public service, for whom ethics education is increasingly recognized as essential preparation; and (3) those scholars, many of whose works are represented in this book or in the earlier edition, who have now become a global community seeking to clarify our understanding of ethical issues and to bring about more ethical management in public and private life throughout the world.

This volume retains the basic structure of the first edition. Part I explores fundamental ethical concepts and introduces readers to classical ethical writings—from Aristotle and Machiavelli to Wilson and Weber—and to contemporary discussions of personal and professional responsibility and accountability. A major purpose of Part I is to provide readers an opportunity to situate themselves and their own ethical orientations within the diverse and ever-evolving tradition of ethical thinkers such as Aristotle, Immanuel Kant, and John Stuart Mill. Part II focuses on management challenges associated with the concepts of fraud, waste, abuse, and corrupt practices. This emphasis should not be perceived as implying that ethics is only concerned with catching or thwarting "wrong-doers." Rather, the issues raised in this section, such as conflict of interest, lying, cheating, and deception, should be seen as problematic practices that may challenge any public managers, often in mundane ways. Part III provides a broad range of management tools and organizational strategies for combating corruption and encouraging ethics.

Each chapter concludes with a case study, discussion questions, and suggestions for further exploration. These suggestions are not intended to be exhaustive but rather to encourage an open-ended journey into other print and Web resources. Those who use the Web may want to use a search engine to explore key terms, such as "ethics codes," "whistle-blowing," or "governmental secrecy."

Many people have helped to make this second edition a reality. Jameson W. Doig, our fellow coeditor of the first edition, was unavailable to join us in the second, but it nonetheless reflects his valuable insights and advice. Several other colleagues read part or all of the manuscript at various stages and offered very valuable comments, including James S. Bowman, J. Patrick Dobel, David Schultz, James Pfiffner, Donald Menzel, Kathryn Denhardt, Linda Richter, Robert Bateman, James Svara, and Renu Khator.

Two teams of organizational and editorial staff have been essential to this project. At ASPA, Mary Hamilton and Christine McCrehin played key roles in the initial stages, and Matthew Rankin's active involvement in the final stages has been wonderful. Similarly, Rowman & Littlefield editors Niels Aaboe and Christopher Anzalone and their staff, especially Asa Johnson and Claire Rojstaczer, have been outstanding. We also wish to express appreciation to our local support systems, especially the staff of The Boston Athenaeum, Kansas State University, and Suffolk University. We hope that others not mentioned by name, including other ASPA staff, members of the ASPA Publications Committee, authors of many of the selections in this book, and editors who provided permission to reprint specific selections, are aware of how much their contributions have been appreciated.

We know that ethics—whether in the public, nonprofit, or private sector—is a dynamic subject. We have attempted to provide students, scholars, practitioners, and other readers with practical tools to address both present and future challenges. We hope that we have succeeded.

Frances Burke	William L. Richter
Boston, MA	Manhattan, KS
integrityintal@yahoo.com	wrichter@ksu.edu

PART I

ETHICS: FOUNDATIONS AND CHALLENGES

WHAT HAS CHANGED?

"September 11 changed everything," or so some people—including United States President George W. Bush—would have us believe. One thing that has not changed is the prominence of corruption and ethics as topics of public discourse. News media continue to be filled with stories of unethical behavior and ethical issues in virtually every aspect of public life: in government and politics, sports, business, religion, education, and other arenas. Bush's predecessor, William J. Clinton, became only the second president in U.S. history to be impeached, for lying concerning his relationship with intern Monica Lewinsky. Bush and British Prime Minister Tony Blair have both been accused of lying to their people in their arguments for initiating the invasion of Iraq in 2003. Scandals in the legal and accounting professions, the Catholic Church, charitable nonprofits, and major universities suggest that combating corruption and encouraging ethics are as timely and challenging endeavors in the twenty-first century as in 1990, when the first edition of this book was published, or indeed as at any time in the past.

These problems are by no means limited to the United States. Transparency International (TI), a nongovernmental organization established in the 1990s, publishes on its website a daily listing of news stories regarding corrupt activities throughout the world. The United Nations has come under attack for its mismanagement of the oil-for-food program in Iraq. These and other instances suggest that, although individual moral values and standards may vary somewhat from culture to culture, most contemporary societies are vulnerable to problems of government corruption.[1]

Indeed, dishonesty and other forms of unethical activity have plagued human beings from the beginnings of recorded history. Every American presidential administration, from George Washington to the present, has featured one or another form of corruption. Some have been worse than others, with Presidents Grant, Harding, Nixon, and Reagan generally acknowledged to have presided over the most corrupt and unconstitutional administrations. Richard Nixon has the distinction of being the only president to be forced to resign from office. The Reagan administration, however, holds the record for numbers of high-level individuals indicted, including Edwin Meese, who as Reagan's Attorney General served as the chief law enforcement officer of the United States.

It would be difficult to argue, however, that political or administrative behavior is on the whole less ethical at the beginning of the twenty-first century than it was at the beginning of the twentieth. Recall that George Washington Plunkitt, "the sage of Tammany Hall," openly advocated what he called "Honest Graft" and took pride in taking many of the "opportunities" which came his way in New York City government.[2]

There is considerable merit in the argument that the prominence of ethics cases is at least partially a function of increased levels of public awareness, intolerance for wrongdoing, and rigorousness of legal standards. In the post-Watergate era (roughly the last quarter of the twentieth century), ethics legislation was passed at all levels of government. Aggressive investigative journalism and the willingness of greater numbers of governmental, nonprofit, and private-sector personnel to "blow the whistle" on cases of graft and malfeasance have all tended to *publicize* ethics. Rapid technological change—in computers, communications, and life support systems, for example—raised additional substantive ethical issues. Security concerns since the September 11, 2001, terrorist attacks in the United States have identified numerous other ethics considerations. These include privacy implications of the USA PATRIOT Act, lying and deception surrounding the Iraq and Afghanistan conflicts, torture and other abusive interrogation techniques, and corporate corruption in government contracting, accounting, and insider trading.

Today, ethics is a topic of high public prominence and concern throughout the world. International entities like the Organization for Economic Cooperation and Development, the World Bank, and the Asian Development Bank have taken action to encourage member states and development projects to combat corruption and encourage ethical practices.[3] International treaties and conventions have been established to counter corruption generally as well as to exhibit such specific practices as bribery and human trafficking. Nongovernmental organizations like Transparency International, Freedom House, the Carnegie Endowment for International Peace, and the Government Accountability Project widely publicize corrupt behavior. They also seek to develop meaningful cross-national comparative scales and accountability practices.

ETHICAL FOUNDATIONS:
COMPLEMENTARY CORNERS OF A TRIANGLE?

The ethical assumptions that people bring to their professional roles as public administrators rest largely upon how they approach ethics as individual human beings.

It is sometimes surprising, even unsettling, to learn that our co-workers deal with ethical issues from perspectives that are different from our own. Chapter 1 reviews three such approaches, each of which has a respectable heritage and current saliency: ethics as *virtue,* as *consequence,* and as *principle.*

Ethics as Virtue

Although valuable ethical lessons may be gleaned from the writings of Confucius, Homer and the Greek poets (for example, Sophocles' *Antigone),* as well as from the scriptures of most religions, it is from Plato's dialogues (e.g., *Gorgias, Crito, Meno, Republic)* and Aristotle's treatises that we derive both the term *ethics* and the first systematic discussions of the subject. As the selection we have included in this volume indicates, Aristotle regarded ethics as moral virtues, which could be instilled in individuals through training and practice.

Ethics as Consequence

Historically the second major approach to understanding ethics, and the most radical alternative to the classical virtues of Aristotle and Plato, was that of Niccolo Machiavelli. As he warned in *The Prince,* good and well-intentioned people often produce bad policy and bad administration. He argued that people needed to learn "how not to be good" and how to "use good and bad" for beneficial ends. This approach, based upon the assumption that the ethical merit of an act should be judged by its consequences rather than by the virtue or principles of the actor, is termed *teleological* or *consequentialist.*

The best known and most persuasive manifestation of consequentialist thinking concerning ethics is utilitarianism, the doctrine that acts should be judged in terms of providing "the greatest good to the greatest number." Developed in the early nineteenth century primarily by Jeremy Bentham and John Stuart Mill, utilitarianism continues to have a major impact on how people think about the ethics of their actions.

In general, consequentialism raises the means-ends question: whether the goal of an action can justify the means undertaken to achieve it. The question becomes particularly poignant in a constitutional democratic society, where the maintenance of certain procedures (means) is important for the survival of the political system, and where administrators may find themselves faced with choices between major programmatic objectives and important procedural values.

Ethics as Principle

One of the problems with consequentialist theories of ethics is that one cannot always predict accurately the outcome of one's actions. It is also somewhat absurd to imagine that a malevolent act which turns out to have beneficial effects might be considered more ethical than a benevolent one which fails to do so. Moreover, utilitarian calculations of the good of the majority may not provide much protection for the rights of minorities. For such reasons, many ethicists prefer a deontological, or principle-based, theory of ethics.

The most famous deontological theory of ethics was formulated by Immanuel Kant 200 years ago. Kant's *categorical imperative* admonishes us to act on the basis of those principles that we might wish everyone to follow. He also required that other people be treated as ends in themselves and not merely as means to an end.

In his *Theory of Justice* (1971), Harvard philosopher John Rawls developed a set of principles based upon a line of reasoning which resembles the seventeenth-century state of nature theories of Thomas Hobbes and John Locke. In brief, he argued that we should follow those principles that we would design for a society if each of us were ignorant of what our individual position might be in that society. His two basic principles are that rights ought to be distributed as equally as possible and that any inequalities ought to be arranged for the benefit of the least advantaged.[4] Former President Ramon Magsaysay of the Philippines summarized this principle succinctly: Those who have less in life should have more in law.

This list of approaches and the accompanying sets of readings and cases are by no means exhaustive, but they should stimulate the reader to ask some introspective questions:

- Which definition of ethics do I find most acceptable?
- What are the conditions under which one approach might be more appropriate than another?
- What problems might I expect to encounter in "real life" as a result of my ethical preferences?
- Do other people operate on the basis of the same ethical assumptions as my own?

The Ethical Triangle

These approaches to ethics are often treated as either/or options, exclusively alternative to one another. But many individuals act according to some combination of approaches, using one under some circumstances and another under others. For instance, people who generally adhere to the principle that "honesty is the best policy" might withhold information or even lie in order to avoid bringing harm to an innocent person. Dean Geuras and Charles Garofalo argue for a "unified ethic" that combines teleological (consequentalist), deontological (principle), virtue, and intuitionist considerations.[5]

James Svara, in a selection included in chapter 1, suggests that the three approaches might best be considered as corners of an "ethical triangle." Following any one of the three corners of the triangle to an extreme, he argues, can be detrimental, so the balancing of ethical orientations is an important skill for anyone to develop.

ETHICS IN ORGANIZATIONS:
RESPONSIBILITY AND ACCOUNTABILITY

When we move beyond the ethical options faced by individuals in general to consider specifically *administrative* ethics, we encounter an added dimension: that of the responsibility of the public official to multiple sources of authority or legitimacy. Operating within any organization imposes upon individuals certain loyalties and obligations, which may sometimes come into conflict with their personal ethical preferences. Loyalties to one's superior, one's agency, one's professional standards, the Constitution, and the less clearly defined "public interest" all may compete for the administrator's attention.[6]

A focus on ethics as responsibility has been prominent in much of the public administration literature, from Woodrow Wilson and Max Weber to the present. In the last two decades, accountability has become an equally prominent concept for setting the parameters of professional public service. One reason for the growth of the importance of accountability has been concern over waste, inefficiency, and lack of transparency. Constituents want to make certain they are getting their money's worth from the governmental agencies that they are funding through their taxes. Businesses in the private sector, it is argued, are held accountable by market processes. Government and not-for-profit agencies need other mechanisms to ensure accountability.

REASONS FOR ETHICAL MALFEASANCE

Why do some administrators fail to follow ethical imperatives? Even when a person wishes to be ethical, to do right, it is often difficult. This is a recurrent theme in literature and religion. ("The spirit is willing but the flesh is weak.")

There are numerous reasons for this gap between good intentions and actual practice, of which the following is by no means an exhaustive list.

Ethical Imperative Versus Personal Benefit

As Michael Josephson notes: "Perhaps the main reason that people fail to act ethically is that it usually meets immediate self interest to do the unethical or less ethical thing. Simply put, it is easier."[7] Individuals perceive that the benefits to themselves or to friends or relatives, or to causes that they favor, neutralize their ethical principles. Great is the human capacity for rationalization.

Ethical Imperative Versus Personal Danger

Sometimes people fail to do what is right because of the anticipated harm such actions might cause to themselves or others. Whistle-blowing, a typical example, can often be dangerous, despite all of the whistle-blower protection legislation that has been developed in recent years.

Ethical Imperative Versus Other Responsibilities

What is "right" by one standard may conflict with other obligations. The person who believes that lying is wrong, but who is asked to present false information on behalf of his or her superior, agency, or country faces just this sort of dilemma.

Ethical Imperative Versus "Reasonableness"

Many problems arise when a person's ethical standards come into conflict with practices that have become firmly established and now seem natural to most of the community. One is expected to "go along to get along."

The "Dirty Hands" Problem

One rationalization for engaging in unethical behavior in public life is the argument that one cannot succeed without getting one's hands dirty. As Machiavelli argues in *The Prince,* good (e.g., ethical) people are likely to "come to grief" among so many who are not good. This argument is particularly seductive when the objective of the unethical activity is not personal gain but benefits for one's agency, program, or operation.[8]

The "Many Hands" Problem

In organizations, particularly large organizations, there is the temptation not to assume personal responsibility for the ethics of one's actions when a person is regarded as only a small part of the overall operation, only a "cog in the wheel" or sees the decision as "above my pay grade." If "many hands" are involved in a decision or set of decisions (such as the *Challenger* and *Columbia* spaceship disasters, the management of the Iraq War, or undertaking public "megaprojects" like subway systems, bridges, and airports), can any individuals be held responsible?[9]

Insensitivity to Ethical Considerations

Perhaps the most insidious and ubiquitous problem is simply the failure to think about the ethical considerations of the many decisions each of us faces in our daily work.

TWENTY-FIRST CENTURY CHALLENGES: GLOBAL DIMENSIONS/CHANGING BOUNDARIES

Ethical challenges derive partially from changing perceptions, issues, and ideals that help to define what is ethical and what is not. Many principles ("one should tell the truth") and practices (lying, bribery) have been part of the terrain of ethics discourse for centuries. Many of these principles can be noted in the Foundations selections in Chapters 1 and 2. Others are of more recent vintage ("one should not engage in sexual harassment," for instance, or "one should not download copyrighted music from the Internet").

Administrative history is replete with traditions and reforms that were regarded as ethical in one era and unethical in another. The practice of rewarding party faithful with public office once led to the winning U.S. president's campaign manager always being appointed to the office of postmaster general. Defended by Andrew Jackson as a means of providing broader access to government positions, the practice of patronage came to be regarded as the "spoils system" and was viewed by many as an odious form of political corruption. Hiring friends and relatives also led at one time to nepotism rules, which among other consequences, barred spouses from working in the same institution or agency. Later, such rules came to be regarded as discriminatory against women and were replaced by other structural arrangements. Inclusion of racial and ethnic information on application forms was eliminated at one point because it was seen as discriminatory, but revived later in order to facilitate affirmative action programs. Affirmative action itself has become a controversial battleground of competing claims of fairness and unfairness.

"New occasions teach new duties," James Russell Lowell wrote in the 1840s, in the midst of the deepening crisis over slavery in America. "Time makes ancient youth uncouth."[10] Clearly, the twenty-first century is replete with "new occasions" that challenge the ethical performance of even the most thoughtful public and private sector managers in virtually every country in the world. Chapter 3 focuses on ethics and the changing global infrastructure, international ideas and worldwide issues. Three broad types of changes are evident in shaping the "now" and the future.

First, the nature of government itself has changed over the past quarter century, especially since the early 1990s. Government has become "governance" and has been severely impacted by "downsizing," "privatization," and "outsourcing" (Starks), the need for "global governance" and accountability (Grant and Keohane), and the "end of geography" (Flyvbjerg et al.). Public Administration has become "public management," again reflecting the complex mixture of public, private, and not-for-profit elements involved in conducting public affairs. Even the facile boundary between *public* and *private* enterprise has become increasingly blurred. Public managers in the twenty-first century will find themselves facing broader and more diffuse responsibilities with greater accountability and fewer human and fiscal resources than in the past. As Patricia Ingraham warns, democratic accountability is outdated, fuzzy, and "perhaps broken."[11]

A second dimension of change is technological, with information technology the most dramatic example, including the Web, WiFi, e-mail, e-government, cell phones (with cameras and other technologies), and global positioning systems. Technological change enhances the capacity for corruption, but also increases the capacity for combating corruption and encouraging ethics. The Web can be a vehicle for scams and viruses, but also can provide online ethics training and accountability.

One aspect of technological change is the increased capacity for megaprojects, usually substantial construction projects, but also including such massive undertakings as large-scale cyberspace and medical enterprises. As Bent Flyvbjerg and his colleagues explain, the very size—the enormity—of these projects makes public accountability difficult. The contracting out or privatization by the George W. Bush administration of many aspects of the Iraq War and reconstruction to private contractors, especially Halliburton and its subsidiaries, constitutes a megaproject with all sorts of ethical challenges.

A third dimension of contemporary change is globalization. Technology, as everyone knows, has made the world a smaller place. This has undermined long-standing government assumptions and perceptions, even the nation-state system that has been the predominant reliable framework for governments and politics for the last few centuries. How, for instance, can countries deal with companies that let offshore subsidiaries handle operations that the parent companies are prohibited by law from doing? How can a government be held accountable for its treatment of prisoners at an offshore site like Guantanamo Bay or in the hands of allies whose methods of interrogation may be less subject to legal or ethical restraint?

Who sets the rules? Robert Dahl in 1961 wrote an insightful book on New Haven government titled *Who Governs?* In the twenty-first century, the International Institute of Administrative Sciences (IIAS) has established a worldwide working group that is exploring the question of today which will help govern us internationally tomorrow: Who governs the complex system of global governance? Duggett and Maron (see chapter 4) set the parameters of the long-range IIAS inquiry; noting that global governance is based on "a vast number of actors, different kinds of organizations, diverse authorities and levels of decision makers." The path toward identifying *who governs globally* is vital for establishing the ethical guidelines and standards needed for the future.

What has changed since 9/11? Some of the contemporary ethical challenges facing public servants are related to the need for managing increased security issues and the ongoing conflicts in the Middle East and elsewhere. Many more ethical challenges are simply a function of rapid technological change (email transparency?) and global span (SARS, avian flu and other biomedical issues with no jurisdictional boundaries). Perhaps the most fundamental ethical challenges have arisen out of the changing nature of government, evidenced by the selections in chapter 4.

Fortunately, the ethical resources available to managers have also expanded. National laws, international conventions, and global professional standards and codes, as well as cyberspace ethics publications, have been developed to assist in defining ethical expectations. Journals, conferences, scholars, and academic programs in many countries have made administrative ethics a global dialogue. The individual manager—in Boston and Bahrain, Topeka and Timbuktu, Manhattan (KS) and Manhattan (NY)—has access to a valuable array of concepts and tools to deal with the ethical challenges of a severely changing world. The basic ethical challenge is to develop the practical and applicable concepts and tools, skills and expertise to deal with the rapid change in the world as we know it today.

NOTES

1. For discussions of public service ethics in several different national settings, see Kenneth Kernaghan and C. P. Dwivedi, eds., *Ethics in the Public Service: Comparative Perspectives* (Brussels: International Institute of Administrative Sciences, 1983); and Special Issue on Bureaucratic Morality, *International Political Science Review* 9:3 (July 1988), pp. 163–242.

2. William L. Riordan, *Plunkitt of Tammany Hall* (New York: E. P. Dutton, 1963), pp. 3–6. See Joan Joseph, *Political Corruption* (New York: Pocket Books, 1974); and C. Vann Woodward, ed., *Responses of the Presidents to Charges of Misconduct* (New York: Dell Publishing, 1974).

3. See, for instance, *Trust in Government: Ethics Measures in OECD Countries* (Paris: Organisation for Economic Cooperation and Development, 2000).

4. John Rawls, *A Theory of Justice* (Cambridge, MA: Harvard University Press, 1971).

5. Dean Geuras and Charles Garofalo, *Practical Ethics in Public Administration* (Vienna, VA: Management Concepts, 2005), pp. 60–62.

6. See, for example, essays by Woodrow Wilson and Max Weber in chapter 2 of this volume.

7. Michael Josephson, *Ethics: Easier Said Than Done*, 1:1, p. 4.

8. The problem of dirty hands is widely discussed in the ethics literature. Cf. Michael Walzer, "Political Action: The Problem of Dirty Hands," *Philosophy and Public Affairs*, 2:2

(Winter, 1973), pp. 160–180; W. Kenneth Howard, "Must Public Hands be Dirty?" *Journal of Value Inquiry* 11 (Spring 1977), pp. 29–40; and Dennis F. Thompson, *Political Ethics and Public Office* (Cambridge, MA: Harvard University Press, 1987), pp. 11–39.

   9. One response to this position, as Debra Stewart argues below, is the assertion that individuals remain morally responsible for their actions regardless of the size and complexity of their organizations. See also Dennis F. Thompson, *Restoring Responsibility: Ethics in Government, Business, and Healthcare* (Cambridge, MA: Cambridge University Press, 2005), pp. 11–32.

   10. James Russell Lowell, "The Present Crisis" (1844), in *The Complete Poetical Works of James Russell Lowell* (Boston and New York: Houghton Mifflin, 1897), p. 68.

   11. Patricia Wallace Ingraham, "'You Talking to Me?' Accountability and the Modern Public Service," *PS: Political Science and Politics* 38:1 (January 2005), pp. 17–26.

Chapter 1

ETHICAL FOUNDATIONS:
VIRTUE, CONSEQUENCE, PRINCIPLE

VIRTUE, HABIT, AND ETHICS
ARISTOTLE

The Nicomachean Ethics serves as the base point for the systematic consideration of the subject of ethics. In this selection from that work, Aristotle (384–322 B.C.) establishes the notion that ethics consists of virtues, which are forms of habits, and therefore can be learned.

Moral virtue comes about as a result of habit, whence also its name *ethike* is one that is formed by a slight variation from the word ethos (habit). From this it is also plain that none of the moral virtues arises in us by nature; for nothing that exists by nature can form a habit contrary to its nature. For instance, the stone which by nature moves downwards cannot be habituated to move upwards, not even if one tries to train it by throwing it up ten thousand times; nor can fire be habituated to move downwards, nor can anything else that by nature behaves in one way be trained to behave in another. Neither by nature, then, nor contrary to nature do the virtues arise in us; rather we are adapted by nature to receive them, and are made perfect by habit.

. . . The things we have to learn before we can do them, we learn by doing them, e.g. men become builders by building and lyre players by playing the lyre, so too we become just by doing just acts, temperate by doing temperate acts, brave by doing brave acts.

This is confirmed by what happens in states; for legislators make the citizens good by forming habits in them, and this is the wish of every legislator, and those who do not effect it miss their mark, and it is in this that a good constitution differs from a bad one.

Again, it is from the same causes and by the same means that every virtue is both produced and destroyed, and similarly every art; for it is from playing the lyre that both

Source: "Ethics Nicomachea," pp. 331–332 in *Introduction to Aristotle* based on Oxford Translation of Aristotle (W. D. Ross, ed.), edited by McKeon, R. (1925). By permission of Oxford University Press.

good and bad lyre-players are produced. And the corresponding statement is true of builders and of all the rest; men will be good or bad builders as a result of building well or badly. For if this were not so, there would have been no need of a teacher, but all men would have been born good or bad at their craft. This, then, is the case with the virtues also; by doing the acts that we do in our transactions with other men we become just or unjust, and by doing the acts that we do in the presence of danger, and being habituated to feel fear or confidence, we become brave or cowardly. The same is true of appetites and feelings of anger; some men become temperate and good-tempered, others self-indulgent and irascible, by behaving in one way or the other in the appropriate circumstances. Thus, in one word, states of character arise out of like activities. This is why the activities we exhibit must be of a certain kind; it is because the states of character correspond to the differences between these.

ON VIRTUE
TERRY COOPER

In his introductory comments to his coedited book, Exemplary Public Administra-tors, *Terry Cooper reflects on the meaning and origin of virtue as an ethical concept, and its resurgence in contemporary thinking about administrative ethics.*

There is a popular tendency to assume that the ancient Greek meaning of virtue was homogeneously understood, but that does not seem to have been true. The Greek word translated into English as *virtue* is *arete.* In Homeric times (eighth century B.C.), it referred to goodness or excellence of any kind without any specifically moral significance. In Homer's poems, *arete* suggested what were then considered "manly" qualities, such as valor and bravery in battle or endurance and skill in athletics, which enabled one to carry out obligations to society. However, by the time of Socrates, Plato, and Aristotle in the fourth and fifth centuries B.C., there was general disagreement over a single meaning of the word. Among the Sophists, the tragedians, Plato, and Aristotle, the same terms were used for specific attributes of virtue such as friendship, courage, self-restraint, wisdom, and justice, but without unanimity over what kind of conduct they required (MacIntyre, 1984).

It was Aristotle's treatment of virtue that "decisively constitutes the classical tradition as a tradition of moral thought" (MacIntyre, 1984, p. 147). Although Aristotle considered the virtues qualities that made possible human fulfillment, he did not view them in the utilitarian sense—as means to achieve certain specific ends. To him,

Source: Terry L. Cooper, "Prologue," pp. 1–7 in *Exemplary Public Administrators: Character and Leadership in Government,* Terry L. Cooper and N. Dale Wright, eds. (San Francisco: Jossey-Bass Publishers, 1992). Reprinted with permission of John Wiley & Sons, Inc.

the patterns of thought and behavior through which one sought the good life were as important as that end and could not be separated from it (Sherman, 1989). Cultivating virtues was the way one lived the good life; they brought *eudaimonia* (blessedness, happiness, prosperity). The important caveat was that those states of being should not be pursued directly; they were byproducts of a search for the good throughout one's life (MacIntyre, 1984).

As Nancy Sherman explains, for Aristotle the virtues "comprise just and decent ways of living as a social being." She points out that excellences of character for Aristotle include more than those we would likely think of as moral, such as benevolence and good will. They encompass traits like wit and humor that are essential to a whole life among other human beings in a political community. She maintains that moral thought and conduct are only one aspect of the balanced, integrated, and well-rounded life of the virtuous person who cultivates generosity, temperance and courage, but also the more earthly qualities of wit, humor, and conviviality . . . recognizes a moment for laughter, and knows how to make other people see it, without becoming offensive or slavishly dependent upon an audience . . . [and] is personable, prizing not merely good action but the qualities of friendliness and emotional candor. To lead a good life is to lead a life in which these non-moral but human pursuits have some ineliminable place . . . within the best example of a good life is the recognition of an activity of superior worth and pleasure that is not itself the exercise of moral virtue or intellect in its practical aspect. The life which cultivates this excellence, jointly with other human virtues, is the happiest life. The life devoted exclusively to morality, which finds no leisure for the speculative pursuits of the mind, will only be second best. It will lack something [1989, p. 103].

In Aristotelian terms, virtues are acquired character traits that include the full range of human faculties—dispositions to think, act, and feel in certain ways. . . .

Christian thought in the Middle Ages placed its own stamp on the Aristotelian tradition. In the theology of Thomas Aquinas, the meaning of virtue betrayed its earlier roots but was adapted to Christian concepts of a cosmic divine order as the end toward which life should be directed. Character traits that served to shape life in accordance with that order were formulated in terms of four traditional cardinal virtues (prudence, justice, temperance, and courage), which go back to Plato and were carried into the doctrine of the church by Ambrose and Augustine. To these were added the three supernatural or theological virtues (faith, hope, and love), which reflect Christianity's ultimate concern for the life of faith (MacIntyre, 1984).

Moving very rapidly into the modern era, with great omissions of twists and turns in the evolution of meanings, we find the concept fragmenting into a variety of understandings. By the early eighteenth century, virtue was often seen as little more than a notion of good breeding, with good humor and natural kindliness as the central desired qualities (Berthoff, 1986, p. 59). MacIntyre points to a tendency during that time for virtue to shift from the plural (referring to specific traits such as prudence, fairness, and so on), to the singular, becoming almost synonymous with moral.

Furthermore, with a loss of a coherent ultimate end, either in the Aristotelian or the Christian sense, virtue increasingly became an end in itself (1984).

When we examine the early American context, we discover that Benjamin Franklin advanced a somewhat different view than any mentioned so far. He proposed traits such as cleanliness, silence, and industry that were not found in the earlier tradition; he also saw the drive to acquire wealth as virtuous. . . .

Virtue in the hands of the Federalists became heavily rule-oriented, a perspective quite consistent with [David] Hume's thinking. Under the sway of these assumptions about the unvirtuous drives behind human action, the "new science" of the Federalists was concerned with "supplying the defect of better motives" (Hanson, 1985, p. 74). Crafting a constitution then became a different problem than it had been for the older republican tradition: "Whereas constitution-making was traditionally conceived as a practical exercise in organizing particular virtues, Madison began to treat it as a science of rule formation. Hence, the inculcation of virtues no longer required a practical education, though of course a willingness to obey rules was still a minimal condition for political success. Hamilton found this willingness in the desire of individuals for fame. This was not so much the glory that animated classical republicans, as it was vainglory. However, it did provide a reliable motive for obeying the constitutional rules and pursuing the common good" (Hanson, 1985, p. 73).

This minimalist, rule-oriented understanding of virtue held by the Federalists is a far cry from Aristotle's notion of excellence in all of those qualities essential to humanness. Aristotle recognized the lack of virtues among people but sought through politics to cultivate them; the Federalists saw that lack as inherent in human nature and able to be overcome only in the form of obedience to prescription and regulation. Institutional arrangements were designed to make human "interests and duties coincide, and for limiting the harmful effects that might result from any disjunction between interest and duty" (Hanson, 1985, p. 73). . . .

Renewed interest in virtue among public administration ethicists seems to have come largely from three sources in particular. First, Mark T. Lilla's article "Ethos, Ethics, and Public Service" (1981), with its attack on the tendency to focus almost exclusively on rational analysis and decision making in the teaching of administrative ethics, struck a responsive chord. Lilla feared that this narrow approach, apart from attention to the ethos of public service, might simply lead to more sophisticated rationalizing rather than genuinely ethical conduct. Second, Alasdair MacIntyre's *After Virtue,* published in the same year as Lilla's article, advocated a return to an Aristotelian ethic of virtue couched in terms that were adaptable to the needs of public administrators. MacIntyre saw one important function of virtues as protecting the "internal goods" of "practices" from the "external goods" of institutions. If public administration could be understood as a "practice," then understanding virtue as certain character traits might be a key element in supporting ethical conduct in the face of organizational pressures to act otherwise. Third, Edmund L. Pincoffs, in *Quandaries and Ethics* (1986), criticized the preoccupation with ethical theories and the emphasis on ethical dilemmas in the teaching of professional ethics, advocating instead an ethic of virtue as a sounder basis for ethical decision making and conduct.

REFERENCES

Berthoff, W. *Literature and the Continuances of Virtue*. Princeton, NJ: Princeton University Press, 1986.

Hanson, R. L. *The Democratic Imagination in America: Conversations with Our Past*. Princeton, NJ: Princeton University Press, 1985.

Lilla, M. T. "Ethos, 'Ethics,' and Public Service," *The Public Interest 63* (1981), 3–17.

McIntyre, A. *After Virtue* (2nd ed.) Notre Dame, IN: Notre Dame University Press, 1984.

Pincoffs, E. L. *Quandaries and Virtues: Against Reductivism in Ethics*. Lawrence: University Press of Kansas, 1986.

Sherman, N. *The Fabric of Character: Aristotle's Theory of Virtue*. Oxford, England: Clarendon Press, 1989.

THE PRINCE
Niccolo Machiavelli

Niccolo Machiavelli (1462–1527) is regarded by many as a great political philosopher whose writings mark the beginning of modern political thought. Others regard Machiavelli's ideas as so evil that his very name has become an adjective to designate unprincipled and unethical behavior. He argued that acts should be judged good or bad in relationship to their consequences or results, rather than their intentions or the characteristics of the actor.

ON THOSE THINGS FOR WHICH MEN, AND PARTICULARLY PRINCES, ARE PRAISED OR BLAMED

. . . [T]here is such a gap between how one lives and how one ought to live that anyone who abandons what is done for what ought to be done learns his ruin rather than his preservation; for a man who wishes to profess goodness at all times will come to ruin among so many who are not good. Hence it is necessary for a prince who wishes to maintain his position to learn how not to be good, and use this knowledge or not according to necessity.

Source: Niccolo Machiavelli, *The Prince*, ed. and trans. by Peter Bondanella (Oxford: Oxford University Press, 1984), chapters 15 and 18. By permission of Oxford University Press.

Leaving aside, therefore, the imagined things concerning a prince, and taking into account those that are true, I say that all men, when they are spoken of, and particularly princes, since they are placed on a higher level, are judged by some of these qualities which bring them either blame or praise. And this is why one is considered generous, another miserly (to use a Tuscan word, since "avaricious" in our language is still used to mean one who wishes to acquire by means of theft; we call "miserly" one who excessively avoids using what he has); one is considered a giver, the other rapacious; one cruel, another merciful; one treacherous, another faithful; one effeminate and cowardly, another bold and courageous; one humane, another haughty; one lascivious, another chaste; one trustworthy, another frivolous; one religious, another unbelieving; and the like. And I know that everyone will admit that it would be a very praiseworthy thing to find in a prince, of the qualities mentioned above, those that are held to be good; but since it is neither possible to have them nor to observe them all completely, because the human condition does not permit it, a prince must be prudent enough to know how to escape the bad reputation of those vices that would lose the state for him, and must protect himself from those that will not lose it for him, if this is possible; but if he cannot, he need not concern himself unduly if he ignores these less serious vices. And, moreover, he need not worry about incurring the bad reputation of those vices without which it would be difficult to hold his state; since carefully taking everything into account he will discover that something which appears to be a virtue, if pursued, will end in destruction; while some other thing which seems to be a vice, if pursued will result in his safety and his well-being.

HOW A PRINCE SHOULD KEEP HIS WORD

How praiseworthy it is for a prince to keep his word and to live by integrity and not by deceit everyone knows; nevertheless, one sees from the experience of our times that the princes who have accomplished great deeds are those who have cared little for keeping their promises and who have known how to manipulate the minds of men by shrewdness; and in the end they have surpassed those who laid their foundations upon loyalty.

You must, therefore, know that there are two means of fighting: one according to the laws, the other with force; the first way is proper to man, the second to beasts; but because the first, in many cases, is not sufficient, it becomes necessary to have recourse to the second. Therefore, a prince must know how to use wisely the natures of the beast and the man. . . .

Since, then, a prince must know how to make good use of the nature of the beast, he should choose from among the beasts the fox and the lion; for the lion cannot defend itself from the traps and the fox cannot protect itself from the wolves. It is therefore necessary to be a fox in order to recognize the traps and a lion in order to frighten the wolves. Those who play only the part of the lion do not understand matters. A wise ruler, therefore, cannot and should not keep his word when such an observance of faith would be to his disadvantage and when the reasons which made him promise are removed. And if men were all good, this rule would not be good; but since men are a contemptible lot and will not keep their promises to you, you likewise need not keep yours to them. A prince never lacks legitimate reasons to break his promise. Of this one could cite an endless number of modern examples to show how many pacts, how many promises have been made null and void because of the infidelity of princes; and he who has known best how to use the fox has come to a better end. But it is necessary to know how to disguise this nature well and to be a great hypocrite and a liar; and men are so simple-minded and so controlled by their present needs that one who deceives will always find another who will allow himself to be deceived. . . .

Therefore, it is not necessary for a prince to have all of the above-mentioned qualities, but it is very necessary for him to appear to have them. Furthermore, I shall be so bold to assert this: that having them and practicing them at all times is harmful; and appearing to have them is useful; for instance, to seem merciful, faithful, humane, trustworthy, religious, and to be so; but his mind should be disposed in such a way that should it become necessary not to be so, he will be able and know how to change to the contrary. And it is essential to understand this: that a prince, and especially a new prince, cannot observe all those things for which men are considered good, for in order to maintain the state he is often obliged to act against his promise, against charity, against humanity, and against religion. And therefore, it is necessary that he have a mind ready to turn itself according to the way the winds of fortune and the changeability of affairs require him; and, as I said above, as long as it is possible, he should not stray from the good, but he should know how to enter into evil when necessity commands.

A prince, therefore, must be very careful never to let anything slip from his lips which is not full of the five qualities mentioned above: he should appear, upon seeing and hearing him, to be all mercy, all faithfulness, all integrity, all kindness, all religion. And there is nothing more necessary than to seem to possess this last quality. And men in general judge more by their eyes than their hands; for everyone can see but few can feel. Everyone sees what you seem to be, few touch upon what you are, and those few do not dare to contradict the opinion of the many who have the majesty of the state to defend them; and in the actions of all men, and especially of princes, where there is no impartial arbiter, one must consider the final result. Let a prince therefore act to conquer and to maintain the state; his methods will always be judged honorable and will be praised by all.

UTILITARIANISM
John Stuart Mill

John Stuart Mill (1806–1873), like Machiavelli, judged actions on the basis of their consequences, particularly insofar as they contributed to human happiness, broadly conceived.

Source: John Stuart Mill, *Utilitarianism* (Peterborough, ONT: Broadview Press, 2000), pp. 20, 29, 34–35, 46, 50, 69, and 79.

According to the Greatest Happiness Principle, . . . the ultimate end, with reference to and for the sake of which all other things are desirable (whether we are considering our own good or that of other people), is an existence exempt as far as possible from pain, and as rich as possible in enjoyments, both in point of quantity and quality; the test of quality, and the rule for measuring it against quantity, being the preference felt by those who, in their opportunities of experience, to which must be added their habits of self-consciousness and self-observation, are best furnished with the means of comparison. This, being, according to the utilitarian opinion, the end of human action, is necessarily also the standard of morality; which may accordingly be defined, the rules and precepts for human conduct, by the observance of which an existence such as has been described might be, to the greatest extent possible, secured to all mankind; and not to them only, but, so far as the nature of things admits, to the whole sentient creation. . . .

Utilitarians are quite aware that there are other desirable possessions and qualities besides virtue, and are perfectly willing to allow to all of them their full worth. They are also aware that a right action does not necessarily indicate a virtuous character, and that actions, which are blamable, often proceed from qualities entitled to praise. When this is apparent in any particular case, it modifies their estimation, not certainly of the act, but of the agent. I grant that they are, notwithstanding, of opinion, that in the long run the best proof of a good character is good actions; and resolutely refuse to consider any mental disposition as good, of which the predominant tendency is to produce bad conduct. This makes them unpopular with many people; but it is an unpopularity which they must share with every one who regards the distinction between right and wrong in a serious light; and the reproach is not one which a conscientious utilitarian need be anxious to repel. . . .

We are told that a utilitarian will be apt to make his own particular case an exception to moral rules, and, when under temptation, will see an utility in the breach of a rule, greater than he will see in its observance. But is utility the only creed which is able to furnish us with excuses for evil doing, and means of cheating our own conscience? They are afforded in abundance by all doctrines which recognize as a fact in morals the existence of conflicting considerations; which all doctrines do, that have been believed by sane persons. It is not the fault of any creed, but of the complicated nature of human affairs, that rules of conduct cannot be so framed as to require no exceptions, and that hardly any kind of action can safely be laid down as either always obligatory or always condemnable. There is no ethical creed which does not temper the rigidity of its laws, by giving a certain latitude, under the moral responsibility of the agent, for accommodation to peculiarities of circumstances; and under every creed, at the opening thus made, self-deception and dishonest casuistry get in. There exists no moral system under which there do not arise unequivocal cases of conflicting obligation. These are the real difficulties, the knotty points both in the theory of ethics, and in the conscientious guidance of personal conduct. They are overcome practically, with greater or with less success according to the intellect and virtue of the individual; but it can hardly be pretended that anyone will be the less qualified for dealing with them, from possessing an ultimate standard to which conflicting rights and duties can be referred. If utility is the ultimate source of moral obligations, utility may be invoked to decide between them when their demands are incompatible. Though the application of the standard may be difficult, it is better than none at all: while in other systems, the moral laws all claiming independent authority, there is no common umpire entitled to interfere between them; their claims to precedence one over another rest on little better than sophistry, and unless determined, as they generally are, by the unacknowledged influence of considerations of utility, afford a free scope for the action of personal desires and partialities. . . .

Questions about ends are, in other words, questions about what things are desirable. The utilitarian doctrine is, that happiness is desirable, and the only thing desirable, as an end. . . .

It results from the preceding considerations, that there is in reality nothing desired except happiness. Whatever is desired otherwise than as a means to some end beyond itself, and ultimately to happiness, is desired as itself a part of happiness, and is not desired for itself until it has become so. Those who desire virtue for its own sake, desire it either because the consciousness of it is a pleasure, or because the consciousness of being without it is a pain, or for both reasons united; as in truth the pleasure and pain seldom exist separately, but almost always together, the same person feeling pleasure in the degree of virtue attained, and pain in not having attained more. If one of these gave him no pleasure, and the other no pain, he would not love or desire virtue, or would desire it only for the other benefits which it might produce to himself or to persons whom he cared for. . . .

We are continually informed that utility is an uncertain standard, which every different person interprets differently, and that there is no safety but in the immutable, ineffaceable, and unmistakable dictates of justice, which carry their evidence in themselves, and are independent of the fluctuations of opinion. One would suppose from this that on questions of justice there could be no controversy; that if we take that for our rule, its application to any given case could leave us in as little doubt as a mathematical demonstration. So far is this from being the fact, that there is as much difference of opinion, and as fierce discussion, about what is just, as about what is useful to society. Not only have different nations and individuals different notions of justice, but in the mind of one and the same individual, justice is not some one rule, principle, or maxim, but many, which do not always coincide in their dictates, and in choosing between which, he is guided either by some extraneous standard, or by his own personal predilections. . . .

It appears from what has been said, that justice is a name for certain moral requirements, which, regarded collectively, stand higher in the scale of social utility, and are therefore of more paramount obligation, than any others; though particular cases may occur in which some other social duty is so important, as to over-rule any one of the general maxims of justice. Thus, to save a life, it may not only be allowable, but a duty, to steal, or take by force, the necessary food or medicine, or to kidnap, and compel to officiate, the only qualified medical practitioner. In such cases, as we do not call anything justice which is not a virtue, we usually say, not that justice must give way to some other moral principle, but that what is just in ordinary cases is, by reason of that other principle, not just in the particular case.

PRINCIPLE: THE CATEGORICAL IMPERATIVE
Immanuel Kant

Immanuel Kant (1724–1804) approached the question of ethics from a very different angle from Machiavelli or Mill. In the following passages he outlines his categorical imperative, the fundamental principle he sees as the ultimate basis of ethical action. In real-life ethical situations, do you act primarily on the basis of principle or on the basis of expected consequences?

Everything in nature works according to laws. Rational beings alone have the faculty of acting according *to the conception* of laws, that is, according to principles, i.e., have a *will*. Since the deduction of actions from principles requires *reason*, the will is nothing but practical reason. . . .

The conception of an objective principle, in so far as it is obligatory for a will, is called a command (of reason), and the formula of the command is called an Imperative. . . .

Now all *imperatives* command either *hypothetically* or *categorically*. The former represent the practical necessity of a possible action as means to something else that is willed (or at least which one might possibly will). The categorical imperative would be that which represented an action as necessary of itself without reference to another end, i.e., as objectively necessary. . . .

There is therefore but one categorical imperative, namely this: Act only on that maxim whereby thou canst at the same time will that it should become a universal law.

Source: *Kant's Critique of Practical Reason and Other Works on the Theory of Ethics*, trans. Thomas Kingsmill Abbott, B. D., Fellow and Tutor of Trinity College, Dublin, 4th revised ed. (London: Longmans, Green and Co., 1889), pp. 36–38, 47–49. The full text is available online at the Online Library of Liberty, oll.libertyfund.org.

Now if all imperatives of duty can be deduced from this one imperative as from their principle, then, although it should remain undecided whether what is called duty is not merely a vain notion, yet at least we shall be able to show what we understand by it and what this notion means.

Since the universality of the law according to which effects are produced constitutes what is properly called *nature* in the most general sense (as to form), that is the existence of things so far as it is determined by general laws, the imperative of duty may be expressed thus: Act as if the maxim of thy action were to become by thy will a Universal Law of Nature.

We will now enumerate a few duties. . . .

A man reduced to despair by a series of misfortunes feels wearied of life, but is still so far in possession of his reason that he can ask himself whether it would not be contrary to his duty to himself to take his own life. Now he inquires whether the maxim of his action could become a universal law of nature. His maxim is: From self-love I adopt it as a principle to shorten my life when its longer duration is likely to bring more evil than satisfaction. It is asked then simply whether this principle founded on self-love can become a universal law of nature. Now we see at once that a system of nature of which it should be a law to destroy life by means of the very feeling whose special nature it is to impel to the improvement of life would contradict itself, and therefore could not exist as a system of nature; hence that maxim cannot possibly exist as a universal law of nature, and consequently would be wholly inconsistent with the supreme principle of all duty.

Another finds himself forced by necessity to borrow money. He knows that he will not be able to repay it, but sees also that nothing will be lent to him, unless he promises stoutly to repay it in a definite time. He desires to make this promise, but he has still so much conscience as to ask himself: Is it not unlawful and inconsistent with duty to get out of a difficulty in this way? Suppose however that he resolves to do so, then the maxim of his action would be expressed thus: When I think myself in want of money, I will borrow money and promise to repay it, although I know that I never can do so. Now this principle of self-love or of one's own advantage may perhaps be consistent with my whole future welfare; but the question now is, Is it right? I change then the suggestion of self-love into a universal law, and state the question thus: How would it be if my maxim were a universal law? Then I see at once that it could never hold as a universal law of nature, but would necessarily contradict itself. For supposing it to be a universal law that everyone when he thinks himself in a difficulty should be able to promise whatever he pleases, with the purpose of not keeping his promise, the promise itself would become impossible, as well as the end that one might have in view in it, since no one would consider that anything was promised to him, but would ridicule all such statements as vain pretenses.

THE ETHICAL TRIANGLE
James Svara

James Svara treats virtue, consequence, and principle as complementary and compet-
ing claims on ethical commitments, in effect three corners of an ethical triangle. This
device helps to identify some types of ethical dilemmas and suggests paths to ethical
decision-making.

A source of continuing debate and disagreement in public administration is identifying the philosophical basis of administrative ethics. Although there is recognition of
the importance of filling one's office in a way that is accountable, promotes the public interest, and obeys the constitution and the law, it is not clear how public administrators ground their ethical thinking when they act as moral agents. For example,
how are they guided when they ponder whether an order is appropriate, when they
make discretionary choices about what best serves the public interest, and when they
seek to determine whether a constitutional right is being jeopardized? Decisions
might be simply grounded in a core set of "governmental ethics" with no philosophical content. For example, the Code of Ethics for Government Service has a
simplicity and directness which does not acknowledge any broader set of ideas about
ethics beyond the Constitution, law, and general standards of work performance. As
might be expected given most of these sources, the values contained in this code are
shallow. Identifying so-called higher ethical standards, however, gets public administrators embroiled in the confusing task of sorting out the competing ethical models
which could form the philosophical basis for ethical action. . . .

   The major contenders for the base of administrative ethics are virtue, principle,
and consequences. These approaches have been summarized . . . by Richter, Burke,
and Doig (1990, pp. 2–3) in . . . *Combating Corruption/Encouraging Ethics.* The first,
which looks to the qualities of the good person for the standards of ethical conduct,
has been advanced by Cooper (1987) and the Josephson Institute among others. The
second, the principle-based approach, applies universal principles to determine ethical choices, as advocated by Chandler (1994) and by Hart (1974) drawing on Rawls'
theory of justice. Although she is reluctant to make a clear-cut choice between deontological and teleological approaches to ethics, Denhardt (1988, p. 53) acknowledges that she considers the former approach to be "more defensible." The consequences approach, a third perspective, looks at the results of actions and seeks to
promote some end, such as the greatest good, drawing on utilitarian ethics. It has few
proponents but many practitioners. Reviewing the three ethical approaches supports
the conclusion that use of all of them helps to avoid the shortcomings and potential
misuse of any of the models used singly. One is best grounded when operating
within an ethical triangle formed by the three approaches.

Source: James Svara, "The Ethical Triangle: Synthesizing the Bases of Administrative Ethics," *Public Integrity Annual 1997*, pp. 33–41. Reprinted with permission from the American Society for Public Administration.

ALTERNATIVE APPROACHES TO
ADMINISTRATIVE ETHICS: VIRTUE AND INTUITION

Two distinct but related elements are included in this approach. First, the basis of ethics is a set of qualities that defines what a good person is. The virtuous person manifests and acts on the characteristics that mark one as a person of character and integrity. Second, the nature of ethical decision-making is intuitive. One grasps in a holistic way what a good person would do in a given situation. The sense that "I know what I have to do" comes from one's being, rather than being derived from an analysis of the situation (a decision-making mode that is necessary in the next two approaches). In so far as there is critical examination, it is guided by the question "What would a good person do?" This in turn may lead to considering how different aspects of one's nature might impel one to choose alternative courses of action. The guiding impulse, however, is the feeling that one should act based on one's character.

For administrators to be virtuous, they can develop their own values. "Virtues exist innately, as potentialities, within each individual," Hart (1994, pp. 113–4) has argued, "and they push for actualization in the life of the individual." Still, there is considerable debate about which virtues are most important or essential to others, i.e., the cardinal virtues, and Hart acknowledges that the cardinal virtues must be "intentionally cultivated" (p. 118). Some argue for the minimal number of virtues with others being derived from these cardinal virtues. Frankena (1963, p. 50) takes this approach and uses benevolence and justice as the essential virtues. The Josephson Institute, on the other hand, has developed a long list of "values and principles." The following are the traits that we would expect to find in a person of character:[1]

Honesty	Caring for others (Benevolence)
Integrity	Respect for others
Promise-keeping (Trustworthiness)	Responsible citizenship
Loyalty (Fidelity)	Pursuit of excellence
Fairness	Accountability

Beyond these, Cooper (1987, 324) adds rationality, prudence, respect for law, self-discipline, civility, and independence.

Advantages of the Virtuous Approach

As noted above, one of the advantages of ethics based on virtue is that ethical choice is intuitive. Essentially, one asks the question "what shall I be?" This gives what Mayo (in Sommers, 1985) has called a "unity to our answer." It is not the logical unity that a set of principles would purport to provide, but rather "the unity of character. A person's character is not merely a list of dispositions; it has the organic unity of something that is more than the sum of its parts." (175) Thus, whether one's list of virtues is short or long, it should have coherence if one has mastered the settled habits and dispositions that help one achieve an active life in accord with excellence. . . .

The chief advantage is easy accessibility to ethical standards. Virtues commonly draw on the core societal values that are inculcated from childhood. Thus, the administrator does not have to learn how to be virtuous, although his or her virtue must be practiced and honed. Hart (1994, 114) reminds us that one pursues virtue rather than ever achieving it. The final advantage is that acting virtuously reflects an intention by the individual to be good. . . .

Disadvantages of the Virtuous Approach

Disadvantages of the virtuous approach are several. An administrator may want to be good, but does he or she know how to do good, i.e., what actions are appropriate for each of the virtues. Definitions of virtues may be circular. For example, Mayo (in Sommers, 1985, 172) defines the virtue of justice as "a quality of character, and a just action is one such as a just man would do." To decide what a just man would do without consulting a principle of justice (or even considering what consequences would be "fair") is difficult. In addition, how does one choose among alternative virtues which may lead one to act in different ways, i.e., choosing between competing "goods"? . . .

ALTERNATIVE APPROACHES: DEONTOLOGY AND THE PRINCIPLE-BASED APPROACH

If administrators are principled rather than virtuous, they base their ethical decision-making on the application of principles. To use this approach, administrators must have a set of principles and the deductive capacity to appropriately apply those principles to actual situations. Deontologists use agreed upon or settled values to determine one's moral obligation to act. Principles identify "kinds of action that are right or obligatory" (Frankena, 1963, 49). Rule-deontologists seek to establish principles that will apply to a variety of situations.[2] The most commonly cited example in the literature on public administration ethics is Kantianism. In Kant's approach (adapted from Chandler, 1994, p. 149), consequences or the ends attained by actions are not what determines moral obligation. The moral worth of an action is determined by the principle from which the action is performed. As a guide to developing principles, Kant provided the categorical imperative: One should act only as if one were legislating a universal law for everyone to follow in a preferred world. The Kantian position is that principles are universally and invariably applicable.

Issues in the Principle-Based Approach

There are several issues that need to be resolved regarding the deontological approach before proceeding to an assessment. They are the source of principles, conflict among principles, and exceptions to principles. The source of principles is an important issue but not an unsolvable one for public administration. The nature of public service requires that regime values be a primary source of principles (Rohr, 1989; Chandler, 1994, p. 149; Fox, 1994, p. 92). Furthermore, Denhardt (1988, p. 45) argues that certain principles are widely accepted in western society. Examples are:

truth telling
promise keeping
the sanctity of the individual
the sanctity of life
justice

The deontological approach requires a set of principles which constitute "a system and not merely an aggregate," as Mayo (in Sommers, 1985, p. 175) has argued, and "the attempt to construct a deductive moral system is notoriously difficult." Public administrators, acknowledging their dependence on the Constitution as a major—but not only—source of principles, may be able to create such a system.[3] Rosenbloom (1992) has identified the Constitution's protection of substantive rights, e.g., freedom of speech, due process, and equal protection as ethical guides. He also points out, however, that the Constitution which once supported slavery and still permits capital punishment and has no protection for women's rights cannot be relied on exclusively as a source of ethical principles. . . .

ALTERNATIVE APPROACHES: UTILITARIAN APPROACH

The teleological approach generally and utilitarianism specifically holds that there are no moral principles which provide justification for an action a priori. An action is right or wrong depending on its consequences. Mill (quoted in Richter et al., 1990, p. 23) rejected the other two approaches when he criticized applying a "sense of instinct, informing us of right and wrong" or a general principle to a specific case. An action is good in so far as it contributes to good ends. Although there are various ways of calculating benefits depending on whether the individual or society as a whole is the referent, it is generally "ethical universalism," as Frankena (1963, p. 14) has called it, or utilitarianism that is incorporated into thinking about administrative ethics. When examining utilities for society as a whole, the preferred choice is that which produces the greatest good for the greatest number. One can either assess the consequences of each separate act or of rules which will persist as long as they produce the greatest net good. The problem with the first of these approaches—act utilitarianism—is that one cannot learn from experience in order to formulate general rules (Frankena, 1963, p. 51), although it is presumably this form to which discussions of administrative ethics typically refer. . . .

THE ETHICAL TRIANGLE

Public administrators should actively utilize the key ideas of each of the three major approaches. Denhardt (1988, p. 53) concluded that if philosophers cannot agree on a choice between the competing ethical models, why should public administrators try to do so? She suggests that using various approaches can be helpful. Lewis's three circle approach (1991, p. 41) assesses decisions in terms of ethical, legal, and effectiveness considerations.

LOGIC OF COMBINING APPROACHES

There are other scholars on ethics who recommend combining approaches. Bok (1989, p. 55) sorts out her position on the practice of lying by starting with the "principle of veracity": Telling the truth is preferred and doing so normally requires no justification whereas lying does. Lies are not necessarily ruled out, but the principle has been framed to permit exceptions. For a lie to ever be justified, it needs to produce clear balance of benefit over harm. Stewart and Sprinthall (1994, pp. 344–345) advocate principled ethical reasoning consistent with the highest stages of moral development, and they recognize the importance of both principle and virtue to ethical reasoning. Such a balance is reflected in Kohlberg's definition of stage six of moral development which refers to "orientation to *conscience or principles*, not only to ordained social rules but to principles of choice appealing to *logical universality and consistency; conscience is a directing agent*, together with mutual respect and trust" (in Stewart and Sprinthall, 1994, pp. 327, italics added).

Frankena provides a convincing argument for the complementarity of all three approaches. There are three major parts. First, utilitarianism is not acceptable without a deontological mooring. If we would agree that "a less beneficent rule which is more just" is preferable to one that produces greater net utility but is less just, then the criterion for determining the rules of morality combines justice and utility (1963, p. 33).

Second, he argues that the deontological approach, though superior to others, depends as well on utilitarianism. Deontologists are not sufficiently concerned about the "promotion of good." (p. 29) He prefers a "mixed deontological theory, since it recognizes the principle of utility as a valid one, but insists that another principle is required as well."

Third, Frankena sees principle and virtue as interdependent. It is not necessary to choose one or the other.

USING THE THREE APPROACHES TO CREATE AN ETHICAL TRIANGLE

Another way of recognizing the complementarity among the approaches is to use all three. The three approaches provide distinct "filters" that reveal different aspects of a situation requiring an ethical choice. Used independently, they help to clarify the options and ethical considerations associated with each. Furthermore, the three approaches reinforce and support each other and help to prevent the shortcomings of using any of the models alone.

These advantages come from synthesizing the three models into an ethical triangle, presented in Figure 1.1. The core ideas of each approach—justice, greatest good, and integrity—are largely reinforcing and mutually supportive.

Although there are troubling instances in which the dictates of principle lead to bad consequences and achieving good ends compromise principles, these are rare. When such a classic trade-off must be faced, the considerations of adhering to the virtue of, for example, benevolence may well help to resolve the dilemma in a public serving way. . . .

As one moves "out" from the triangle, the ethical basis for action is weakened and unethical actions may seem justifiable. In addition, reinforcement from other bases is decreased. As one moves "in" toward the triangle, the reinforcement among bases is increased.

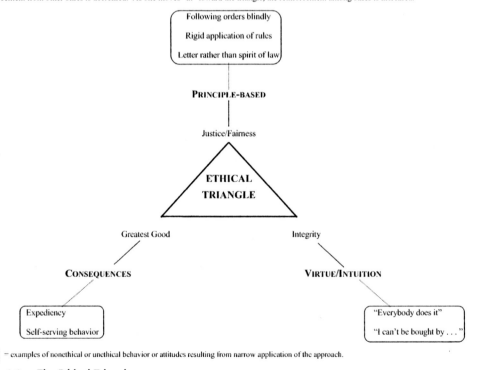

□ = examples of nonethical or unethical behavior or attitudes resulting from narrow application of the approach.

Figure 1.1.   The Ethical Triangle.

NOTES

1. Adapted from "Ethical Values and Principles," *Easier Said Than Done,* Winter, 1988, p. 69.

2. In contrast, act-deontologists argue that "basic judgments of obligation are all purely particular ones like 'In this situation I should do so and so.'" (Frankena, 1963, p. 15)

3. It will not be an easy process, but it can be done. Chandler (1994, p. 149) offers an example of how a constitutional protection can be reframed as a principle. Due process is an important value. For it to be an "organizing value, however, we would need a deontological principle which could show us what pattern of action would comply with this value. A common form of the due process *principle* (italics added), for example, is that 'law must be just, fair, and equal,' and it should not be 'oppressive, fanciful, or biased.' Under this principle, therefore, all accused persons have the protections of the Bill of Rights and the guarantees of the Fourteenth Amendment."

REFERENCES

Bok, Sissela, 1989. *Lying: Moral Choice in Public and Private Life.* New York: Vintage Books.

Chandler, Ralph Clark, 1994. "Deontological Dimensions of Administrative Ethics," in *Handbook of Administrative Ethics,* ed. Terry L. Cooper. New York: Marcel Dekker, 1994. Pp. 147–56.

Cooper, Terry L., 1987. "Hierarchy, Virtue, and the Practice of Public Administration: A Perspective for Normative Ethics," *Public Administration Review* 47 (July/August): 320–328.

Denhardt, Kathryn G. 1988. *The Ethics of Public Administration: Resolving Moral Dilemmas in Public Organizations.* New York: Greenwood.

Fox, Charles J. 1994. "The Use of Philosophy in Administrative Ethics," in *Handbook of Administrative Ethics,* ed. Terry L. Cooper. New York: Marcel Dekker, 1994. Pp. 83–106.

Frankena, William, 1963. *Ethics.* Englewood Cliffs, NJ: Prentice-Hall.

Hart, David K., 1974. "Social Equity, Justice, and the Equitable Administrator," *Public Administration Review* 34 (January/February): 3–11.

———, 1994. "Adminstration and the Ethics of Virtue: In All Things, Choose First for Good Character and Then for Technical Expertise," in Terry L. Cooper, ed., *Handbook of Administrative Ethics.* New York: Marcel Dekker, pp. 107–23.

Lewis, Carol W., 1991. *The Ethics Challenge in Public Service.* San Francisco: Jossey-Bass.

Mayo, Bernard, "Ethics and Moral Life," excerpted in Sommers (1985), pp. 171–176.

Richter, William L., Frances Burke, and Jameson W. Doig, eds., 1990. *Combating Corruption/Encouraging Ethics: Sourcebook for PA Ethics.* Washington, DC: American Society for Public Administration.

Rohr, John A. 1989. *Ethics for Bureaucrats,* 2nd edition. New York: Marcel Dekker.

Rosenbloom, David H. 1992. "The Constitution as a Basis for Public Administrative Ethics," in *Essentials of Government Ethics,* ed. Peter Madsen and Jay M. Shafritz. New York: Meridian Book.

Sommers, Christina Hoff, 1985. *Vice and Virtue in Everyday Life.* New York: Harcourt Brace Jovanovich.

Stewart, Debra W. and Norman A. Sprinthall, 1994. "Moral Development in Public Administration," in *Handbook of Administrative Ethics,* ed. Terry L. Cooper. New York: Marcel Dekker, 1994. Pp. 325–48.

CASE 1: GYGES'S RING

In Book II of the *Republic*, Plato tells the story of an ancestor of Gyges, the Lydian, who came into possession of an unusual ring. When the ring was turned on the wearer's finger, it would make the person invisible. Realizing the ring's power, the man became a messenger to the king, then "committed adultery with the king's wife and, along with her, set upon the king and killed him. And so he took over the rule." (Plato, *Republic*, 359d–360b, Bloom trans.)

American philosopher Mortimer Adler used to put these questions to participants in his Aspen Institute seminars: "If you were walking along the street and saw a sign in a store window: 'Ring of Gyges, enquire within,' would you ask about it? Would you buy it? If you did, what would you do with it?"

Both Plato and Adler used this story to raise ethical questions. What would our actions be if we had no fear of being observed? What are the implications of our responses to these questions for administrative ethics? What are the implications for ethics education?

CHAPTER DISCUSSION QUESTIONS

1. With which approach to ethics (virtue, principle, consequences) do you identify most? If you follow a combination of approaches, what are the circumstances in which you use each approach?

2. Discuss these categories with a friend, a co-worker, or a fellow student. Do you have the same ethical assumptions? If not, how do you differ?

3. Do you use different ethical approaches in different circumstances? Are you likely to follow rules under some circumstances and regard consequences as more important at other times?

4. Is the "ethics triangle" a useful tool for resolving ethical dilemmas? Why? Why not?

FOR FURTHER EXPLORATION

Berman, Evan M., Jonathan P. West, and Stephen J. Bonczek, eds. *The Ethics Edge*. Washington, DC: International City/County Management Association, 1998. Chapter 3 ("The Ethical Professional: Cultivating Scruples," pp. 60–86) includes a discussion of Svara's Ethical Triangle.

Bowman, James S., ed. *Ethical Frontiers in Public Management: Seeking New Strategies for Resolving Ethical Dilemmas*. San Francisco: Jossey-Bass, 1991.

Source: William L. Richter, adapted from discussions between Bill Moyers and Mortimer Adler in "Justice," an episode in Moyers's PBS series, *Six Great Ideas*.

Bowman, James S., Jonathan P. West, Evan M. Berman, and Montgomery Van Wart. *The Professional Edge: Competencies in Public Service.* Armonk, NY: M. E. Sharpe, 2004.

Bruce, Willa M., ed. *Classics of Administrative Ethics.* Boulder: Westview Press, 2001.

Chapman, Richard A., ed. *Ethics in Public Service.* Edinburgh, UK: Edinburgh University Press, 1993.

———. *Ethics in Public Service for the New Millennium.* Aldershot: Ashgate, 2000.

Cody, W. J. Michael, and Richardson R. Lynn. *Honest Government: An Ethics Guide for Public Service.* Westport, CT: Praeger, 1992.

Cooper, Terry L., *Handbook of Administrative Ethics.* New York: M. Dekker, 1994.

Denhardt, Kathryn G., *The Ethics of Public Service: Resolving Moral Dilemmas in Public Organizations.* New York: Greenwood Press, 1988.

Dobel, J. Patrick. *Compromise and Political Action: Political Morality in Liberal and Democratic Life.* Lanham, MD: Rowman & Littlefield, 1990.

———. *Public Integrity.* Baltimore: The Johns Hopkins University Press, 1999.

Frederickson, H. George, ed. *Ethics and Public Administration.* Armonk, NY: M. E. Sharpe, 1993.

Lewis, Carol W. *The Ethics Challenge in Public Service: A Problem-Solving Guide.* San Francisco: Jossey-Bass, 1991.

Reynolds, Harry W. ed. *Ethics in American Public Service.* Thousand Oaks, CA: Sage, 1995.

Richardson, William D. *Democracy, Bureaucracy, and Character: Founding Thought.* Lawrence: University Press of Kansas, 1997.

Richardson, William D., J. Michael Martinez, and Kerry Stewart, eds. *Ethics and Character: The Pursuit of Democratic Virtues.* Durham, NC: Carolina Academic Press, 1999.

Richter, William L., Frances Burke, and Jameson W. Doig, eds. *Combating Corruption/Encouraging Ethics: A Sourcebook for Public Service Ethics.* Washington, DC: American Society for Public Administration, 1990.

Rohr, John A. *Public Service, Ethics, and Constitutional Practice.* Lawrence: University Press of Kansas, 1998.

———. *Ethics for Bureaucrats: An Essay on Law and Values,* second edition. New York: M. Dekker, 1989.

David H. Rosenbloom, "The Constitution as a Basis for Public Administrative Ethics," pp. 48–64 in *Essentials of Government Ethics,* ed. P. Madsen and J. Shafritz. New York: Meridian Books, 1992.

WEBSITES

Ethics Today: Online Journal of the ASPA Section on Ethics, www.unpan.org/namerica-aspa-ethics.asp

Josephson Institute of Ethics, www.josephsoninstitute.org

Making Ethical Decisions (Josephson Institute). www.josephsoninstitute.org/MED/MED intro+toc.htm

ASPA Ethics Section, www.aspaonline.org/ethicscommunity/

Internet Classics/Aristotle's *Nicomachean Ethics.* http://classics.mit.edu/Aristotle/nicomachaen.html

Online copy of Machiavelli's *The Prince.* www.constitution.org/mac/prince00.htm

Chapter 2

RESPONSIBILITY AND ACCOUNTABILITY

THE STUDY OF ADMINISTRATION
Woodrow Wilson

This seminal essay by Woodrow Wilson (1856–1924) is widely regarded as a classic in the profession of public administration. In the second section of the essay, reprinted here, Wilson emphasizes two types of administrative responsibility: that of civil servants to elected officials and that of civil servants to the public interest.

The field of administration is a field of business. It is removed from the hurry and strife of politics; it at most points stands apart even from the debatable ground of constitutional study. It is a part of political life only as the methods of the counting-house are a part of the life of society; only as machinery is part of the manufactured product. But it is, at the same time, raised very far above the dull level of mere technical detail by the fact that through its greater principles it is directly connected with the lasting maxims of political wisdom, the permanent truths of political progress.

The object of administrative study is to rescue executive methods from the confusion and costliness of empirical experiment and set them upon foundations laid deep in stable principle.

It is for this reason that we must regard civil-service reform in its present stages as but a prelude to a fuller administrative reform. We are now rectifying methods of appointment; we must go on to adjust executive functions more fitly and to prescribe better methods of executive organization and action. Civil-service reform is thus but a moral preparation for what is to follow. It is clearing the moral atmosphere of official life by establishing the sanctity of public office as a public trust, and, by making the service unpartisan, it is opening the way for making it businesslike. By sweetening its motives it is rendering it capable of improving its methods of work.

Source: Woodrow Wilson, "The Study of Administration," *Political Science Quarterly* 2:2 (June 1887), 209–217. Also available in *The Papers of Woodrow Wilson*, ed. Arthur S. Link (Princeton, NJ: Princeton University Press, 1966) V, 370–76.

Let me expand a little what I have said of the province of administration. Most important to be observed is the truth already so much and so fortunately insisted upon by our civil-service reformers; namely, that administration lies outside the proper sphere of politics. Administrative questions are not political questions. Although politics sets the tasks for administration, it should not be suffered to manipulate its offices. . . .

There is another distinction which must be worked into all our conclusions, which, though but another side of that between administration and politics, is not quite so easy to keep sight of: I mean the distinction between constitutional and administrative questions, between those governmental adjustments which are essential to constitutional principle and those which are merely instrumental to the possibly changing purposes of a wisely adapting convenience. . . .

To discover the best principle for the distribution of authority is of greater importance, possibly, under a democratic system, where officials serve many masters, than under others where they serve but a few. All sovereigns are suspicious of their servants, and the sovereign people is no exception to the rule; but how is its suspicion to be allayed by knowledge? If that suspicion could be clarified into wise vigilance, it would be altogether salutary; if that vigilance could be aided by the unmistakable placing of responsibility, it would be altogether beneficent. Suspicion in itself is never healthful either in the private or in the public mind. Trust is strength in all relations of life; and, as it is the office of the constitutional reformer to create conditions of trustfulness, so it is the office of the administrative organizer to fit administration with conditions of clear-cut responsibility which shall insure trustworthiness.

And let me say that large powers and unhampered discretion seem to me the indispensable conditions of responsibility. Public attention must be easily directed, in each case of good or bad administration, to just the man deserving of praise or blame. There is not danger in power, if only it be not irresponsible. If it be divided, dealt out in shares to many, it is obscured; and if it obscured, it is made irresponsible. But if it be centered in heads of the service and in heads of branches of the service, it is easily watched and brought to book. If to keep his office a man must achieve open and honest success, and if at the same time he feels himself intrusted with large freedom of discretion, the greater his power the less likely is he to abuse it, the more is he nerved and sobered and elevated by it. The less his power, the more safely obscure and unnoticed does he feel his position to be, and the more readily does he relapse into remissness.

Just here we manifestly emerge upon the field of that still larger question—the proper relations between public opinion and administration.

To whom is official trustworthiness to be disclosed, and by whom is it to be rewarded? Is the official to look to the public for his need of praise and his push of promotion, or only to his superior in office?

Are the people to be called in to settle constitutional principles? These questions evidently find their root in what is undoubtedly the fundamental problem of this whole study. That problem is: What part shall public opinion take in the conduct of administration?

The right answer seems to be, that public opinion shall play the part of author-itative critic.

But the method by which its authority shall be made to tell? Our peculiar Ameri-can difficulty in organizing administration is not the danger of losing liberty, but the danger of not being able or willing to separate its essentials from its accidents. Our suc-cess is made doubtful by that besetting error of ours, the error of trying to do too much by vote. Self-government does not consist in having a hand in everything, any more than housekeeping consists necessarily in cooking dinner with one's own hands. The cook must be trusted with a large discretion as to the management of the fires and the ovens.

In those countries in which public opinion has yet to be instructed in its privi-leges, yet to be accustomed to having its own way, this question as to the province of public opinion is much more readily soluble than in this country, where public opinion is wide awake and quite intent upon having its own way anyhow. It is pa-thetic to see a whole book written by a German professor of political science for the purpose of saying to his countrymen, "Please try to have an opinion about national affairs"; but a public which is so modest may at least be expected to be very docile and acquiescent in learning what things it has not a right to think and speak about imperatively. It may be sluggish, but it will not be meddlesome. It will submit to be instructed before it tries to instruct. Its political education will come before its polit-ical activity. In trying to instruct our own public opinion, we are dealing with a pupil apt to think itself quite sufficiently instructed beforehand.

The problem is to make public opinion efficient without suffering it to be med-dlesome. Directly exercised, in the oversight of the daily details and in the choice of daily means of government, public criticism is of course a clumsy nuisance, a rustic handling delicate machinery. But as superintending the greater forces of formative policy alike in politics and administration, public criticism is altogether safe and beneficent, altogether indispensable. Let administrative study find the best means for giving public criticism this control and for shutting it out from all other interference.

POLITICS AS A VOCATION
MAX WEBER

Like Wilson, Max Weber (1864–1920) wrote seminal discussions of bureaucracy and public service that continue to influence thinking a century later. The following selections include his comments on the ethical roles of public officials. What would Weber's posi-tion be with respect to the "ethical triangle" discussed in the previous chapter?

Source: Max Weber, "Politics as a Vocation," pp. 95, 118–122, 198–199, in *From Max Weber: Essays in So-ciology*, ed. and trans. H. H. Gerth and C. Wright Mills, copyright 1946, 1958, 1973 by H. H. Gerth and C. Wright Mills (New York: Oxford University Press, 1958). Used by permission of Oxford University Press, Inc.

According to his proper vocation, the genuine official—and this is decisive for the evaluation of our former regime—will not engage in politics. Rather, he should engage in impartial "administration." This also holds for the so-called political administrator, at least officially, in so far as the *raison d'etat,* that is, the vital interests of the ruling order, are not in question. *Sine ira et studio,* "without scorn and bias," he shall administer his office. Hence, he shall not do precisely what the politician, the leader as well as his following, must always and necessarily do, namely, *fight.*

To take a stand; to be passionate—*ira et studium*—is the politician's element, and above all the element of the political *leader.* His conduct is subject to quite a different, indeed, exactly the opposite, principle of responsibility from that of the civil servant. The honor of the civil servant is vested in his ability to execute conscientiously the order of the superior authorities, exactly as if the order agreed with his own conviction. This holds even if the order appears wrong to him and if, despite the civil servant's remonstrances, the authority insists on the order. Without this moral discipline and self-denial, in the highest sense, the whole apparatus would fall to pieces. The honor of the political leader, of the leading statesman, however, lies precisely in an exclusive *personal* responsibility for what he does, a responsibility he cannot and must not reject or transfer. It is in the nature of officials of high moral standing to be poor politicians, and above all, in the political sense of the word, to be irresponsible politicians. . . .

Now then, what relations do ethics and politics actually have? Have the two nothing whatever to do with one another, as has occasionally been said? Or, is the reverse true: that the ethic of political conduct is identical with that of any other conduct? Occasionally an exclusive choice has been believed to exist between the two propositions-either the one or the other proposition must be correct. But is it true that any ethic of the world could establish commandments of identical content for erotic, business, familial, and official relations; for the relations to one's wife, to the greengrocer, the son, the competitor, the friend, the defendant? Should it really matter so little for the ethical demands on politics that politics operates with very special means, namely, power backed up by *violence?* . . .

We must be clear about the fact that all ethically oriented conduct may be guided by one of two fundamentally differing and irreconcilably opposed maxims: conduct can be oriented to an "ethic of ultimate ends" or, to an "ethic of responsibility." This is not to say that an ethic of ultimate ends is identical with irresponsibility, or that an ethic of responsibility is identical with unprincipled opportunism. Naturally nobody says that. However, there is an abysmal contrast between conduct that follows the maxim of an ethic of ultimate ends—that is, in religious terms, "The Christian does rightly and leaves the results with the Lord"—and conduct that follows the maxim of an ethic of responsibility, in which case one has to give an account of the foreseeable results of one's action.

The ethic of ultimate ends apparently must go to pieces on the problem of the justification of means by ends. As a matter of fact, logically it has only the possibility of rejecting all action that employs morally dangerous means—in theory! In the world of realities, as a rule, we encounter the ever-renewed experience that the adherent of an ethic of ultimate ends suddenly turns into a chiliastic prophet. . . . The proponent of an ethic of absolute ends cannot stand up under the ethical irrationality of the world.

THE FRIEDRICH-FINER DEBATE

Several of the issues of responsibility raised by Wilson and Weber were echoed later in an interchange which has come to be known as the Friedrich-Finer debate. Friedrich's position placed much greater emphasis on a public servant's moral responsibility, rather than upon accountability to democratically elected leaders.

PUBLIC POLICY AND THE NATURE OF ADMINISTRATIVE RESPONSIBILITY
CARL JOACHIM FRIEDRICH

It has long been customary to distinguish between policymaking and policy execution. Frank J. Goodnow, in his well-known work, *Politics and Administration*, undertook to build an almost absolute distinction upon this functional difference.

There are, then, in all governmental systems two primary or ultimate functions of government, viz. the expression of the will of the state and the execution of that will. There are also in all states separate organs, each of which is mainly busied with the discharge of one of these functions. These functions are respectively, Politics and Administration.[1]

But while the distinction has a great deal of value as a relative matter of emphasis, it cannot any longer be accepted in this absolute form. . . . The reason for making this distinction an absolute antithesis is probably to be found in building it upon the

Source: Reprinted from *Public Policy* 1 (1940), ed. Carl J. Friedrich and Edward S. Mason, Cambridge, MA: Harvard University Press, Copyright 1940 by the President and Fellows of Harvard College, pp. 5–6, 19–20. Reprinted by permission of the publishers.

metaphysical, if not abstruse, idea of a will of the state. This neo-Hegelian (and Fascist) notion is purely speculative. Even if the concept "state" is retained—and I personally see no good ground for it—the idea that this state has a will immediately entangles one in all the difficulties of assuming a group personality or something akin to it.[2] In other words, a problem which is already complicated enough by itself—that is, how a public policy is adopted and carried out—is bogged down by a vast ideological superstructure which contributes little or nothing to its solution. The concrete patterns of public policy formation and execution reveal that politics and administration are not two mutually exclusive boxes, or absolute distinctions, but that they are two closely linked pieces of the same process. Public policy, to put it flatly, is a continuous process, the formation of which is inseparable from its execution. Public policy is being formed as it is being executed, and it likewise being executed as it is being formed. Politics and administration play a continuous role in both formation and execution, though there is probably more politics in the formation of policy, more administration in the execution of it. Insofar as particular individuals or groups are gaining or losing power or control in a given area, there is politics; insofar as officials act or propose action in the name of public interest, there is administration. . . .

SHALL WE ENFORCE OR ELICIT RESPONSIBLE CONDUCT?

The old-timers who are enamored of strict subserviency undoubtedly will be inclined to argue that the foregoing is very well. But that it depends entirely for its effectiveness upon the goodwill of the administrator, and that as soon as he is indifferent or hostile to such public reactions he can and will discard them. There is unquestionably some truth in this objection. Responsible conduct of administrative functions is not so much enforced as it is elicited. But it has been the contention all along that responsible conduct of administrative functions is never strictly enforceable, that even under the most tyrannical despot administrative officials will escape effective control—in short, that the problem of how to bring about responsible conduct of the administrative staff of a large organization is, particularly in a democratic society, very largely a question of sound work rules and effective morale. As an able student of great practical experience has put it:

> The matter of administrative power commensurate with administrative responsibility, or the administrator's freedom from control, is not, under our system of government, anything absolute or complete: It is a question of degree. . . . Nothing which has been said should be construed to mean that preservation of administrative freedom, initiative and resourcefulness is not an important factor to be considered in organization: quite the contrary, it is one of the major factors.[3]

The whole range of activities involving constant direct contact of the administrator with the public and its problems show that our conception of administrative responsibility is undergoing profound change. The emphasis is shifting; instead of subserviency to arbitrary will we require responsiveness to commonly felt needs and wants. The trend of the creative evolution of American democracy from a negative conception to a positive ideal of social service posits such a transformation. As the range of government services expands, we are all becoming each other's servants in the common endeavor of operating our complex industrial society.

NOTES

1. Frank J. Goodnow, *Politics and Administration* (New York: Macmillan, 1900), p. 22.

2. See Carl J. Friedrich, *Constitutional Government and Politics* (New York: Harper, 1936), pp. 29ff and elsewhere.

3. Lewis Meriam, *Public Personnel Problems* (Washington, DC: Brookings Institution, 1938), p. 340.

ADMINISTRATIVE RESPONSIBILITY IN DEMOCRATIC GOVERNMENT
HERMAN FINER

Are the servants of the public to decide their own course, or is their course of action to be decided by a body outside themselves? My answer is that the servants of the public are not to decide their own course; they are to be responsible to the elected representatives of the public, and these are to determine the course of action of the public servants to the most minute degree that is technically feasible. Both of these propositions are important: the main proposition of responsibility, as well as the limitation and auxiliary institutions implied in the phrase, "that is technically feasible." This kind of responsibility is what democracy means; and though there may be other devices which provide "good" government, I cannot yield on the cardinal issue of democratic government. . . .

Never was the political responsibility of officials so momentous a necessity as in our own era. Moral responsibility is likely to operate in direct proportion to the strictness and efficiency of political responsibility, and to fall away into all sorts of perversions when the latter is weakly enforced. While professional standards, duty to the public, and pursuit of technological efficiency are factors in sound administrative operation, they are but ingredients, and not continuously motivating factors, of sound policy, and they require public and political control and direction. . . .

Source: Herman Finer, "Administrative Responsibility in Democratic Government," *Public Administration Review* 1 (1941), pp. 336–50. Reprinted with permission from the American Society for Public Administration.

Contemporary devices to secure closer cooperation of officials with public and legislatures are properly auxiliaries to and not substitutes for political control of public officials through exertion of the proper sovereign authority of the public. Thus, political responsibility is the major concern of those who work for healthy relationships between the officials and the public, and moral responsibility, although a valuable conception and institutional form, is minor and subsidiary.

ETHICS AND THE PUBLIC SERVICE
STEPHEN K. BAILEY

Stephen K. Bailey (1916–1982), in this memorial essay on Paul Appleby, suggests "optimism, courage, and fairness tempered by justice" as key ethical qualities. Is this, in effect, an "ethics as virtue" argument posed against Appleby's "ethics as responsibility"? Or does it reassert Friedrich's "personal responsibility" position from the Friedrich-Finer debate?

NORMATIVE MODEL FOR PERSONAL ETHICS

[Dean Paul Appleby's] normative model ran something as follows: politics and hierarchy force public servants to refer private and special interests to higher and broader public interests. Politics does this through the discipline of the majority ballot which forces both political executives and legislators to insert a majoritarian calculus into the consideration of private claims. Hierarchy does it by placing in the hands of top officials both the responsibility and the necessity of homogenizing and moralizing the special interests inevitably represented by and through the lower echelons of organizational pyramids.[1] Both politics and hierarchy are devices for assuring accountability to the public as a whole. . . .

Government is moral in so far as it induces public servants to relate the specific to the general, the private to the public, the precise interest to the inchoate moral judgment. Within this context, amoral public decision becomes one in which:

> the action conforms to the processes and symbols thus far developed for the general protection of political freedom as the agent of more general freedom; . . . leaves open the way for modification or reversal by public determination; . . . is taken within a hierarchy of controls in which responsibility for action may be readily identified by the public; . . . and embodies as contributions of leadership the concrete structuring of response to popularly felt needs, and not merely responses to the private and personal needs of leaders.

Source: Stephen K. Bailey, "Ethics and the Public Service," *Public Administration Review* 24:4 (December 1964), 234–243. Reprinted with permission from the American Society for Public Administration.

It is no disparagement of Dean Appleby's contributions to a normative theory of democratic governance to point out that he dealt only intermittently and unsystematically with the moral problems of the individual public servant. The moral system intrigued him far more consistently than the moral actor. . . .

Dean Appleby's fragments suggest that personal ethics in the public service is compounded of mental attitudes and moral qualities. Both ingredients are essential. Virtue without understanding can be quite as disastrous as understanding without virtue.

The three essential mental attitudes are: (1) a recognition of the moral ambiguity of all men and of all public policies; (2) a recognition of the contextual forces which condition moral priorities in the public service; and (3) a recognition of the paradoxes of procedures.

The essential moral qualities of the ethical public servant are: (1) optimism; (2) courage; and (3) fairness tempered by charity.

These mental attitudes and moral qualities are relevant to all public servants in every branch and at every level of government. They are as germane to judges and legislators as they are to executives and administrators. They are as essential to line officers as to staff officers. They apply to state and local officials as well as to national and international officials. They are needed in military, foreign, and other specialized services quite as much as they are needed in the career civil service and among political executives. They, of course, assume the virtue of probity and the institutional checks upon venality, which Dean Appleby has so brilliantly elaborated. They are the generic attitudes and qualities without which big democracy cannot meaningfully survive. . . .

OVERCOMING AMBIGUITY AND PARADOX

Optimism is an inadequate term. It connotes euphoria, and public life deals harshly with the euphoric. But optimism is a better word than realism, for the latter dampens the fires of possibility. Optimism, to paraphrase Emerson, is the capacity to settle with some consistency on the "sunnier side of doubt." It is the quality which enables man to face ambiguity and paradox without becoming immobilized. It is essential to purposive, as distinct from reactive behavior. Hanna Arendt once commented that the essence of politics is natality not mortality. Politics involves creative responses to the shifting conflicts and the gross discomfitures of mankind. Without optimism on the part of the public servants, the political function is incapable of being performed. There is no incentive to create policies to better the condition of mankind if the quality of human life is in fact unviable, and if mankind is in any case unworthy of the trouble.

Optimism has not been the religious, philosophical, or literary mood of the twentieth century. But, in spite of a series of almost cataclysmic absurdities, it has been the prevailing mood of science, education, and politics. It is the mood of the emerging nations; it is the mood of the space technologist; it is the mood of the urban renewer. Government without the leavening of optimistic public servants quickly becomes a cynical game of manipulation, personal aggrandizement, and parasitic security. The ultimate corruption of free government comes not from the hopelessly venal but from the persistently cynical. Institutional decadence has set in when the optimism of leadership becomes a ploy rather than an honest mood and a moral commitment. True optimism is not Mr. Micawber's passive assumption that something will turn up; true optimism is the affirmation of the worth of taking risks. It is not a belief in sure things; it is the capacity to see the possibilities for good in the uncertain, the ambiguous, and the inscrutable. . . .

A CAPACITY FOR IMPERSONALITY AND DECISION

The second essential moral quality needed in the public service is courage. Personal and public life are so shot through with ambiguities and paradoxes that timidity and withdrawal are quite natural and normal responses for those confronted with them. The only three friends of courage in the public service are ambition, a sense of duty, and a recognition that inaction may be quite as painful as action.

Courage in government and politics takes many forms. The late President John F. Kennedy sketched a series of profiles of one type of courage—abiding by principle in an unpopular cause. But most calls upon courage are less insistent and more pervasive. In public administration, for example, courage is needed to insure that degree of impersonality without which friendship oozes into inequities and special favors. Dean Appleby relates a relevant story about George Washington. Washington told a friend seeking an appointment: "You are welcome to my house; you are welcome to my heart . . . my personal feelings have nothing to do with the present case. I am not George Washington, but President of the United States. As George Washington, I would do anything in my power for you. As President, I can do nothing."[2] Normally it takes less courage to deal impersonally with identifiable interest groups than with long standing associates and colleagues upon whom one has depended over the years for affection and for professional and personal support. This is true in relationship to those inside as well as those outside the organization. Part of the loneliness of authority comes from the fact, again in the words of Dean Appleby, that "to a distinctly uncomfortable degree [the administrator] must make work relationships impersonal."[3] Appleby was quick to see that impersonality invites the danger of arrogance, but he also saw that the courage to be impersonal in complicated organizational performance is generally valuable as far as the affected public is concerned. "Its tendency is to systematize fair dealing and to avoid whimsy and discrimination—in other words to provide a kind of administrative due process."[4] . . .

Perhaps the most essential courage in the public service is the courage to decide. For if it is true that all policies have bittersweet consequences, decisions invariably produce hurt. President Eliot of Harvard once felt constrained to say that the prime requisite of an executive was his willingness to give pain. Much buck-passing in public life is the prudent consequence of the need for multiple clearances in large and complex institutions. But buck-passing which stems from lack of moral courage is the enemy of efficient and responsible government. The inner satisfactions which come from the courage to decide are substantial; but so are the slings and arrows which are invariably let loose by those who are aggrieved by each separate decision. The issues become especially acute in personnel decisions. Courage to fire, to demote, to withhold advancement, or to shift assignments against the wishes of the person involved, is often the courage most needed and the most difficult to raise.

MAN'S SENSE OF INJUSTICE

The third and perhaps most essential moral quality needed in the public service is fairness tempered by charity. The courage to be impersonal and disinterested is of no value unless it results in just and charitable actions and attitudes. Government in a free society is the authoritative allocator of values in terms of partly ineffable standards of justice and the public zeal. It requires the approximation of moving targets partly camouflaged by the shadows of an unknowable future. The success or failure of policies bravely conceived to meet particular social evils is more frequently obscured than clarified by the passage of time. . . . Justice was the only positive heritage of the Roman World. The establishment of justice follows directly behind the formation of union itself in the Preamble to the American Constitution.

But the moral imperative to be just—to be fair—is a limited virtue without charity. Absolute justice presupposes omniscience and total disinterestedness. Public servants are always faced with making decisions based upon both imperfect information and the inarticulate insinuations of self-interest into the decisional calculus. Charity is the virtue that compensates for inadequate information and for the subtle importunities of self in the making of judgments designed to be fair. Charity is not a soft virtue. To the contrary, it involves the ultimate moral toughness. For its exercise involves the disciplining of self and the sublimation of persistent inner claims for personal recognition, power, and status. It is the principle above principle. . . .

NOTES

1. The intellectual as distinct from the moral implications of hierarchy have been suggested by Kenneth Underwood in his contention that "The policy-making executive is to be distinguished from the middle management-supervisor levels most basically in the excessively cognitive, abstract dimensions of his work." See his paper "The New Ethic of Personal and Corporate Responsibility," presented at the Third Centennial Symposium on *The Responsible Individual*, April 8, 1964, University of Denver.

2. Paul H. Appleby, *Morality and Administration in Democratic Government* (Baton Rouge: Louisiana State University Press, 1952), p. 130.

3. Op. cit., p. 221.
4. Op. cit., p. 149.

— —

ACCOUNTABILITY AND ABUSES OF POWER IN WORLD POLITICS
Ruth W. Grant and Robert O. Keohane

This article urges rethinking of the usual idea of nation-state accountability to pro-vide a stronger understanding of global accountability particularly in the absence of democracy in many nations. Grant & Keohane suggest mechanisms that draw on "participation" and "delegation" models of accountability. Are these helpful when ex-amining accountability in countries with little or no democratic system?

Accountability, as we use the term, implies that some actors have the right to hold other actors to a set of standards, to judge whether they have fulfilled their respon-sibilities in light of these standards, and to impose sanctions if they determine that these responsibilities have not been met. Accountability presupposes a relationship between power-wielders and those holding them accountable where there is a gen-eral recognition of the legitimacy of (1) the operative standards for accountability and (2) the authority of the parties to the relationship (one to exercise particular powers and the other to hold them to account). The concept of accountability im-plies that the actors being held accountable have obligations to act in ways that are consistent with accepted standards of behavior and that they will be sanctioned for failures to do so.

Thus, not all constraints on abuses of power in world politics constitute mech-anisms of accountability. Unilateral uses of force, though they are often described as "holding someone accountable," do not qualify as accountability mechanisms in our sense. In the classical, European balance of power system, . . . the principal mecha-nism of constraint was ultimately coercion or the threat of coercion. States were the exclusive sources of legitimate authority, and, though they could legally bind them-selves through international treaties, if treaties were broken, states had to resort to self-help to assert their rights. States in a balance of power system are not "held ac-countable" in any meaningful sense, although they may be constrained by coercion or the threat thereof. Similarly, the economic interdependence of states creates con-straints, but states that are bargaining for advantage on economic issues are not nec-essarily held accountable to one another. States in the nineteenth century engaged in bilateral tariff negotiations, confronting limits on their ability to achieve their objec-tives. But since they had undertaken no prior obligations by joining multilateral in-stitutions, there was no accountability process involved.

Source: Ruth W. Grant and Robert O. Keohane, "Accountability and Abuses of Power in World Poli-tics," *American Political Science Review* 99, no. 1 (February 2005), pp. 29–45. Selection is from pp. 29–30, 35–37. Reprinted with the permission of Cambridge University Press.

There is another important mode of constraining the powerful that must be distinguished from accountability. "Checks and balances" are mechanisms designed to *prevent* action that oversteps legitimate boundaries by requiring the cooperation of actors with different institutional interests to produce an authoritative decision. Accountability mechanisms, on the other hand, always operate after the fact: exposing actions to view, judging and sanctioning them. The executive veto power in the U.S. Constitution is part of a system of checks and balances. The impeachment power is an accountability mechanism. Of course, though they always operate *ex post*, accountability mechanisms can exert effects *ex ante*, since the anticipation of sanctions may deter the powerful from abusing their positions in the first place.

SEVEN ACCOUNTABILITY MECHANISMS

[The] question, "Who is entitled to hold power-wielders accountable for abuses?" receives a variety of answers in the practice of global politics. We have identified seven discrete accountability mechanisms that actually operate in world politics on the basis of which improved practices of accountability could be built. . . . Some operate most effectively when standards of legitimacy are formally encoded in law; others enforce less formal norms. Four of these mechanisms rely heavily on delegation: hierarchical, supervisory, fiscal, and legal accountability. The remaining three—market, peer, and reputational accountability—involve forms of participation, although the participants in each of these forms of accountability are different. It should be noted that these categories should not be too rigidly applied: Legal accountability, for example, involves a participatory element in any legal system that allows citizens to sue powerful entities for failures of responsibility.

Hierarchical accountability is a characteristic of bureaucracies and of virtually any large organization. Superiors can remove subordinates from office, constrain their tasks and room for discretion, and adjust their financial compensation. Hierarchical accountability as we use the term applies to relationships within organizations, including multilateral organizations such as the United Nations or the World Bank.

Supervisory accountability refers to relations between organizations where one organization acts as principal with respect to specified agents. For instance, the World Bank and IMF are subject to supervision by states and by institutions within states, such as courts. These supervisory relationships are more or less democratic as states are more or less democratic. Indeed, courts in democracies could demand that international organizations such as the IMF and World Bank follow procedures that meet due process standards of international law (Stewart 2003, p. 459). Advocacy groups within states can put pressure on such organizations as the IMF and World Bank through domestic political institutions, as environmentalists did with respect to World Bank loans for dam projects in the1980s (Fox and Brown 1998). Firms also hold state agencies accountable, through the political process, for their policies in international organizations, such as the WTO, whose decisions are relevant to the firms' interests.

Fiscal accountability describes mechanisms through which funding agencies can demand reports from, and ultimately sanction, agencies that are recipients of funding. This form of accountability was fundamental to the emergence of parliamentary power in England during the seventeenth century and is particularly important for international organizations such as the United Nations and the World Bank, which rely on government appropriations to fund substantial parts of their activities.

Legal accountability refers to the requirement that agents abide by formal rules and be prepared to justify their actions in those terms, in courts or quasi-judicial arenas. Public officials, like anyone else, can be "held accountable" for their actions both through administrative and criminal law. Courts do not have the broad general authority of governments or of electorates in democracies. Instead, the courts apply a narrow version of the trusteeship model . . . , asking whether the power-wielders performed the duties of their offices faithfully in a limited sense: whether they obeyed the law. Legal accountability has long been important in constitutional democracies and has become increasingly important in world politics during recent years (Goldstein et al. 2001). The WTO Dispute Settlement Mechanism, the operations of the Hague Tribunal on the Former Yugoslavia, and the creation of a new International Criminal Court all illustrate the incursions that conceptions of legal accountability have made in world politics.

Market accountability is a less familiar category, but an important one. We want to emphasize that this form of accountability is not to an abstract force called "the market," but to investors and consumers, whose influence is exercised in whole or in part through markets. Investors may stop investing in countries whose policies they dislike or, at least, demand higher rates of interest (Mosley 2003). Consumers may refuse to buy products from companies with bad reputations for labor standards or other practices, as well as from companies with inferior or costly products.

Peer accountability arises as the result of mutual evaluation of organizations by their counterparts. NGOs, for example, evaluate the quality of information they receive from other NGOs and the ease of cooperating with them. Organizations that are poorly rated by their peers are likely to have difficulty in persuading them to cooperate and, therefore, to have trouble achieving their own purposes.

Public reputational accountability is pervasive because reputation is involved in all the other forms of accountability. Superiors, supervisory boards, courts, fiscal watchdogs, markets, and peers all take the reputations of agents into account. Indeed, reputation is a form of "soft power," defined as "the ability to shape the preferences of others" (Nye 2004, 5). The category of public reputational accountability is meant to apply to situations in which reputation, widely and publicly known, provides a mechanism for accountability even in the absence of other mechanisms as well as in conjunction with them.

There are also processes that do not meet the standards for accountability but that serve to constrain power. As in a system of checks and balances, overlapping jurisdictions or interest areas may require actors to compromise with one another to secure the cooperation necessary to define or implement policy. Such a situation is characterized by *negotiation constraints.* Since our ultimate goal is to provide greater restraints on the abuse of power, negotiation constraints are properly included in this analysis, though they are not accountability mechanisms. . . .

REFERENCES

Fox, Jonathan A., and L. David Brown, eds. 1998. *The Struggle for Accountability: The World Bank, NGOs and Grassroots Movements.* Cambridge, MA: MIT Press.

Goldstein, Judith, et al. 2001. *Legalization and World Politics.* Cambridge, MA: MIT Press.

Mosley, Layna. 2003. *Global Capital and National Governments.* Cambridge, MA: Cambridge University Press.

Nye, Joseph S. 2004. *Soft Power: The Means to Success in World Politics.* New York: Public Affairs Press.

Stewart, Richard. 2003. "Administrative Law in the Twenty-First Century," *New York University Law Review* 78, no. 2.

CASE 2: FOLLOWING ORDERS

My office provides benefits to welfare recipients, some of whom are not always able to document their needs as fully as they should. In the past, we have generally been accepting a client's assurances if we felt that the person was telling us the truth (that is, if we had no reason to doubt his or her veracity). We have thus far had no instances, as far as we know, of fraud or lying using this procedure.

The new director of our agency, however, has recently urged us to be much more stringent in requiring documentation from possible clients. I suspect that she has done so as part of a general movement in the state to reduce the welfare rolls.

I am concerned that several deserving people are going to be hurt by our imposing stricter requirements. I don't think that confronting my agency director would do any good. I could probably get by doing what we have been doing, if I am careful about it, but I have the feeling I might be running some personal risk in doing so.

What should I do? Do I have an obligation to follow orders even if I think they will have harmful consequences? On the other hand, do I have a right to substitute my notions of justice and fair play for the directions coming to our office from the state government?

CHAPTER DISCUSSION QUESTIONS

1. What ethical issues arise from the roles people play *in organizations*? Do the concepts of responsibility and accountability adequately represent these issues? How well do responsibility and accountability "fit" with the earlier-considered concepts of virtue, principle, and consequence?

Source: Eileen Houltberg and William L. Richter, Kansas State University.

2. If you were trying to fit responsibility and accountability into the "ethics triangle" discussed in the previous chapter, would it become an "ethics quadrangle" or some other geometric figure?

3. Should responsibility and accountability be different in different cultures? If so, how?

4. What happens when organizational responsibilities conflict with personal ethical positions? Have you experienced this in your own work? If so, how have you dealt with the conflict?

FOR FURTHER EXPLORATION

Behn, Robert D. *Rethinking Democratic Accountability.* Washington, DC: Brookings Institution Press, 2001.

Brenkert, George G., ed. *Corporate Integrity & Accountability.* Thousand Oaks, CA: Sage, 2004.

Burke, John P. *Bureaucratic Responsibility.* Baltimore and London: Johns Hopkins University Press, 1986.

Cooper, Terry L., *The Responsible Administrator: An Approach to Ethics for the Administrative Role,* 4th edition. San Francisco, CA: Jossey-Bass Publishers, 1998.

Ingraham, Patricia Wallace. "'You Talking to Me?' Accountability and the Modern Public Service," *PS: Political Science and Politics* 38, no. 1 (January 2005), pp. 17–21.

Jabbra, Joseph G., and O. P. Dwivedi, *Public Service Accountability: A Comparative Perspective.* West Hartford, CT: Kumarian Press, 1988.

Kearns, Kevin P. *Managing for Accountability: Preserving the Public Trust in Public and Nonprofit Organizations.* San Francisco: Jossey-Bass, 1996.

Kernaghan, Kenneth, and John W. Langford. *The Responsible Public Servant.* Halifax, Nova Scotia: Institute for Research on Public Policy, Institute of Public Administration of Canada, 1991.

Michael, Bryane. "Questioning Public Sector Accountability," *Public Integrity* 7, no. 2 (Spring 2005), pp. 95–109.

Van Wart, Montgomery. "Codes of Ethics as Living Documents: The Case of the American Society for Public Administration," *Public Integrity* 5, no. 4 (Fall 2003), pp. 331–46.

WEBSITES

AccountAbility (Institute of Social and Ethical Accountability), www.accountability.org.uk

Florida Government Accountability Report, www.oppaga.state.fl.us/government

Governmental Accountability Project (GAP), www.whistleblower.org

Government Accountability Project (Mercatus Center, George Mason University), www.mercatus.org/governmentaccountability

U.S. Government Accountability Office, www.gao.gov

Chapter 3

TWENTY-FIRST CENTURY CHALLENGES: GLOBAL DIMENSIONS/ CHANGING BOUNDARIES

THE NEW PUBLIC ADMINISTRATOR
GLENN L. STARKS

American public administrators in the twenty-first century work in an environment that has seen, in the previous decade or so, massive government downsizing coupled with extensive federal employee retirements. Starks provides an eight-point dynamic strategy to cope with the dramatically changing work environment. The changes he describes are characteristic of many other countries. Are his prescriptions enough? Are there ethical strategies that would ease the rigors of dramatic change?

The federal public administrators of the twenty-first century can no longer rely on the same staples of management their predecessors employed. Obstacles of the past two decades have created an atmosphere where today's administrators must employ dynamic strategies in order to meet their agencies' missions, which are growing ever more varied and complex. Some of these obstacles have included continual downsizing, growing levels of employee turnover, a pending mass exodus of retiring employees, and the inability of agencies to attract young employees to replace these generations of experience, knowledge, and skills. The administrators of the 1960s and 1970s never saw these obstacles coming, and some agencies have found themselves ill equipped to proactively deal with them. Instead, they are reactively developing strategies to cope, and often ill effectively. . . .

THE AGE OF CHANGE

The 1990s was the decade of government downsizing; the federal workforce was reduced by an average of 2.4 percent per year from 1991 through 2000. While agencies were making efforts to make the government leaner in terms of employment

---

Source: Glenn L. Starks, "The New Public Administrator," *The Public Manager* 33:2 (Fall 2004), pp. 17–21. Reprinted with the permission of *The Public Manager.*

levels, dual efforts were not being employed to ensure a highly skilled workforce was being maintained. Nor were efforts being made to develop strategies to fill future vacancies with highly skilled employees.

The efforts of the National Performance Review (NPR) in the 1990s transformed the federal government into a leaner entity, but not a more efficient one. Under the NPR, federal agencies were mandated to make cuts in personnel, but were not mandated to develop strategies to meet the dynamic challenges of serving the interests of its customers, the American people. Tom Shoop (1994) reported that the NPR's efforts were less of a reform movement and more of a movement just to eliminate jobs. He reported:

> Last October (1993), when Administration officials trooped to Capitol Hill to try to sell the NPR's initial round of legislative proposals, they talked less about systems reform and more about getting rid of twelve percent of the government's civilian employees—252,000 jobs—by cutting layers of management. . . .
>
> On September 11 (1993), shortly after the NPR report was released, Clinton sent all agency heads a memo telling them to prepare streamlining plans by December 1, "consistent with the National Performance Review's recommendation to reduce the executive branch civilian workforce by 252,000."

GAO CONCLUSIONS

The General Accounting Office (2001) concluded the following in reviewing the effects of downsizing efforts on the federal workforce:

> Today's non-postal civilian federal workforce is smaller than it was a decade ago. The federal workforce was reduced from approximately 2.3 million federal employees in fiscal year 1990 to fewer than 1.9 million by fiscal year 1999. At the same time, federal outlays grew from $1.5 trillion in fiscal year 1990 to $1.7 trillion in fiscal year 1999. But what happened—or more importantly, did not happen—as this downsizing was being accomplished was just as significant as the downsizing itself. For example, initial rounds of the downsizing were set in motion without sufficient planning relating to the longer term effects on agencies' performance capacity. At the same time, the federal government reduced permanent new hires from 118,000 in fiscal year 1990 to about 74,000 in fiscal year 1999. A number of individual agencies drastically reduced or froze their hiring efforts for extended periods. This helped reduce the size of agencies' workforces, but it also reduced the influx of new people with new skills, new knowledge, new energy, and new ideas-the reservoir of future agency leaders and managers.

Coupled with the downsizing of the workforce was growing employee turnover. In cabinet-level departments in 1996, 1998, and 2000, the number of new hires to federal service (492,815) was exceeded by the number of employees separating

(564,131) in all three years. The majority of those separating were quitting, and the majority of those quitting were under 40 years of age. The primary reason is that young employees today want more. They want the higher salaries, greater promotion opportunities, and the mobility offered in the private sector. Stephen Barr (2000) reported on the generation gap of recent college graduates compared with those prior to the 1970s. He stated,

> The federal workforce entrants in the 1930s became experts at interpreting and enforcing a series of laws that expanded the influence of government. Most of them retired in the 1960s. They were followed by a new crop of civil servants inspired by John F. Kennedy's New Frontier and Lyndon B. Johnson's War on Poverty. Now it is their turn to depart. Many of them took to government for lifelong careers.

Barr referenced statements from federal personnel experts in stating that (today)

> many talented young people do not see the government offering what they want: high starting pay, training that gives them an edge, a casual work environment and high-impact assignments.

The future of the federal government looks even bleaker when analyzing pending retirements. In 1999, 15 percent of the federal workforce was eligible for retirement, compared with only 8 percent in 1989. Over the next five to ten years, 50 percent of the federal workforce will either have retired or be eligible for retirement. A report excerpt from the Subcommittee on Oversight of Government Management, Restructuring, and the District of Columbia (Voinovich 2000) illustrates the future of the federal workforce:

> Today, the average Federal employee is 45 years old and more than half the workforce is between 45 and 69 years old. By 2004, 32 percent of the Federal workforce will be eligible for regular retirement, and an additional 21 percent will be eligible for early retirement.

Senator Voinovich does not expect them all to rush for the exit at once. Nevertheless, it is fair to assume that by 2010, at least 500,000 employees will have retired, taking with them valuable and perhaps irreplaceable institutional knowledge, which threatens to leave the government with an inexperienced and ineffective workforce. The government must develop a comprehensive plan to address the problem. . . .

STRATEGIES FOR EFFECTIVE ADMINISTRATION

In the face of all these obstacles is the pressure for administrators within the federal government to become more innovative and efficient in meeting the missions of their respective organizations. The following eight recommendations are critical considerations for effective and efficient public administrators. . . .

1. Act Like a Business

Public administrators that do not employ private-sector business practices in today's environment of outsourcing will find themselves replaced. Private contractors have assumed an array of historically government roles, from supporting troops on the front line to awarding government contracts to even administering government contracts. In addition, many agencies cannot rely on congressional budget allocations. For example, the Defense Logistics Agency's annual budget is based upon retaining a percentage of its annual sales from the prior year. If sales are not generated to meet its budgetary needs, the agency must reduce manpower or make financial reductions in some other areas. The primary area of targeted budget cuts would be in personnel reductions. Many government agencies are also competing with the private sector to retain their customers. Within the Department of Defense, weapon system program managers are awarding full service and parts contracts to private companies instead of relying on support from within the government. For example, the Navy awarded a multimillion-dollar contract to Boeing for full support of the F/A-18 E and F models of aircraft. Historically this support would have come from within the Navy, the Defense Logistics Agency, and other federal agencies.

2. Manage the Whole Person

Public administrators manage a diverse workforce. Their workforces have varied cultural backgrounds, interests, and experiences. They also comprise personnel from various age groups, ranging from Generation Xers to the GI Generation. Administrators cannot apply the same managerial approach to all employees. They must recognize the uniqueness of each person and capitalize on the ability of each individual to provide unique viewpoints and inputs to problems.

Administrators must also recognize the importance of managing the whole person. Employees carry problems from work into their personal lives, and bring personal problems into their professional lives. While employees are expected to maintain a certain degree of professionalism at all times, administrators cannot ignore the effects of employees' personal lives at work. . . .

3. Empower Employees

Effective administrators allow their employees to make decisions and have input into major decisions. Empowering employees also requires listening to them, giving them room to develop teamwork, using their ideas, and sharing the credit. While this may be especially difficult in an era of e-mail and teleworking, administrators cannot ignore the importance of empowerment coupled with personal communication.

4. Expect More Out of Employees

As the federal workforce gets smaller, existing employees must be expected to perform more efficiently, take on more responsibility, and be much more accountable with less supervision. In order to deal with these challenges, however, employees must be offered training and incentives. Behavior modification that results in a more efficient employee results from a combination of training and rewards. . . .

5. Avoid Politics

Many administrators have been trained to believe they must engage in politics in order to advance in their careers. They are told how important it is to never question top management decisions, become a team player at all costs, and gain top management favor through schmoozing. Administrators who blindly follow top management without question and devote more time to organizational politics than hard work will only hurt their organizations. A prime example of this occurred in a leading Defense agency. Administrators never questioned the decisions of their commander, who was a military officer stationed to the agency for two years. When the commander left the agency, administrators spent the next decade overcoming the negative repercussions of the commander's two years of command. These repercussions included a loss of employee morale, suppliers who doubted the agency's integrity, and customers who doubted the agency's ability to meet their demands.

6. Become Educated

While it is important to take advantage of all the training opportunities offered by an organization, it is equally important to gain training from outside sources. Mentor programs, on-the-job training, and leadership programs offered by federal agencies provide excellent opportunities for their employees to gain extensive knowledge on how the organization functions. They are often major contributors to career advancement. However, these programs often do not expand the knowledge of employees to make them more competitive with employees from other federal organizations and the private sector. Thus, the organization is not more competitive and efficient. Outside training, particularly from accredited universities and certified private companies that provide professional training, enable employees to continually sharpen their skills, and stay abreast of current business practices and technologies. . . .

7. Remember for Whom You Work

Federal administrators should always remember for whom they are ultimately working, the taxpayer. As an administrator, always remember the taxpayers struggling to make a living to support their families who are trusting federal agencies to be efficient and effective. While this trust was once blind, today federal agencies are closely scrutinized by the media, lobbyists, and better-educated taxpayers. . . .

8. Be a Manager and a Leader

Federal administrators today are expected to also be effective managers and leaders. They must independently set tactical and strategic goals to meet the missions of their agencies, be responsible and accountable, be able to access the organization and make the most of what is available, and be able to prove their value in the organization. Federal administrators must display and exude the same capabilities expected of private sector managers.

REFERENCES

Barr, Stephen. "Retirement Wave Creates Vacuum." *The Washington Post*, A-01, May 7, 2000.
Shoop, Tom. "Targeting Middle Managers." *Government Executive*, January 1994.
U.S. General Accounting Office. *Major Management Challenges and Program Risks: Department of Defense*. Performance and Accountability Series, January 2001.
Voinovich, George V. *Report to the President: The Crisis in Human Capital*. Chairman: Subcommittee on Oversight of Government Management, Restructuring, and the District of Columbia, December 2000.

MEGAPROJECTS AND RISK
Bent B. Flyvbjerg, Nils Bruzelius, and Werner Rothengatter

The sheer magnitude of public-funded infrastructure projects world-wide creates not only engineering challenges, but also projects ethical conundrums. What difference will "the end of geography," "the death of distance," or "frictionless capitalism" make in management operations? Are unethical, wasteful, abusive, and corrupt practices a "natural" part of megaproject operations?

A NEW ANIMAL

Wherever we go in the world, we are confronted with a new political and physical animal: the multibillion-dollar mega infrastructure project. In Europe we have the

Source: Bent Flyvbjerg, Nils Bruzelius, and Werner Rothengatter, *Megaprojects and Risk: An Anatomy of Ambition* (Cambridge: Cambridge University Press, 2003), pp. 1–5. Reprinted with the permission of Cambridge University Press.

Channel tunnel; the Øresund bridge between Denmark and Sweden; the Vasco da Gama bridge in Portugal; the German MAGLEV train between Berlin and Hamburg; the creation of an interconnected high-speed rail network for all of Europe; cross-national motorway systems; the Alps tunnels; the fixed link across the Baltic Sea between Germany and Denmark; plans for airports to become gateways to Europe; enormous investments in new freight container harbors; DM 200 billion worth of transport infrastructure projects related to German unification alone; links across the straits of Gibraltar and Messina; and the world's longest road tunnel in Norway—not to speak of new and extended telecommunications networks; systems of cross-border pipelines for transport of oil and gas; and cross-national electrical power networks to meet the growing demand in an emerging European energy market. It seems as if every country—and pair of neighboring countries—is in the business of promoting this new animal, the megaproject, on the European policy-making scene. And the European Union, with its grand scheme for creating so-called Trans-European Networks, is an ardent supporter and even initiator of such projects, just as it is the driving force in creating the regulatory, and deregulatory regimes that are meant to make the projects viable.[1]

The situation is similar in industrialized and industrializing countries in other parts of the world, from Asia to the Americas. There are, for example, Hong Kong's Chek Lap Kok airport; China's Quinling tunnel; the Akashi Kaikyo Bridge in Japan; Sydney's harbor tunnel; Malaysia's North-South Expressway; Thailand's Second Stage Expressway; and proposals for an integrated Eurasian transport network. In the Americas there are Boston's Big Dig; freeways and railways in California; Denver's new international airport; Canada's Confederation Bridge; Sao Paulo-Buenos Aires Superhighway; the Bi-Oceanic highway right across South America from the Atlantic to the Pacific; and the Venezuela-Brazil highway. Even a proposed US $50 billion project to link the USA and Russia across the Bering Strait—the "biggest project in history" according to its promoters—is not missing in the megaproject scheme of things.[2] Outside the field of transport infrastructure there are the Three Gorges Dam in China; Russia's natural gas pipelines; the Pergau Dam in Malaysia; flood control in Bangladesh; the Bolivia-Brazil gas pipeline; the Venezuela-Brazil power line; and, again and everywhere, the ultimate megaproject, the Internet with associated infrastructure and telecommunications projects.

ZERO-FRICTION SOCIETY

Megaprojects form part of a remarkably coherent story. Sociologist Zygmunt Bauman perceptively calls it the "great war of independence from space," and he sees the resulting new mobility as the most powerful and most coveted stratifying factor in contemporary society.[3] Paul Virilio speaks of the "end of geography" while others talk of the "death of distance."[4] Bill Gates, founder and chair of Microsoft Corporation, has dubbed the phenomenon "frictionless capitalism" and sees it as a novel stage in capitalist evolution.[5] When Microsoft and Gates single out a concept or a product, one is well advised to pay attention. "Frictionless society" may sound like an advertiser's slogan in the context of its usage. It is not. The term signifies a qualitatively different stage of social and economic development.

In this development, "infrastructure" has become a catchword on par with "technology." Infrastructure has rapidly moved from being a simple precondition for production and consumption to being at the very core of these activities, with just-in-time delivery and instant Internet access being two spectacular examples of this. Infrastructure is the great space shrinker, and power, wealth, and status increasingly belong to those who know how to shrink space, or know how to benefit from space being shrunk.[6]

Today infrastructure plays a key role in nothing less than the creation of what many see as a new world order where people, goods, energy, information and money move about with unprecedented ease. Here the politics of distance is the elimination of distance. The name of it is Zero-Friction Society. And even if we can never achieve utopian frictionlessness, we may get close, as is currently happening with the spread of the Internet. Modern humans clearly have a preference for independence from space and are consistently undercutting the friction of distance by building more and improved infrastructure for transport, including telecommunications and energy.

Megaprojects are central to the new politics of distance because infrastructure is increasingly being built as megaprojects. Thus the past decade has seen a sharp increase in the magnitude and frequency of major infrastructure projects, supported by a mixture of national and supranational government, private capital and development banks.

PERFORMANCE PARADOX

There is a paradox here, however. At the same time as many more and much larger infrastructure projects are being proposed and built around the world, it is becoming clear that many such projects have strikingly poor performance records in terms of economy, environment, and public support.[7] Cost overruns and lower-than-predicted revenues frequently place project viability at risk and redefine projects that were initially promoted as effective vehicles to economic growth as possible obstacles to such growth. The Channel tunnel, opened in 1994 at a construction cost of £4.7 billion, is a case in point, with several near-bankruptcies caused by construction cost overruns of 80 percent, financing costs that are 140 percent higher than those forecast and revenues less than half of those projected. . . . The cost overrun for Denver's US $5 billion new international airport, opened in 1995, was close to 200 percent and passenger traffic in the opening year was only half of that projected. Operating problems with Hong Kong's new US $20 billion Chek Lap Kok airport, which opened in 1998, initially caused havoc not only to costs and revenues at the airport; the problems spread to the Hong Kong economy as such with negative effects on growth in gross domestic product.[8] After nine months of operations, *The Economist* dubbed the airport a "fiasco," said to have cost the Hong Kong economy US $600 million.[9] The fiasco may have been only a start-up problem, albeit an expensive one, but it is the typical expense that is rarely taken into account when planning megaprojects.

Some may argue that in the long term cost overruns do not really matter and that most monumental projects that excite the world's imagination had large overruns. This line of argument is too facile, however. The physical and economic scale of today's megaprojects is such that whole nations may be affected in both the medium and long term by the success or failure of just a single project. As observed by Edward Merrow in a RAND study of megaprojects:

> Such enormous sums of money ride on the success of megaprojects that company balance sheets and even government balance-of-payments accounts can be affected for years by the outcomes. . . . The success of these projects is so important to their sponsors that firms and even governments can collapse when they fail.[10]

Even for a large country such as China, analysts warn that the economic ramifications of an individual megaproject such as the Three Gorges Dam "could likely hinder the economic viability of the country as a whole."[11] Stated in more general terms, the Oxford-based Major Projects Association, an organization of contractors, consultants, banks and others interested in megaproject development, in a recent publication speaks of the "calamitous history of previous cost overruns of very large projects in the public sector." In another study sponsored by the Association the conclusion is, "too many projects proceed that should not have [been] done."[12] We would add to this that regarding cost overruns there is no indication that the calamity identified by the Major Projects Association is limited to the public sector. Private sector cost overruns are also common.

For environmental and social effects of projects, one similarly finds that such effects often have not been taken into account during project development, or they have been severely miscalculated.[13] In Scandinavia, promoters of the Øresund and Great Belt links at first tried to ignore or downplay environmental issues, but were eventually forced by environmental groups and public protest to accept such issues on the decision-making agenda. . . . In Germany, high-speed rail projects have been criticized for not considering environmental disruption. Dams are routinely criticized for the same thing. However, environmental problems that are not taken into account during project preparation tend to surface during construction and operations; and such problems often destabilize habitats, communities, and megaprojects themselves, if not dealt with carefully. Moreover, positive regional development effects, typically much touted by project promoters to gain political acceptance for their projects, repeatedly turn out to be non-measurable, insignificant or even negative. . . .

In consequence, the cost-benefit analyses, financial analyses, and environmental and social impact statements that are routinely carried out as part of megaproject preparation are called into question, criticized, and denounced more often and more dramatically than analyses in any other professional field we know. Megaproject development today is not a field of what has been called "honest numbers."[14] It is a field where you will see one group of professionals calling the work of another not only "biased" and "seriously flawed" but a "grave embarrassment" to the profession.[15] And that is when things have not yet turned unfriendly. In more antagonistic situations the words used in the mud-slinging accompanying many megaprojects are "deception," "manipulation," and even "lies" and "prostitution."[16] Whether we like it or not, megaproject development is currently a field where little can be trusted, not even— some would say especially not—numbers produced by analysts.

Finally, project promoters often avoid and violate established practices of good governance, transparency, and participation in political and administrative decision-making, either out of ignorance or because they see such practices as counterproductive to getting projects started. Civil society does not have the same say in this arena of public life as it does in others; citizens are typically kept at a substantial distance from megaproject decision-making. In some countries this state of affairs may be slowly changing, but so far megaprojects often come draped in a politics of mistrust. People fear that the political inequality in access to decision-making processes will lead to an unequal distribution of risks, burdens, and benefits from projects.[17] The general public is often skeptical or negative towards projects; citizens and interest groups orchestrate hostile protests; and occasionally secret underground groups even encourage or carry out downright sabotage on projects, though this is not much talked about in public for fear of inciting others to similar guerrilla activities.[18] Scandinavians, who like other people around the world have experienced the construction of one megaproject after another during the past decade, have coined a term to describe the lack in megaproject decision-making of accustomed transparency and involvement of civil society: "democracy deficit." The fact that a special term has come into popular usage to describe what is going on in megaproject decision-making is indicative of the extent to which large groups in the population see the current state of affairs as unsatisfactory.

NOTES

1. On the role of the European Union as a promoter of megaprojects, see John F. L. Ross, *Linking Europe: Transport Policies and Politics in the European Union* (Westport, CT: Praeger Publishers, 1998). See also OECD, *Infrastructure Policies for the 1990s* (Paris: OECD, 1993); and

Roger W. Vickerman, "Transport Infrastructure and Region Building in the European Community," *Journal of Common Market Studies*, vol. 32, no. 1, March 1994, pp. 1–24.

2. *The Economist*, 19 August 1995, p. 84.

3. Zygmunt Bauman, *Globalization: The Human Consequences* (Cambridge: Polity Press, 1998); here quoted from Bauman, "Time and Class: New Dimensions of Stratification," *Sociologisk Rapportserie*, no. 7, Department of Sociology, University of Copenhagen, 1998, pp. 2–3.

4. Paul Virilio, "Un monde surexposé: fin de l'histoire, ou fin de la geographie?," in *Le Monde Diplomatique,* vol. 44, no. 521, August 1997, p. 17, here quoted from Bauman "Time and Class." According to Bauman, the idea of the "end of geography" was first advanced by Richard O'Brien, in *Global Financial Integration: The End of Geography* (London: Chatham House/Pinter, 1992). See Frances Cairncross, *The Death of Distance: How the Communications Revolution Will Change Our Lives* (Boston, MA: Harvard Business School Press, 1997). See also Linda McDowell, ed., *Undoing Place? A Geographical Reader* (London: Arnold, 1997).

5. *Time,* 3 August 1998.

6. Although dams are not part of transport and communication infrastructure as such, we consider the building of dams to be part of the war of independence from space. Dams typically involve the production of electricity and electricity is one of the most effective ways of freeing industry from localized sources of energy and thus for making industry "footloose," that is, independent from space.

7. Peter W. G. Morris and George H. Hough, *The Anatomy of Major Projects: A Study of the Reality of Project Management* (New York: John Wiley & Sons, 1987); Mads Christoffersen, Bent Flyvbjerg, and Jørgen Lindgaard Pedersen, "The Lack of Technology Assessment in Relation to Big Infrastructural Decisions," in *Technology and Democracy: The Use and Impact of Technology Assessment in Europe. Proceedings from the 3rd European Congress on Technology Assessment*, vol. I, Copenhagen: n. p., 4–7 November 1992, pp. 54–75; David Collingridge, *The Management of Scale: Big Organizations, Big Decisions, Big Mistakes* (London: Routledge, 1992); Joseph S. Szyliowicz and Andrew R. Goetz, "Getting Realistic About Megaproject Planning: The Case of the New Denver International Airport," *Policy Sciences,* vol. 28, no. 4, 1995, pp. 347–67; Mark Bovens and Paul Hart, *Understanding Policy Fiascoes* (New Brunswick, NJ: Transaction Publishers, 1996); Peter Hall, "Great Planning Disasters Revisited," paper, Bartlett School, London, undated.

8. CNN, *Financial News,* 16 July 1998. . . . See also Elinor Ostrom, Larry Schroeder, and Susan Wynne, *Institutional Incentives and Sustainable Development: Infrastructure Policies in Perspective* (Boulder, CO: Westview Press, 1993).

9. *The Economist,* 28 August 1999, p. 47.

10. Edward W. Merrow, *Understanding the Outcomes of Megaprojects: A Quantitative Analysis of Very Large Civilian Projects* (Santa Monica, CA: RAND Corporation, 1988), pp. 2–3.

11. Joanna Gail Salazar, "Damning the Child of the Ocean: The Three Gorges Project," *Journal of Environment and Development,* vol. 9, no. 2, June 2000, p. 173.

12. Major Projects Association, *Beyond 2000: A Source Book for Major Projects* (Oxford: Major Projects Association, 1994), p. 172; Morris and Hough, *The Anatomy of Major Projects,* p. 214.

13. Ralf C. Buckley, "How Accurate Are Environmental Impact Predictions?" *Ambio,* vol. 20, nos. 3–4, 1993.

14. Walter Williams, *Honest Numbers and Democracy* (Washington, DC: Georgetown University Press, 1998).

15. Paul C. Huszar, "Overestimated Benefits and Underestimated Costs: The Case of the Paraguay-Paraná Navigation Study," *Impact Assessment and Project Appraisal,* vol. 16, no. 4, December 1998, p. 303; Philip M. Fearnside, "The Canadian Feasibility Study of the Three Gorges Dam Proposed for China's Yangtze River: A Grave Embarrassment to the Impact Assessment Profession," *Impact Assessment,* vol. 12, no. 1, spring 1994, pp. 21–57; C. Alvares and R. Billorey, *Damming the Narmada: India's Greatest Planned Environmental Disaster* (Penang, Malaysia: Third World Network and Asia-Pacific People's Environment Network, APPEN, 1988).

16. John F. Kain, "Deception in Dallas: Strategic Misrepresentation in Rail Transit Promotion and Evaluation," *Journal of the American Planning Association,* vol. 56, no. 2, (Spring 1990), pp. 184–96; Alan Whitworth and Christopher Cheatham, "Appraisal Manipulation: Appraisal of the Yonki Dam Hydroelectric Project," *Project Appraisal,* vol. 3, no. 1, March 1988, pp. 13–20; Martin Wachs, "When Planners Lie with Numbers," *Journal of the American Planning Association,* vol. 55, no. 4, autumn 1989, pp. 476–79; R. Teichroeb, "Canadian Blessing for Chinese Dam Called "Prostitution," *Winnipeg Free Press,* 20 September 1990, p. 9.

17. For an empirical case, see Åsa Boholm and Ragnar Löfstedt, "Issues of Risk, Trust and Knowledge: The Hallandsås Tunnel Case," *Ambio,* vol. 28, no. 6, September 1999, pp. 556–61. For the theoretical argument, see James Bohman, *Public Deliberation: Pluralism, Complexity, and Democracy* (Cambridge, MA: MIT Press, 1996), chap. 3.

18. Brian Doherty, "Paving the Way: The Rise of Direct Action Against Road-Building and the Changing Character of British Environmentalism," *Political Studies,* vol. 47, no. 2, June 1999, pp. 275–91; Andrea D. Luery, Luis Vega, and Jorge Gastelumendi de Rossi, *Sabotage in Santa Valley: The Environmental Implications of Water Mismanagement in a Large-Scale Irrigation Project in Peru* (Norwalk, CT: Technoserve, 1991); Jon Teigland, "Predictions and Realities: Impacts on Tourism and Recreation from Hydropower and Major Road Developments," *Impact Assessment and Project Appraisal,* vol. 17, no. 1, March 1999, p. 67; "Svensk webbsida uppmanar till sabotage" (Swedish website is encouraging sabotage) and "Sabotage för miljoner" (sabotage for millions), *Svensk Vagtidning,* vol. 84, no. 2, 1997, p. 3, and vol. 85, no. 1, 1998, p. 7. One of the authors of the present book has similarly come across sabotage of a large-scale irrigation project in the Kilimanjaro region in Tanzania: see Bent Flyvbjerg, *Making Social Science Matter: Why Social Inquiry Fails and How It Can Succeed Again* (Cambridge: Cambridge University Press, 2001), chap. 10.

— · —

THE WORLD WE COULD WIN
Michael Duggett and Fabienne Maron

Examining the complex idea of "global governance," Duggett and Maron posit a crisis which the International Institute of Administrative Sciences (IIAS) proposes resolving by establishing a "Charter of Good Global Governance" at the end of the research study. Identify the elements of good governance.

Source: Michael Duggett and Fabienne Maron, "Administering Global Governance: Making It Work," *IIAS Newsletter* 23, no. 1 (2004). Reprinted by permission of IIAS.

When Peter Laslett wrote his famous book, *The World We Have Lost*, he was appealing to a certain kind of nostalgia for a once-warmer and safer world before the hard modern times of atomized families and heartless markets. Many people see the international scene today as like that—no one in charge except maybe a big brother whose motives are doubted, or a kind uncle whose powers are only notional. States, international organizations, networks, and civil society are becoming involved in an increasingly complex system of "global governance" as they seek global solutions. What many see as a crisis of the United Nations, of the post-war settlement, with weakened international regulatory mechanisms facing a threat they cannot master, is the context of our new Working Group on *Administering Global Governance*. We begin with a simple question: Who Governs Our World? Who sets the rules for an unruly world community?

CRISIS

This perceived crisis in the ability to govern has stimulated much research and deliberation on the new concept of "global governance." Today, experts question the way this "global governance" should be administered, especially as it relies on a vast number of actors, different kinds of organization, diverse authorities, and levels of decision-making. . . .

QUESTIONS

There are many possible issues to examine:

- Where are we in this historical process, what has the turbulent turn of the millennium left behind?
- How should the current system be described? Is it a "system" at all?
- If the question of administration of global governance is so important, are structures, processes, cultures, and visions really working together in synergy or not?
- How can a voice be given to the voiceless, those actors in states or even states themselves who are at present excluded from the process or have, as at Cancun, or at Genoa or in Porto Alegre and Mumbai, to make their presence felt in ways that others see as negative?
- How should regions and interregional policies be formulated in the context of global governance?
- And lastly, how can we make global governance work?

NEW PATHS OF THOUGHT

We will be ambitious but practical, focused but we hope idealistic. We will need to talk about inclusion and exclusion, about respect for the rule of law and due process, what we mean by difficult concepts like legitimacy, subsidiarity, sustainability, professionalism, and integrity. . . . [We shall take] some small steps today toward the well-ordered world we could win if we wanted.

THE CAUX ROUND TABLE PRINCIPLES FOR BUSINESS
CAUX ROUND TABLE

Does business, particularly global commerce, have responsibility for, and to, government? If so, is this responsibility reflected in the CAUX Round Table Principles? Is accountability to government clearly stated?

These principles are rooted in two basic ethical ideals: *kyosei* and human dignity. The Japanese concept of *kyosei* means living and working together for the common good—enabling cooperation and mutual prosperity to coexist with healthy and fair competition. "Human dignity" refers to the sacredness or value of each person as an end, not simply as a means to the fulfillment of other's purposes or even majority prescription. The General Principles in Section 2 seek to clarify the spirit of *kyosei* and "human dignity," while the specific Stakeholder Principles in Section 3 are concerned with their application.

SECTION 1. PREAMBLE

The mobility of employment, capital products, and technology is making business increasingly global in its transactions and its effects.

Laws and market forces are necessary, but insufficient guides for conduct.

Responsibility for the policies and actions of business and respect for the dignity and interests of its stakeholders are fundamental.

Shared values, including a commitment of shared prosperity, are as important for a global community as for communities of smaller scale.

For these reasons, and because business can be a powerful agent of positive social change, we offer the following Principles as a foundation for dialogue and action by business leaders in search of business responsibility. In so doing, we affirm the necessity for moral values in business decision-making. Without them, stable business relationships and a sustainable world community are impossible.

Source: "The CAUX Round Table Principles for Business: An International Ethics Statement for Business," special reprint prepared by *Business Ethics*, n.d. Copies of this supplement are available from *Business Ethics* magazine.

SECTION 2. GENERAL PRINCIPLES

Principle 1. The Responsibilities of Businesses: Beyond Shareholders Toward Stakeholders

Businesses have a role to play in improving the lives of all their customers, employees, and shareholders by sharing with them the wealth they have created. Suppliers and competitors as well should expect businesses to honor their obligations in a spirit of honesty and fairness. As responsible citizens of the local, national, regional, and global communities in which they operate, businesses share a part in shaping the future of those communities. . . .

SECTION 3. STAKEHOLDER PRINCIPLES

Customers

We believe in treating all customers with dignity, irrespective of whether they purchase our products and services directly from us or otherwise acquire them in the market. . . .

Employees

We believe in the dignity of every employee and in taking employee interests seriously. . . .

Owners / Investors

We believe in honoring the trust our investors place in us. . . .

Suppliers

Our relationship with suppliers and subcontractors must be based on mutual respect. . . .

Competitors

We believe that fair economic competition is one of the basic requirements for increasing the wealth of nations and, ultimately for making possible the just distribution of goods and services. . . .

Communities

We believe that as global corporate citizens, we can contribute to such forces of reform and human rights as are at work in the communities in which we operate. We therefore have a responsibility in those communities to:

- respect human rights and democratic institutions, and promote them wherever practicable;
- recognize government's legitimate obligation to the society at large and support public policies and practices that promote human development through harmonious relations between business and other segments of society;
- collaborate with those forces in the community dedicated to raising standards of health, education, workplace safety, and economic well-being;
- promote and stimulate sustainable development and play a leading role in preserving and enhancing the physical environment and conserving the earth's resources;
- support peace, security, diversity, and social integration;
- respect the integrity of local cultures; and
- be a good corporate citizen through charitable donations, educational and cultural contributions, and employee participation in community and civic affairs.

BALANCE BETWEEN ELECTRONIC ACCESS AND PRIVACY RIGHTS
Blake Harris

Privacy issues arise in other areas of public policy and affairs than national security. In what areas in the United States is the issue of privacy vital to protect? How public, for instance, should court documents be? Has information technology transformed the ethics of public information?

Nowhere has the rise of the Internet posed so complex a challenge to public policy as it has to the tradition of public access to judicial processes and records. Traditionally, most court files are available to anyone willing to go to the courthouse and look at them.

But the Internet and other technological innovations have made court records available in electronic form, offering access that is easier and more widespread than

Source: Blake Harris, "Hung Jury: State Courts Struggle to Find Balance Between Electronic Access and Privacy Rights," *Government Technology*, April 2003, pp. 36–37. Reprinted with permission of *Government Technology*.

ever before. Simply following rules developed in the era of paper files can result in controversy—as Manatee County, FL, recently discovered. The county made scans of all unsealed court documents available on its website . . . but a public outcry soon led to their removal from the site, at least for the time being.

Many have argued that open courts are a fundamental aspect of maintaining a working democracy. Open court records produce accountability and public confidence in the operation of the judiciary, the operation of other government agencies and the uniform enforcement of laws. Only through public access, for instance, can citizens be assured courts are fulfilling their role of protecting the rule of law.

Yet privacy concerns certainly are legitimate. Information on the Internet is available internationally to virtually anyone, regardless of the person's purpose for seeking the material. Such information also can be compiled into entire databases and distributed independently without any access controls. Court documents often contain personal information of those found guilty of a crime, those found innocent, and even witnesses called to testify. Moreover, civil suits brought on the basis of unproven allegations frequently bring people into court, even when they have not acted improperly.

So it is not surprising that in the last few years, many state courts grappled with these issues, seeking the proper balance between public access, personal privacy, and public safety—all while maintaining the integrity of the judicial process. This resulted in different approaches in different states, none of which seem to resolve all concerns or provide a model example.

POTPOURRI OF SOLUTIONS

New Jersey courts were among the first to explore these issues comprehensively. In 1996, the New Jersey Supreme Court created a committee that held public hearings to consider both privacy and public access, which resulted in a published report titled *The Report of the Public Access Subcommittee of the Judiciary Information Systems Policy Committee*. Although the Internet was not as developed as it is today, the committee considered many implications it would have.

"Practical barriers to information use and dissemination imposed by traditional paper documents disappear when information is stored in electronic bits and bytes, susceptible to manipulation and capable of being easily transferred around the globe via computer networks such as the Internet," the report said. "This qualitative difference between paper and electronic records gives rise to an argument that the dissemination of public records in computer readable form should be restricted."

Despite the clear recognition that Internet-accessible records could trigger abuses, the committee rejected the notion that "restricting access to nonconfidential court records is an effective or appropriate solution to a societal problem rooted in our in-formation-fueled economy." Concerns about privacy, the report continued, were best dealt with legislatively through the enactment of laws controlling the use of publicly available data, similar to protections afforded by the Fair Credit Reporting Act.

The Vermont Supreme Court followed New Jersey and formed a committee; it published *Rules for Public Access* to Court Records in 2000. Apart from integrating various previous policies on access, the committee also put forth the principle that different rules shouldn't exist for access to paper records versus electronic records. But in 2001, that rule was amended to say that record custodians have the authority to deny access electronically.

In 2000, Chief Judge Robert M. Bell of the Maryland Court of Appeals drafted an administrative order restricting access to criminal trial records to lawyers and court officers. Internet access to these records was unavailable at the time of Bell's order; however, the court offered dial-up access and access from terminals within the court building.

The order—which received widespread bad press and public criticism—eventu-ally triggered a report from the Reporters Committee for Freedom of the Press, an organization formed to protect First Amendment rights. The committee's report—*Comments on Draft Model Policy on Public Access to Court Records,* released in 2002—ar-gued that access should be the same for paper and electronic court records, and that courts should not ask who wants the information or why they want it. The com-mittee added that other state laws already provide criminal sanctions for identity theft, harassment, stalking and other crimes that result from information acquired from the Internet.

Arizona, on the other hand, took a different approach, and in 2000 released rules that focused largely on financial privacy. The rules specifically identified data such as Social Security numbers, credit card numbers, and financial account numbers said to be private and confidential, and therefore, should be unavailable to the public in ei-ther paper or electronic form.

Washington state also restricted certain data elements, but in addition to finan-cial information, included address and identity information as confidential. These, the state decided, should not be publicly available in paper or electronic form.

Meanwhile, California makes civil cases available on the Internet. Citizens also may electronically access other types of cases, such as criminal, family, and mental health hearings, but they must walk into the courthouse to do so.

Many other states are now tackling the issue, so new approaches may emerge in the next few years.

NEW GUIDELINES

To provide the states direction in setting access policy, the National Center for State Courts and the Justice Management Institute, on behalf of the Conference of Chief

Justices (CCJ) and Conference of State Court Administrators (COSCA), recently released recommendations for formulating access policies for court records.

"Originally, when they formed a committee, they were calling for a 'model policy' for all state courts," said Susan Larson, a lawyer with Boos, Grajczyk & Larson who has consulted with courts in several states on access issues. "However, as the drafting process and public hearings progressed, they changed that to policy guidelines for states. A lot of people had been hoping there would be some teeth or some mandates within this document, but really it is just a starting point for states to consider the various issues."

The document—*Developing CCJ/COSCA Guidelines for Public Access to Court Records: A National Project to Assist State Courts*—does not spell out exactly what should and should not be accessible electronically. It concludes that, ultimately, the issue must be settled by individual states within their own judicial and legislative frameworks.

Committee members also were split on how to approach the topic. "Many members of the advisory committee expressed the view that the presumption of openness is constitutionally based, requiring a 'compelling interest' to overcome the presumption," the report said. "Other members expressed the view that the law in this area is evolving."

Nevertheless, many principles advocated in the guidelines seemed to fall more toward openness of electronic records. The premise underlying the guidelines is that "court records should generally be open and accessible to the public," according to the report's final draft. "Court records have historically been open to public access at the courthouse, with limited exceptions. This tradition is continued in the CCJ/COSCA guidelines. Open access serves many public purposes."

CASE 3: INTEGRITY AT THE UNITED NATIONS

United Nations workers are subject to many rules and regulations intended to insure that their behavior is beyond reproach, including a responsibility to report and combat corruption. But do they take this responsibility seriously? This question has gained prominence as a result of the possible involvement of UN officials in the now defunct Iraq oil-for-food program where billions of dollars are alleged to have been diverted in kickbacks and overcharges. Did UN staffers know about such corruption? If so, did they do anything to combat it? No one knows the answers to these questions but a UN commissioned study of the attitudes and perceptions about integrity among UN staff is suggestive.

Source: Donald C. Menzel, "Ethics Moment: Integrity at the United Nations?" *PA Times*, October 2004. The survey is online at www.un.org. Reprinted with permission from the American Society for Public Administration.

The UN survey canvassed all UN staff and leaders in the Secretariat, a population of 18,035, to find out what they thought about a core UN value, integrity. One-third (6,086) of the employees responded. The results indicate that staffers are very satisfied with their work and committed to the organization's goals. This is the good news. The not-so-good news is that many are reluctant to become whistle-blowers or report misconduct. The report states "staff members feel unprotected from reprisals for reporting violations of the codes of conduct." Not surprisingly, staff members are uncomfortable about approaching their managers with ethical concerns and many do not feel that their supervisors and colleagues regularly discuss ethical issues that arise in the workplace.

You have been invited to make recommendations to the UN on how it might strengthen ethical practices within the organization. Where would you begin and what more would you want to know in order to make good recommendations?

CHAPTER DISCUSSION QUESTIONS

1. What do you see as the twenty-first century changes that present the greatest challenges to ethical management? Can you support all of Starks' eight reforms?

2. Do you think that ethical assumptions and ethical principles differ significantly from country to country and culture to culture? If so, what might be the implications for international organizations like the United Nations?

3. Do you think the world is in "a qualitatively different stage of social and economic development" as Flyvbjerg et al. suggest? How do you think this might impact management ethics?

FOR FURTHER EXPLORATION

Cohen, David B. and John W. Wells, eds. *American National Security and Civil Liberties in an Era of Terrorism.* New York: Palgrave Macmillan, 2004.

Gawthrop, Louis C. "Public Administration in a Global Mode: With Sympathy and Compassion," *Public Integrity,* 7:3 (Summer 2005), pp. 241–59.

Gawthrop, Louis C. *Public Service and Democracy: Ethical Imperatives for the 21st Century.* New York: Chatham House, 1998.

Gunatilleke, Godfrey, Tiruchelvam, Neelan, and Coomaraswamy, Radhika, eds. *Ethical Dilemmas of Development in Asia.* Lexington, MA: Lexington Books, 1983.

Ignatieff, Michael. *The Lesser Evil: Political Ethics in an Age of Terror.* The Gifford Lectures. Edinburgh: Edinburgh University Press, 2004.

Light, Paul C. *The New Public Service.* Washington, DC: Brookings Institution Press, 1999.

Montefiore, Alan, and David Vines, eds. *Integrity in the Public and Private Domains.* London and New York: Routledge, 1999.

Reforming Public Institutions and Strengthening Governance: A World Bank Strategy Implementation Update. Washington, DC: The World Bank, 2003.

Schultz, David. "Professional Ethics in a Postmodern Society," *Public Integrity* 6:4 (Fall 2004), pp. 279–297.

Stanislawski, Bartosz H. "Transnational 'Bads' in the Globalized World: The Case of Transnational Organized Crime," *Public Integrity* 6:2 (Spring 2004), pp. 155–170.

WEBSITES

Institute for Global Ethics, Ethics Newsline, www.globalethics.org/newsline/members/index.tmpl

Urgent Business for America: Revitalizing the Federal Government for the 21st Century. Report of the National Commission on the Public Service, January 2003, www.uscourts.gov/newsroom/VolckerRpt.pdf

United Nations Online Network on Public Administration and Finance, www.unpan.org/discover.asp. UNPAN ethics links and contacts, www.unpan.org/EthicsWebSite/inc/contactspg.htm

Business Ethics magazine, www.business-ethics.com

PART II

ETHICAL PROBLEMS:
SOME BLATANT,
SOME NOT SO OBVIOUS

Public officials confront a wide variety of ethical issues and dilemmas. The problems discussed in this volume—lying and other forms of deception, graft and fraud, secrecy, abuse of authority—form only a part of the total landscape of administrative ethics. It is, however, an important part, for these patterns of misbehavior have long been prominent features of the American political scene, at all levels of government. Indeed, they have become matters of recent public debate not only in the United States but in virtually every country of the world. Problems of corruption and deceptive practices are not limited, certainly, to government officials, but in the citizens' minds these issues may be more readily associated with the public service, in part because it *is* public.

In thinking about ethical problems of these kinds, we can usefully distinguish among three important perspectives from which a decision—or a pattern of behavior—might be viewed as raising ethical concerns. The first perspective is that of the *individual* government official, who may, for example, be offered a free plane ticket to a business convention. From this point of view, the problem is often that of identifying and clarifying the ethical issue. For instance: Are some of my future program decisions likely to help—or harm—the businesses holding this convention? If so, will the free plane ride incline me to view their interests more favorably than I should, in relation to overall program goals? And if, on reflection, I conclude that my objectivity will *not* be contaminated by the gift, would I still risk damage to my personal reputation for objectivity and to my effectiveness if that free ride is later reported by the media? Thus, the individual official must be sensitive to the conditions under which one's objectivity may be compromised in reality, and also to the question of whether the person's behavior might reasonably *appear to others* to be unethical.

A second perspective is that of the manager, who is not only responsible for her own behavior but also for that of others within the agency. Here, in addition to her concerns regarding whether she is behaving ethically, the manager must consider whether existing practices and rules encourage ethical behavior or whether external pressures, together with the "organizational culture" within the agency, encourage behavior that might reasonably be criticized on ethical grounds. For example, the manager might want to ensure that her agency has rules regarding free airplane rides and the acceptance of other gifts, and that the importance of these rules—and "gray areas" that need to be clarified—are *regularly* discussed in meetings of the agency's staff.

The third perspective is that of the public, who have entrusted government officials with a portion of their society's affairs and well-being. Public opinion on an issue—such as conditions under which gifts can be properly received by public officials—will frequently be unclear or divided. Even so, there often are fundamental standards that can be applied in judging particular cases. First, particularly in a democratic society, the citizenry need to be *well informed,* so that officials are fully accountable to the public. Secondly, citizens need to have a *sense of trust* in public officials, based on their judgment that officials are acting in the public interest.

The purpose of Part II of this volume is to describe a range of problem areas, together with specific examples, in which public officials confront ethical issues—including some where officials have acted in violation of law or against acceptable ethical standards. Our aim is not, however, to showcase "public horrors." There would be little benefit if the situations described here merely appalled the reader or lent grim satisfaction to the critic who believes that government must inevitably do more harm than good.

As the title of this book indicates, we see corruption as both a significant component of ethical concerns and a continuing problem of considerable magnitude in public administration and in public life generally. As many of the readings in Part II of this volume illustrate, it is sometimes difficult to determine whether a specific act *is* unethical. Is a policeman acting unethically when he regularly accepts a free cup of coffee from a restaurant owner while on duty? Is the person who makes photocopies of personal papers at the office without reimbursing the organization engaged in corruption? There is also the problem of awareness: How many administrators unknowingly commit acts that they would regard as wrong if they thought through the implications?

To focus upon the problems of graft, lying, and other aspects of corrupt behavior is not to deny the importance of other types of ethical concerns. It is valuable at this point to recall the distinction made by Amy Gutmann and Dennis Thompson between *policy ethics* and *process ethics*.[1] "Policy ethics" is concerned with questions of distributive justice, the sanctity of life, and other ultimate moral choices, as illustrated by the continuing controversies over welfare policy and abortion. "Process ethics" deals with those problems encountered in the administrative process, regardless of policy issues: secrecy, abuse of authority, and graft. It is often difficult to separate these two types of ethical questions. For the most part, however, this volume focuses upon the ethics of process rather than the ethics of policy choices.

Our primary goals are two: first, to illustrate and analyze pressures which give rise to unethical or questionable behavior; and second, to encourage our readers to exercise both their analytical skills in exploring the sources of ethical lapses, and their own judgment in considering how the officials in the cases should have behaved if they had thought systematically and carefully about the issues. Our hope is that by reading these essays and cases, and debating them with others, readers might be in a better position to understand the ethical risks and implications of their own behavior, and to make choices that will be ethically defensible.

From the perspective of the manager, some of the articles and cases illustrate the importance of the agency's traditions in encouraging or undermining ethical behavior, as well as suggesting strategies that managers may be able to use in order to improve the ethical climate within their agencies. Finally, the selections in Part II illustrate some of the pressures that can erode public trust in government action, and that can weaken the capacity of the citizenry to be well informed and thus able to hold government officials accountable for their rhetoric and their actions. These examples will also suggest some steps that might be used to protect these elements of the public interest. In Part III, then, we turn explicitly to strategies that can be used to encourage ethical behavior when viewed from the perspective of the individual, the manager, and the broader public.

In the remaining paragraphs of this introductory essay, we suggest some ways of sorting out the range of ethical problems that public officials often confront in the course of their duties.

"CLEARLY WRONG" AND "CONDITIONALLY WRONG" BEHAVIOR

It may be useful to divide the kinds of unethical behavior encountered in public life, and in the selections in this volume, into two categories. The first group we might label "clearly wrong." These include those behaviors which are so widely viewed as unethical that few people would attempt to justify them on moral grounds. Some philosophers label these as "*prima facie* wrong." Harassment of co-workers and clients, as well as graft, fraud, and other forms of corruption fit in this category; these behaviors subvert the trust in fair-dealing that is a hallmark of constructive human relationships, and they may also undermine effective accountability in a democratic society. The phrase "fraud, waste and abuse," now widely used in critical assessments of agency programs by the U.S. Government Accountability Office and other evaluators, extends across an even wider terrain of misbehavior.

In the second category, of "conditionally wrong" behaviors, we might place lying and other forms of deception and some aspects of conflict of interest. As to lying and other behavior in the "conditionally wrong" category, the student of ethics begins by asking, "Under what conditions is lying ethically permissible?" The initial challenge, then—for public officials, and for those who would evaluate their activities—is to clarify the conditions that *might* be used to justify such behavior, and then to subject these rationales to close scrutiny, in order to test the persuasiveness of the reason (or excuse). Often that analysis is so challenging and complex that much less attention is given to the questions that must follow: (1) what are the factors that lead to such behavior, and (2) what managerial strategies might be employed to reduce the extent of such unethical behavior in the future?

Are the practices described in the Malek Manual, excerpted in Chapter 8, "clearly wrong" or "conditionally wrong"? Are they simply "standard operating procedures," justified by "getting one's hands dirty" in order to get the job done or an abuse of public office? Are such standard operating procedures a form of "administrative evil," as Guy Adams and Danny Balfour have labeled certain types of endemic organizational ills? Several of the selections in chapter 8 explore these themes.

MOTIVATIONS: HELPING YOURSELF, HELPING YOUR AGENCY, IMPROVING SOCIETY

There is a second distinction that might usefully be made among activities that are labeled unethical, a distinction based on motivation. The dominant motive for exacting a bribe is usually self-interest, narrowly understood: lining one's own pocket with dollars or rubles, or aiding one's family or one's political party. A similar motivation underlies familial or party nepotism. But lying and other forms of deception by public officials are often motivated substantially by other concerns—the desire to advance important program goals; loyalty to co-workers or a desire to keep one's own agency in high public repute; patriotism. Again, lines are blurred: Lies in defense of agency goals may be rewarded by promotion and other benefits for the "loyal" official; to harass clients of a welfare program may reduce agency costs and so earn praise for "efficient" staff activities. Still, in thinking about causes of certain kinds of unethical behavior—and especially in thinking about remedies—it may be helpful to sort out motivations in this way.

For example, deception and other unethical behavior at lower staff levels are often motivated by a desire to meet goals set—implicitly or explicitly—by one's superiors. In such cases, punitive action directed toward lower-level staff members who follow those signals may have very little long-term effect. Penalizing the senior executives, despite their efforts to use "the strategy of deniability," or employing other strategies to change the signals they send down the line may be far more important.

Both of these categories of behavior—lining one's pockets, helping one's organization—place the emphasis on the *active* decision-maker, taking the initiative to uphold or to undermine ethical standards. But often, the situation is otherwise; an individual is required to take little or no action, simply "looking the other way" or "going along" passively while unethical behavior continues. Others may take the initiative; and the organization's "culture" may provide a pervasive environment in which *ethical* behavior is viewed as deviant. What can one do then?

PROFESSIONAL INTEGRITY AND THE POLITICAL ENVIRONMENT

Underlying these comments on the problems of ethics that confront public officials is the assumption of "professional integrity," the expectation that professional expertise and judgment should predominate in shaping and implementing agency programs, and that every agency staff member is expected to adhere to and contribute to this orientation. In a democratic society, other factors must also come into play. Accountability to elected officials will sometimes lead to policies that agency professionals would not favor, and accountability to law will at times require bending professional standards to meet the peculiarity of statutes. But these modifications should carry with them the requirement of *openness* or *transparency*—that the policies and orders of elected officials, and the constraints of statutes, be understood by the public and available for critical review by the media and other observers. With transparency comes the possibility of self-correction, so that "professional integrity" and democratic accountability can fruitfully co-exist.

While these general standards may seem reasonably clear, they mask some important elements in the environment of public officials which often operate against the grain of ethical behavior. Some of these elements are linked directly to the struggle to achieve popular control over a large and expanding public bureaucracy; others are pressures and problems frequently found in private corporations as well as government agencies. In these final paragraphs, we list some aspects of the environment and direct the reader's attention to selections that illustrate them.

The struggle for political control and the desire of party leaders to nurture loyal and active party service will often generate pressures to use government positions and workers on behalf of political-party goals, as the excerpts from the Malek Manual illustrate. The search for ways to overcome the red tape and other alleged inefficiencies of government bureaucracy will sometimes lead to corruption, as the articles by Yadong Luo and by Gerald Caiden demonstrate. The availability of public funds in large amounts—not always carefully supervised—is likely to attract the venal. Also, there will be gray areas, where the *appearance* of conflict of interest may reveal a lack of ethical standards, laxity, or confusion.

The environment of the public official also includes crucial factors, also widely found in private organizations, which press against professional integrity and ethical behavior. These include, for example, a culture of minor fraud, and pressure to cover up professional analyses and findings that senior officials find uncomfortable. These cases show that no individual can safely yield to superiors or organizational pressures in deciding, "Is this ethical?" We must each remain the keeper of the keys to our own individual conscience.

Even so, the prospects for maintaining ethical behavior throughout an organization depend on more than individual self-reflection. Managers and other senior officials can crucially shape the possibilities for ethical behavior throughout their agencies by their own sensitivity—or insensitivity—to ethical concerns, and by the structure of rewards and other incentives they provide within an organization.

NOTE

1. Amy Gutmann and Dennis Thompson, *Ethics & Politics: Cases & Comments*, fourth ed. (Belmont, CA: Thomson Wadsworth, 2006), p. xi.

Chapter 4

UNDERSTANDING FRAUD, WASTE, AND CORRUPT PRACTICES

AN ORGANIZATIONAL PERSPECTIVE ON CORRUPTION
YADONG LUO

One clear indication of the increasing global awareness of corruption as an adminis-trative, political and economic problem is the growing body of writing on the subject by scholars in many countries. Yadong Luo, in this extraction from his article in the inaugural issue of a leading Chinese management journal, defines and clarifies some of the conceptual features of corruption.

Corruption has drawn the enormous attention of scholars in various fields and practitioners around the world. A survey by Transparency International identi-fied 4,000 books and journal articles published in the last ten years with corruption as their main theme. Of those, 74 percent addressed politics and public administra-tion issues, 10 percent took a historical perspective, 9 percent focused on law and the judiciary; 4 percent on economics, 2 percent on ethnographic and culture and 1 percent on business ethics (*Global Corruption Report*, 2001, p. 229). Recent debacles of many well-known companies, from the U.S. companies Enron and WorldCom to China's GITIC and Yuanhua Group, have further raised the profile of corrupt prac-tices and their organizational repercussions.

The disciplines that deal with corruption each have fundamental paradigms, which they bring into the analysis of the phenomenon. Sociologists hold that the roots of corruption are social and cultural, and that corruption hinders public wel-fare and social development. Political scientists maintain that nontransparent institu-tions, low-paid public servants, and a shortage of independent and well-functioning market mechanisms are antecedents of corruption. Legal scholars focus on the type of legal system and its enforcement. Macroeconomists focus on weak economic in-stitutions and lack of transparent economic institutions as root causes. . . .

Source: Yadong Luo, "An Organizational Perspective of Corruption," *Management and Organization Re-view*, July 2005, 119–124. Reprinted with permission of Blackwell Publishing.

DEFINITION OF ORGANIZATIONAL CORRUPTION

Corruption is a complex and multifaceted phenomenon with multiple causes and effects, occurring as it takes on various forms and functions in differing contexts. This article defines corruption as an illegitimate exchange of resources involving the use or abuse of public or collective responsibility for private ends (i.e. gains, benefits, profits, or privileges). This definition includes corruption between organizations and political agencies (when public power is misused) and between organizations and other organizations (when collective responsibility is abused). In a narrow sense, corruption involves a bureaucratic behavior that deviates from the norm or violates rules specified by a given political context, and is motivated by private gains that can be accrued from the public role. . . . The majority of corruption takes place between business organizations and political agencies, both domestically and internationally (U.S. Department of State, 2001). Corrupt practices generally include bribery, fraud, extortion, and favoritism. As the primary form of corruption, bribery is the payment (in money or kind) given or taken in a corrupt relationship. Other terms for bribery include kickbacks, red envelopes, gratuities, baksheesh, grease money, facilitation payment, and expediting fees.

To most companies, bribery of public officials is the most prevalent form of a corrupt act. Fraud is an economic crime that involves some kind of trickery, swindle or deceit. Extortions involve corrupt transactions where money or other resources are violently extracted by those who have the power to do so. Lastly favoritism is a mechanism of power that privatizes public resources; a highly biased distribution of state resources, no matter how the resources were accumulated in the first place. Favoritism is the human proclivity to favor friends, family, and anybody close and trusted, at the expense of public interests. It is a misuse of public responsibilities and implies a corrupted distribution of public resources. It must be noted that the definition of corrupt acts varies across nations. For instance, the U.S. Foreign Corrupt Practices Act 1977 (FCPA) defines bribery as the offer, promise, or gift of undue pecuniary or other advantage, whether made directly or through intermediaries, to a person holding public office for that person to commit an act or refrain from acting in relation to the performance of official duties. This definition has not been effective outside the United States nor with non-U.S. companies (The Conference Board, 2000). . . .

It is necessary to understand the nature of corruption. First, *corruption is context-based*. Depending on the individual, ideology, culture, or other context, the term *corruption* can mean different things to different people. It is particularly important to take into consideration the impact that a changing political environment may have on the term. Politics not only affects the understanding and explanation of corruption, but also produces and identifies certain social behaviors as corrupt.

Therefore, it is necessary to examine not only corrupt practices per se, but also the attitude and performance of the political system toward corruption—such as the exposure of corruption by the press, by the party in power, and by different factions—as well as the reaction of government to corruption, whether administrative or judiciary.

Second, *corruption is norm-deviated*. Although corrupt behavior can arise in a number of different contexts, its essential aspect is an illegal or unauthorized transfer of money or an in-kind substitute. Although there may be a situation where certain behavior is generally considered corruption but no legal precedent has been established for it (in this case, the legalist definition lags behind the moralist definition), law-based norms are the most widely used. This is because the legal definition of corruption is generally more operational, clear-cut, consistent and precise than the moral definition. . . .

Third, *corruption is power-related*. In order to be eligible as a corrupt transaction, a corruptor or bribe-taker must necessarily be in a position of power, created either by market imperfections or an institutional position that grants him discretionary authority. Corruption always depends on power; power, however, does not necessarily spring from the law. People in public service such as physicians in Taiwan, customs clerks in the Philippines, and low-level staff who process bank loans in mainland China gain power not from the law but from the actual influence they exert on procedural costs afforded by businesses. Nevertheless, bureaucratic corruption (involving governmental officials) constitutes the most corruptible and corrupted part in many societies.

Fourth, *corruption is virtually covert*. Because of the nature of the operation, corruption is hidden in the underground informal arena. No formal written contract is delivered. Contact is made through oral communication so that it cannot be documented and used to prosecute a responsible entity. Maneuvers are carried out to conceal the identity of the actors. Overall, corruption is an informal, veiled system transforming benefits derived from one's public roles and power to personal gain. . . .

Fifth, *corruption is intentional*. The motivation of personal gain conveys the very connotation of corruption. Illegal misconduct may not necessarily be corruption if there is no personal gain. Economists generally treat corruption as another means by which to maximize profits or seek optimal economic resources. Addressing its sensitivity to the rationality underlying corruption enables us to differentiate purposive dereliction of duty for personal gain from other careless maladministrative behaviors. . . .

Lastly *corruption is perceptional*. It relates to individual behavior as perceived by public as well as political authorities. Since it is a perceptual term judged by others, the concept becomes dynamic, subject to changes in social attitudes and political ideologies. As such, corruption can be further classified as "white," "black," or "grey." Although all violate legal codes or institutional rules, each of these has different moral implications. White corruption (i.e., some types of misconduct) can be tolerated by mass opinion. However, black corruption is clearly condemned. In between falls grey corruption, which is often ambiguous. Accordingly, the legal definition of corruption remains important for black and grey corruptions, but is not as important for white corruption. Under certain circumstances, the public may reasonably feel that an act legally defined as corruption is a necessary tool to survive. This explains in part why anti-corruption laws and rules in many transition economies, such as China, have been changing so rapidly. . . .

REFERENCES

U.S. Department of State (2001). Fighting global corruption: Business risk management. Washington, DC: Department of State Publication 10731.

Conference Board, The (2000). *Company Programs for Resisting Corrupt Practices: A Global Study*. Research Report 1279-00-RR, New York: The Conference Board.

Global Corruption Report 2001. Berlin: Transparency International.

CORRUPTION AND GOVERNANCE
Gerald E. Caiden

Like Luo, Gerald Caiden provides a definition of corruption and discussion of various factors that condition its incidence. Are there significant differences between Luo's and Caiden's perspectives?

As so often occurs in science, the more attention a subject receives, the more complicated it becomes. Corruption comes in too many forms to permit easy generalization. . . . There is high-level and low-level corruption, and there is predominantly political and predominantly bureaucratic corruption. There are endemic, pervasive forms and isolated, infrequent forms. There are mutually reinforcing networks of complex, indirect, and subtle transactions; and isolated, simple, direct, and bilateral transactions that have contradictory effects.

There is large, disruptive corruption and petty, trivial corruption. Corrupt exchanges may be rare or frequent, open or closed, between equals or nonequals; the stakes may be tangible or intangible, durable or nondurable, routine or extraordinary; and the channels may be legitimate or illegitimate (Johnston 1986). Nonetheless, this confusion does not invalidate certain universal generalizations:

1. Corruption has been found in all political systems, at every level of government, and in the delivery of all scarce public goods and services.
2. Corruption varies in origin, incidence, and importance among different geographic regions, sovereign states, political cultures, economies, and administrative arrangements.
3. Corruption is facilitated or impeded by the societal context (including international and transnational influences) in which public power is exercised.
4. Corruption has multitudinous causes, assumes many different patterns and guises and cannot be accurately measured because of its often indeterminate and conspiratorial nature.
5. Corruption is deeply rooted, cancerous, contaminating, and impossible to eradicate because controls tend to be formalistic, superficial, temporary, and even counterproductive.

Source: Gerald E. Caiden, "Corruption and Governance," in *Where Corruption Lives*, ed. Gerald E. Caiden, O.P. Dwivedi, and Joseph Jabbra (Bloomfield, CT: Kumarian Press, 2001), pp. 17–26. Reprinted by permission.

6. Corruption is directed at real power, key decision points, and discretionary authority. It commands a price for both access to decision makers and influence in decision making.

7. Corruption is facilitated by unstable polities, uncertain economies, maldistributed wealth, unrepresentative government, entrepreneurial ambitions, privatization of public resources, factionalism, personalism, and dependency.

8. Corruption favors those who have (over those who have not), illegal enterprises, underground economies, and organized crime.

9. Corruption persists substantially as long as its perpetrators can coerce participation, public attitudes towards it vary widely, and it greatly benefits a privileged few at the expense of the disadvantaged mass or benefits all participants at the cost of nonparticipants.

10. Corruption can be contained within acceptable limits through political will, democratic ethos, fragmented countervailing power, legal-rational administrative norms, inculcation of personal honesty and integrity, and effective enforcement of public ethics—although its complete elimination is still beyond human capability.

These findings indicate that corruption can be reduced and contained though appropriate countermeasures, but as long as the underlying causes persist, corruption is unlikely to be eliminated altogether. Indeed as long as human beings are imperfect corruption will persist. What anticorruption measures seek to do is drive it out of major areas of governance, reduce its scope, lessen its occurrence, and implement fail-safe devices. These measures should improve the image of governance, increase effectiveness and efficiency, streamline operations, and make for more civic activity and greater public participation.

DEFINITION

The word *corruption* means something spoiled: something sound that has been made defective, debased, and tainted; something that has been pushed off course into a worse or inferior form. Whoever corrupts sets out to make something impure and less capable, an adverse departure from an expected course. When applied to human relations, corruption is a bad influence, an injection of rottenness or decay, a decline in moral conduct and personal integrity attributable to venality or dishonesty. When applied to public office, rather than referring to departures from ideal or even generally expected standards of incumbent behavior, the practice has been to spell out specific acts of misconduct that disgrace public office and make the offenders unfit to remain there. . . .

In the absence of an all-purpose definition, in recent years the public office definition coined by Nye has been the most widely accepted, namely, that corruption is "behavior which deviates from the formal duties of a public role because of private-regarding (personal, close family, private clique) pecuniary or status gains, or violates rules against the exercise of certain types of private-regarding influence" (1967, 419). Nye specifically included bribery, nepotism, and misappropriation. This operational definition—when extended to include unscrupulous performance, undue pressures to influence official decisions, and failure to act—should suffice as a working definition in most instances. It stresses the behavioral element of intentional deviation for personal gain. It covers most market-centered definitions that concentrate on maximizing pecuniary gains (Rose-Ackerman 1978), and it can be stretched to include public interest definitions identifying corrupt acts as those that favor private interests over public concerns. It even includes a strictly Marxist-Leninist interpretation of corruption as all official activities that protect the interests of the dominant (capitalist) class "whether they be spending, taxing, regulating or policing" (Greenberg 1974, 25) but not the public office definitions actually employed in Communist regimes. Perhaps the only area that is not covered is that of "noble" or "patriotic" corruption where public officials supposedly turn their private vices into public benefits (Werner 1983, 147), where they do not personally gain and no improper consideration induce the violation of duty. However, as a result of their noble actions, their ignoring the law and expected public ethics may, in turn, be ignored with impunity, secreted, and viewed as making up inadequate past compensation. . . .

REFERENCES

Greenberg, Edward. 1974. *Serving the Few: Corporate Capitalism and the Bias of Government Policy.* New York: John Wiley and Sons.

Johnston, Michael. 1986, "The Political Consequences of Corruption: A Reassessment." *Comparative Politics* 18 (4): 459–77.

Nye, Joseph S. 1967. "Corruption and Political Development: A Cost-Benefit Analysis." *American Political Science Review* 61 (2): 417–27.

Rose-Ackerman, Susan. 1978. *Corruption: A Study in Political Economy.* New York: Academic Press.

Werner, Simcha. 1983. "New Directions in the Study of Administrative Corruption." *Public Administration Review* 43 (2): 146–54.

WHAT IS CORRUPTION?
U.S. AGENCY FOR INTERNATIONAL DEVELOPMENT

The United States Agency for International Development (USAID) has become increasingly sensitive to corruption issues, especially since the early 1990s. This succinct statement articulates some of the assumptions underlying USAID anti-corruption programs. Identify several of these assumptions.

Source: USAID Democracy and Governance website (downloaded July 14, 2003), www.usaid.gov/democracy/anticorruption/corruption.html.

In broad terms, USAID focuses on corruption as the misuse of public office for private gain. It encompasses abuses by government officials such as embezzlement and nepotism, as well as abuses linking public and private actors such as bribery, extortion, influence peddling, and fraud. Corruption arises in both political and bureaucratic offices and can be petty or grand, organized or unorganized. Though corruption often facilitates criminal activities such as drug trafficking, money laundering, and prostitution, it is not restricted to these activities. For purposes of understanding the problem and devising remedies, it is important to keep crime and corruption analytically distinct. Corruption poses a serious development challenge. In the political realm, it undermines democracy and good governance by subverting formal processes. Corruption in elections and in legislative bodies reduces accountability and representation in policymaking; corruption in the judiciary suspends the rule of law; and corruption in public administration results in the unequal provision of services. More generally, corruption erodes the institutional capacity of government as procedures are disregarded, resources are siphoned off, and officials are hired or promoted without regard to performance. At the same time, corruption undermines the legitimacy of government and such democratic values as trust and tolerance.

Corruption also undermines economic development by generating considerable distortions and inefficiency. In the private sector, corruption increases the cost of business through the price of illicit payments themselves, the management cost of negotiating with officials, and the risk of breached agreements or detection. Although some claim corruption reduces costs by cutting red tape, an emerging consensus holds that the availability of bribes induces officials to contrive new rules and delays. Where corruption inflates the cost of business, it also distorts the playing field, shielding firms with connections from competition and thereby sustaining inefficient firms.

Corruption also generates economic distortions in the public sector by diverting public investment away from education and into capital projects where bribes and kickbacks are more plentiful. Officials may increase the technical complexity of public sector projects to conceal such dealings, thus further distorting investment. Corruption also lowers compliance with construction, environmental, or other regulations; reduces the quality of government services and infrastructure; and increases budgetary pressures on government.

FIGHTING CORRUPTION GLOBALLY
Transparency International

Transparency International (TI) was created in the 1990s as an effort to counter corruption globally. This selection, from TI's website, provides a succinct description of corruption and a summary of the adverse consequences of corruption.

Source: Transparency International, www.transparency.org/about_us

WHAT IS TRANSPARENCY INTERNATIONAL?

Transparency International, the global civil society organization leading the fight against corruption, brings people together in a powerful worldwide coalition to end the devastating impact of corruption on men, women, and children around the world. TI's mission is to *create* change toward a world free of corruption.

Transparency International challenges the inevitability of corruption, and offers hope to its victims. TI plays a lead role in improving the lives of millions around the world, by building momentum for the anti-corruption movement, raising awareness and diminishing apathy and tolerance of corruption, as well as devising and implementing practical actions to address it.

Transparency International is a global network including more than 90 locally established national chapters and chapters-in-formation. These bodies fight corruption in the national arena in a number of ways. They bring together relevant players from government, civil society, business, and the media to promote transparency in elections, in public administration, in procurement, and in business. TI's global network of chapters and contacts also uses advocacy campaigns to lobby governments to implement anti-corruption reforms.

Politically non-partisan, TI does not undertake investigations of alleged corruption or expose individual cases, but at times will work in coalition with organizations that do.

TI has the skills, tools, experience, expertise, and broad participation to fight corruption on the ground, as well as through global and regional initiatives.

Now in its second decade, Transparency International is maturing, intensifying, and diversifying its fight against corruption.

WHAT IS CORRUPTION?

Corruption is the abuse of entrusted power for private gain. It hurts everyone whose life, livelihood, or happiness depends on the integrity of people in a position of authority.

WHY DOES FIGHTING CORRUPTION MATTER?

Corruption hurts everyone, and it harms the poor the most. Sometimes its devastating impact is obvious:

- A father who must do without shoes because his meager wages are used to pay a bribe to get his child into a supposedly free school.
- The unsuspecting sick person who buys useless counterfeit drugs, putting their health in grave danger.
- A small shop owner whose weekly bribe to the local inspector cuts severely into his modest earnings.
- The family trapped for generations in poverty because a corrupt and autocratic leadership has systematically siphoned off a nation's riches.

Other times corruption's impact is less visible:

- The prosperous multinational corporation that secured a contract by buying an unfair advantage in a competitive market through illegal kickbacks to corrupt government officials, at the expense of the honest companies who didn't.
- Post-disaster donations provided by compassionate people, directly or through their governments, that never reach the victims, callously diverted instead into the bank accounts of criminals.
- The faulty buildings, built to lower safety standards because a bribe passed under the table in the construction process that collapse in an earthquake or hurricane.

Corruption has dire global consequences, trapping millions in poverty and misery and breeding social, economic, and political unrest.

Corruption is both a cause of poverty and a barrier to overcoming it. It is one of the most serious obstacles to reducing poverty.

Corruption denies poor people the basic means of survival, forcing them to spend more of their income on bribes. Human rights are denied where corruption is rife, because a fair trial comes with a hefty price tag where courts are corrupted.

Corruption undermines democracy and the rule of law.

Corruption distorts national and international trade.

Corruption jeopardizes sound governance and ethics in the private sector.

Corruption threatens domestic and international security and the sustainability of natural resources.

Those with less power are particularly disadvantaged in corrupt systems, which typically reinforce gender discrimination.

Corruption compounds political exclusion: if votes can be bought, there is little incentive to change the system that sustains poverty.

The conclusion: Corruption hurts everyone.

CORRUPTION IN THE NOT-FOR-PROFIT SECTOR
MIAMI-DADE COUNTY

Corruption in nonprofit organizations gets less scholarly attention than that in business or government, but major scandals in churches, charitable organizations, and other nonprofits demonstrate that it is a prevalent phenomenon. In the context of a much longer paper on ethics issues in Miami-Dade County, this selection discusses the rationale for public oversight of not-for-profit organizations. It also reports on interesting local survey data.

Source: Miami-Dade County "A Community's Resolve to Restore Integrity, Accountability, and Public Trust: The Miami-Dade Experience (1996 to Present)," unpublished paper, Miami-Dade County, Florida, January 2004.

This report is predicated on the belief that corruption is a community crisis, requiring action by all the major sectors in the community. Scant attention has been directed to nonprofits or community-based organizations, but these organizations comprise a significant percentage of the workforce in the County and allocate and receive substantial government funding. Therefore, it stands to reason nonprofit agencies which request and receive public dollars ought to be held accountable for these funds no differently than private companies receiving government contracts. Local governments need to ensure that these grants and awards are going to serve the community and that the funds are not squandered or misallocated by the recipients.

Oversight takes on many forms and government has a responsibility to assure the public that the monies allocated are properly spent and the services are effectively delivered. This is true whether the government is funding multi-million dollar contracts or awarding small community based organizations grants in the thousands. Regardless of the external controls government adopts to watch over its money, recipients must vow to act ethically and responsibly. With this background, a survey was developed to examine internal ethical considerations within nonprofit agencies in Miami-Dade County and the emphasis such organizations placed on ethical behavior and accountability. In part, the survey sought information about trends occurring within the non-profit community that were connected to the concept of ethical governance.

The survey results portray the need for better consistency in ethics information disseminated among the nonprofit sector. More than half of the respondents reported that the subject of ethics is a topic of concern in a majority of professional workshops, seminars, and conferences. Moreover, a little over a third of the respondents cited that their organizations' trade journals were devoting more space to covering the subject of ethics.

One in four respondents reported that their organizations have been affected by ethical lapses in the last five years. Out of these respondents, three-fourths reported that as a result of these ethical lapses their organizations have implemented "stricter rules on accountability, disclosure and financial standards."

Three in four affirmed that their organizations have established written ethics standards or codes of ethics. Nine out of ten of these respondents reported having a code of ethics established longer than one year. Surprisingly, more than half reported that their organizations did not offer ethics training. Furthermore, one in three who claimed that their organizations did offer ethics training listed various examples of training.

Moreover, although three in four respondents affirmed an organizational code of ethics, more than half reveal that there is no institutional mechanism in place to seek guidance on ethical issues; no vehicle for employees to pursue ethics advice. The data reveals an inconsistent message between the adoption of a code of ethics, standardized ethics training and a medium for attaining an ethics opinion.

In addition, the data also indicates that an inconsistency exists between reporting or witnessing organizational misconduct and organizations being affected by ethical lapses within the last five years. This leads to the conclusion that although one in four organizations were affected by ethical lapses only a few actually witnessed the misconduct that may have violated the law.

It is interesting to note that approximately one-quarter of all the nonprofits surveyed acknowledged some type of ethical lapse in the last five years and most developed stricter rules on accountability, disclosure, and financial statements to remedy the situation. However, very few personnel felt pressured by management to compromise standards to meet objectives and those select few who witnessed misconduct did report their observations to management.

It is difficult to decipher how nonprofits in Miami-Dade address ethical lapses, but the most plausible explanation appears to be formulating a written set of ethics standards. In some cases, action against the wrongdoer was taken and the respondents tend to be satisfied with the manner in which their organizations handle reports of misconduct. By the same token, there is no universal commitment to promote ethical behavior in the form of training and workshops. One wonders about the effects of written standards and guidelines that are not properly disseminated and discussed throughout the organization. Finally, given the responsibilities of nonprofit organizations, ethical quandaries are likely to manifest themselves in a variety of different scenarios and it would be prudent for such agencies to encourage employees to seek advice before acting.

CASE 4: THE ADJUNCT PROFESSOR

David is personnel director for a medium-size university town in a Midwestern American state. He was flattered when the MPA director at the local state university invited him to teach a personnel management course as an adjunct professor. "It greatly benefits our students to learn from practitioners," he was told.

Soon after he agreed to take on the course, David was given advice by Julie, one of his new colleagues, on the logistics of course preparation. "You should order all of the books you might need as free exam copies from the publishers," he was told. "They are happy to send them to you for course consideration."

"But I am pretty sure what text I will use for the course," said David. "Isn't there something unethical about asking for free books if I am not likely to use them, and what about the ethics of publishers sending free books to professors to entice sales to students?"

Source: William L. Richter, Kansas State University

"Nobody in academia views it that way," said Julie. "It is just the way publishers do business, and have done so for decades. Some of them charge nominal fees for exam copies, just to discourage frivolous orders, but many send free books even without your requesting them."

David thought for a moment, then added, "There has been a lot of news in the papers recently about the ethics of drug companies that give doctors free samples. How is this any different? Also, our state has an ethics law that applies to state universities as well as public officials. It says we cannot receive gifts worth more than $40. Most of the university textbooks appear to cost more than that, and I am not certain how I can avoid considering exam copies a gift from the publisher."

"I respect your concerns, David," Julie replied, "but I think you are making too much of this matter. I suggest you talk with other colleagues, even with the university attorney, and satisfy yourself that there is nothing wrong with this system. Then go ahead and order your exam copies."

Case Study Questions

1. Is David being overly sensitive or are there real ethical issues facing him?
2. Can this system be seen as corrupt? Does the fact that David seems to be the only one who thinks so make it less so?
3. Is the analogy between exam copies for professors and drug samples for doctors reasonable?
4. What guidance, if any, does the ASPA code provide to resolve David's ethical concern? What should David do?

CHAPTER DISCUSSION QUESTIONS

1. What is your understanding of corruption? Are you largely in agreement with the ways Luo and Caiden have defined and explained it?

2. Are concerns with corruption in health care and other contemporary policy areas a result of increased corruption or changing perceptions?

3. How important do you think corruption is in relationship to your own role as an ethical administrator? Do you consider it irrelevant (e.g., "I don't have to worry about corruption because I am not a corrupt person"), highly relevant (e.g., "I am sure I will encounter corrupt practices and/or risks of wrongdoing, so I need to be prepared") or somewhere in-between?

FOR FURTHER EXPLORATION

Aquino, Belinda A. *Politics of Plunder: The Philippines Under Marcos*, second ed. Quezon City: University of the Philippines, National College of Public Administration and Governance, 1999.

Gerald Caiden, O. P. Dwivedi and Joseph Jabbra, eds. *Where Corruption Lives*. Kumarian Press, 2001.

Elliott, Kimberly Ann, ed. *Corruption and the Global Economy*. Washington, DC: Institute for International Economics, 1997.

Gilman, Stuart C. "An Idea Whose Time Has Come: The International Experience of the U.S. Office of Government Ethics in Developing Anticorruption Systems," *Public Integrity*, 2:2 (Spring 2000), pp. 135–155.

Heffernan, William C., and John Kleinig, eds. *Private and Public Corruption*. Lanham, MD: Rowman & Littlefield, 2004.

Heidenheimer, Arnold J., and Michael Johnston, eds. *Political Corruption: Concepts & Contexts*. New Brunswick, NJ: Transaction Publishers, 2002.

Johnson, Roberta Ann, ed. *The Struggle Against Corruption: A Comparative Study*. New York: Palgrave Macmillan, 2004.

Jones, Peter. *Fraud and Corruption in Public Services: A Guide to Risk and Prevention*. Aldershot, UK: Gower, 2004.

Joaquin, Ernita. "Decentralization and Corruption: The Bumpy Road to Public Sector Integrity in Developing Countries," *Public Integrity*, 6:3 (Summer 2004), pp. 207–219.

Kidd, John, and Frank-Jurgen Richter, eds. *Fighting Corruption in Asia: Causes, Effects, and Remedies*. New Jersey, London, Singapore, Hong Kong: World Scientific, 2003.

Manion, Melanie. *Corruption by Design: Building Clean Government in Mainland China and Hong Kong*. Cambridge, MA: Harvard University Press, 2004.

Quah, Jon S. T. *Curbing Corruption in Asia: A Comparative Study of Six Countries*. Singapore: Eastern Universities Press, 2003.

Rose-Ackerman, Susan. *Corruption: A Study in Political Economy*. New York: Academic Press, 1978.

———. *Corruption and Government: Causes, Consequences, and Reform*. Cambridge, MA: Cambridge University Press, 1999.

Stapenhurst, Rick, and Sahr J. Kpundeh, eds. *Curbing Corruption: Toward a Model for Building National Integrity*. Washington, DC: The World Bank, 1999

Theobold, Robin. *Corruption, Development and Underdevelopment*. Durham, NC: Duke University Press, 1990.

WEBSITES

Global Corruption Report, 2005, available online and in hard copy, www.globalcorruption report.org/download.html

Stability Pact Anti-Corruption Initiative for Southeastern Europe, http://spai-rslo.org/about/spai/mission.asp

Asian Development Bank Integrity and Anti-corruption site, www.adb.org/Integrity

United Nations Development Programme site on public administration reform and anti-corruption, www.undp.org/governance/sl-par.htm

Chapter 5

GRAFT, BRIBERY, AND CONFLICT OF INTEREST

HONEST GRAFT AND DISHONEST GRAFT
WILLIAM L. RIORDAN

Behind George Washington Plunkitt's homespun philosophy in support of "honest graft" and against the "evils" of civil-service reform lie some serious questions. Are all of Plunkitt's cases illustrations of graft, or can we distinguish among the ethical problems raised by the various examples? Is it possible to make a plausible argument in favor of Plunkitt's distinction between "honest graft" and "dishonest graft"?

Everybody is talkin' these days about Tammany men growin' rich on graft, but nobody thinks of drawin' the distinction between honest graft and dishonest graft. There's all the difference in the world between the two. Yes, many of our men have grown rich in politics. I have myself. I've made a big fortune out of the game, and I'm gettin' richer every day, but I've not gone in for dishonest graft—black-mailin' gamblers, saloon-keepers, disorderly people, etc.—and neither has any of the men who have made big fortunes in politics.

There's an honest graft, and I'm an example of how it works. I might sum up the whole thing by sayin': "I seen my opportunities and I took 'em." Just let me explain by examples. My party's in power in the city, and it's goin' to undertake a lot of public improvements. Well, I'm tipped off, say, that they're going to lay out a new park at a certain place.

I see my opportunity and I take it. I go to that place and I buy up all the land I can in the neighborhood. Then the board of this or that makes its plan public, and there is a rush to get my land, which nobody cared particular for before.

Source: William L. Riordon, *Plunkitt of Tammany Hall* (New York: E. P. Dutton & Co., 1963), ch. 1.

Ain't it perfectly honest to charge a good price and make a profit on my invest-ment and foresight? Of course it is. Well that's honest graft.

Or supposin' it's a new bridge they're goin' to build. I get tipped off and I buy as much property as I can that has to be taken for approaches. I sell at my own price later on and drop some more money in the bank.

Wouldn't you? It's just like lookin' ahead in Wall Street or in the coffee or cot-ton market. It's honest graft. and I'm lookin' for it every day in the year. I will tell you frankly that I've got a good lot of it, too.

I'll tell you of one case. They were goin' to fix up a big park, no matter where. I got on to it, and went lookin' about for land in that neighborhood.

I could get nothin' at a bargain but a big piece of swamp, but I took it fast enough and held on to it. What turned out was just what I counted on. They couldn't make the park complete without Plunkitt's swamp, and they had to pay a good price for it. Anything dishonest in that?

Up in the watershed I made some money, too. I bought up several bits of land there some years ago and made a pretty good guess that they would be bought up for water purposes later by the city.

Somehow, I always guessed about right, and shouldn't I enjoy the profit of my foresight? It was rather amusin' when the condemnation commissioners came along and found piece after piece of the land in the name of George Plunkitt of the fif-teenth Assembly District, New York City. They wondered how I knew just what to buy. The answer is—I seen my opportunity and I took it. I haven't confined myself to land; anything that pays is in my line.

For instance, the city is repavin' a street and has several hundred thousand old granite blocks to sell. I am on hand to buy, and I know just what they are worth.

How? Never mind that. I had a sort of monopoly of this business for a while, but once a newspaper tried to do me. It got some outside men to come over from Brooklyn and New Jersey to bid against me.

Was I done? Not much. I went to each of the men and said: "How many of these 250,000 stones do you want?" One said 20,000, and another wanted 15,000, and other wanted 10,000. I said: "All right, let me bid for the lot, and I'll give each of you all you want for nothin'."

They agreed, of course. Then the auctioneer yelled: "How much am I bid for these 250,000 fine pavin' stones?"

"Two dollars and fifty cents," says I.

"Two dollars and fifty cents!" screamed the auctioneer. "Oh, that's a joke! Give me a real bid."

He found the bid was real enough. My rivals stood silent. I got the lot for $2.50 and gave them their share. That's how the attempt to do Plunkitt ended, and that's how all such attempts end.

STRUGGLING AGAINST BRIBERY
John T. Noonan, Jr.

Bribery is an exceptionally widespread and prominent form of corruption around the world. John Noonan reflects in this selection on some of the features, and some of the contradictions, of recent efforts to deal with bribery.

In Shakespeare's day "bribe" in the sense of a payment to an officeholder was relatively new. Its sense was established by Shakespeare's plays and by Francis Bacon's conviction. In this accomplishment the English language did what the classical languages Greek, Hebrew, and Latin had not done: settle on a precise term for a bad gift, a gift that is corrupt and corrupting. No doubt exists as to the principal practices in view when corruption or bribery is denounced.

The problem—the mess—is everywhere. As to kinds of business, the worst have been identified as the arms trade; the sale of aircraft; the procurement and distribution of energy; the building of infrastructure; and the obtaining of telecommunications rights. As to countries, think of Prime Minister Tanaka and the sale of Lockheed aircraft in Japan, of the strenuous methods, including capital punishment, used to contain corruption in China; of the upheavals in government that charges of corruption have caused in Indonesia, Korea, and the Philippines. Asia is no different from Africa, whose richest countries have been held back in their development by corrupt officeholders such as Abacha of Nigeria and Moi of Kenya. The Near East is little better; even Western-style states like Israel have seen bribes affect political life.

In the old Soviet Union the Communist regime had the effect, although not the intention, of promoting a second underground economy governed by bribery. "Moral double standards, the decline of professional ethics, inefficiencies in centralized planning, the necessity of self-defense in an economy of shortages, the lack of a clear distinction between 'private' and 'public,' the lack of transparency in public finance, the lack of independent agencies of control, of stable public institutions, of an independent press"—all these factors, notes a writer at the University of Warsaw, contributed to corruption which, paradoxically functioned as a kind of stabilizer of the system. Russia and other states that have succeeded to the Soviet heritage still suffer from customs that became entrenched.

If one turns to Western Europe, how different is it? The head of Elf, the largest French oil company, testifies to an accepted pattern of payoffs orchestrated by the president of the republic. A former foreign minister is convicted for bribes paid to his mistress, but acquitted on appeal. The present president of France is accused of being part of a corrupt system. The long-time leader of Germany does not explain

Source: John T. Noonan, Jr., "Struggling Against Corruption," in *Private and Public Corruption*, ed. William C. Heffernan and John Kleinig (Lanham, MD: Rowman & Littlefield, 2004), pp. 227–37 (selection from pp. 229–37).

his party's financing by undisclosed contributions. Prior to the OECD Treaty of 1997 none of its members had laws criminalizing bribes paid to officials of foreign governments and none of them denied tax deductibility to bribes. Britain still has not fulfilled its treaty obligation to criminalize overseas bribery. In Italy serious magistrates uncover a mountain of corruption affecting the major parties. *Mani pulite* was a major success. The furor dies, and the electorate elects a prime minister under indictment. Although proving bribery is often difficult and hard documentation is lacking, the extent of European involvement may be inferred from the fact that in the period from 1994 to 2000, the United States government received complaints of bribery occurring in four hundred competitions affecting $200 billion of contracts.[1] The competitors typically complained about were Europeans.

As recent campaign financing and the campaign itself showed, the United States is not immune from illicit influences upon the government. At Global Forum II, one theme of the conference was, "The enemy is us." Did we look out on a mess or into a mirror?

Country after country notorious for its corrupt customs sent to Global Forum I and Global Forum II representatives who aspired to be rid of the prevailing ways. Were they hypocrites? I attended the Eighth International Congress Against Corruption, held in Lima, Peru, in 1997, with the government of Peru as its host. The government had to surround the meeting site with soldiers to prevent an incident, but the government found it easy to be lavish in its support of anti-corruption talk. President Alberto Fujimori delivered an impassioned speech "for a culture of honorableness" because, "corruption is an old wound that subverts the institutions and undermines the progress of the nations."[2] His government issued a postage stamp to commemorate the great occasion. The Minister of Justice even improbably attributed to the Inca an anti-corruption ethic. Today we all know the hypocrisy of our hosts of 1997. Were the delegates to the Hague any better? Some of them, one may be confident, were not. At the same time one could scarcely doubt the pathetic desire, the sincere hope, of other delegates to destroy an incubus that was destroying their country.

Why is international corruption attracting so much hostile attention? One answer must be the self-interest of American businesses which can compete in corruption only by evading the Foreign Corrupt Practices Act; they have an understandable desire to level the playing field. It is indicative of this desire that General Electric and other large American companies are the financial backers of TI [Transparency International]. More generally, as the economy becomes global; more companies enter the international arena without experience in paying bribes. They do not easily fit the pattern set by arms dealers; they do not want to be pressured to make payoffs. The International Chamber of Commerce begins to speak out.

At the same time the economists who have studied developing countries have come to the conclusion that corruption is the greatest barrier to the developing countries' development. Once the social scientists were tolerant of bribery: "It's the way the system works. Bribes are lubricants. Who are we to judge?" Now, although voices are not unanimous, corruption is seen as fatal to function at a productive level.

Disillusion with foreign aid where the money given is drained off by insiders has had an impact on the World Bank and the IMF. Indonesia under Suharto is a case in point. Why finance Third World efforts at economic improvement, if Third World political leaders treat the loans as spoils? So reasoned Peter Eigen, leaving the World Bank after twenty-five years in order to found TI. So reasoned James Wolfensohn when he became the World Bank's president. The United States Agency for International Development has become active in developing strategy to prevent corruption in the countries it helps.

The initiative appears to be from the West and the North. Countries that once were colonies have had two serious complaints: one, that colonialism sponsored and covered up corruption and that ex-colonies are being unfairly blamed for customs that preceded their independence; two, that the colonialists treated the natives as lesser breeds without the law, incapable of grasping the demands of an anti-bribery ethic. These complaints have left a residue of suspicion directed at the Western powers. But now the developing countries are asserting their own responsibility for reform. Under the auspices of the Global Coalition for Africa, fourteen African nations have adopted a set of anti-corruption principles.[3] The Asia-Pacific Economic Cooperation Forum is developing an anti-corruption program for the wide area it embraces. The leadership has, in countries where new leaders have replaced discredited regimes, taken a strong stand for reform. So the message has run from Obasanjo in Nigeria to Fox in Mexico to Macapagal in the Philippines. Internal reform is linked to international approval and increased trade and investment.

TI itself has been a force in bringing corruption to the fore. It has worked to make citizens the censors of corruption in their government. It has encouraged and publicized the work of the national chapters. It has had its heroes and even martyrs for integrity—for example Obasanjo, the president of its honorary directors, was imprisoned by Abacha in Nigeria. It has provided advice to governments. It has had a leading role in the organization of the international conferences. It has issued its annual index of perceptions of corruption. . . .

"Transparency" itself is a term without old baggage, a modern invention, bridging the economic and the moral. It has proved to be a wonderful shibboleth. Who does not want to have clean windows? It has even come to use by the leadership of the Chinese Communist Party, if the translator of the Tiananmen Papers has accurately translated Central Secretary Zhao telling the other leaders: "No doubt about it, getting rid of corruption is the most urgent task before us. We need transparency. . . . The fight for clean government and against corruption has to start with the Politburo." Chairman Deng replied: "We need to tackle the corruption problem head on."[4] . . .

How important, it may be asked at the end of the day, is the movement against corruption? As a world evil, corruption is not as bad as the exploitation of children by child slavery, child prostitution, child pornography, and child labor. Corruption is not as destructive of life as AIDS or as tobacco or some drugs. Corruption control may not be as vital to the planet's health as arms control. All of these subjects may be more important globally than bribery. But the reduction, if not the elimination, of bribery may be the key to reducing each of the other evils.

NOTES

1. U.S. Department of Commerce, International Trade Administration, *The National Export Strategy, 2000,* www.ita.doc.gov.

2. Alberto Fujimori, Presentation at the Eighth Annual Anti-Corruption Conference (September 7, 1997).

3. Global Coalition for Africa, *Corruption and Development* (1997) GCA/PF/N.2/11/1997.

4. Liang Zhang, *The Tiananmen Papers: The Chinese Leadership's Decision to Use Force Against Their Own People—In Their Own Words,* ed. Andrew J. Nathan and Perry Link (New York: Public Affairs, 2001).

CONFLICT OF INTEREST IN NONPROFIT ETHICS
DAVID SCHULTZ

David Schultz argues that the boundaries among the public, private, and nonprofit sectors become increasingly blurred in "postmodern" society. Yet the three sectors have different practices and expectations, particularly with respect to incentives and rewards. Consequently, as his discussion illustrates, managers of nonprofits may face special challenges when dealing with conflict-of-interest issues. How might these challenges be handled?

The nature of the nonprofit sector, which is neither based on market principles nor constrained by constitutional principles, makes it a unique economic sector. Several characteristics contribute to the sector's uniqueness.

One of these is that the independent sector is mission-driven. According to John Carver (1997), the values of a nonprofit entity are defined by the mission statement that lays out the goals of the organization by specifying the social need it seeks to meet or the good it is trying to achieve (Fischer 2000, 22). Unlike the public or private sectors, where missions pertain to serving the public good or maximizing profit, nonprofit entities are relatively free to define their own missions, values, and purposes. In addition, the nonprofit sector is volunteer-based (Scott 2001). Unlike the other sectors, which are primarily based upon paid or compensated labor, much of the nonprofit world is premised upon the voluntary activity of donors and individuals who freely give their money and time to help others. In *Democracy in America,* Alexis de Tocqueville de-

Source: David Schultz, "Professional Ethics in a Postmodern Society," *Public Integrity,* 6:4 (Fall 2004), 285–90. Reprinted with permission from the American Society for Public Administration.

scribed Americans as unique in their propensity to form voluntary associations to address a variety of social ills and needs (Tocqueville [1835] 1974). These associations serve not only to enhance the social capital of individuals (Putnam 2000) but also perform critical social tasks that might not otherwise be secured if left to the marketplace.

Marilyn Fischer adds the insight that the nonprofit sector is a gift economy. Unlike the market economy, which is based upon interest and an expectation of quid pro quo, the gift economy is different: "The most important feature is that the exchange is not *quid pro quo,* and while reciprocity is expected, the return is not given directly to the original giver. . . . The gift, or another item in its place, is to be passed on to a third person, and then on to another so that the gift circulates widely" (Fischer 2000, 10–12). Such gifts serve to bind people, build communities, and forge a sense of interdependence and connectedness. In her discussion Fischer invokes the Maori word *hau* to underscore that gifts have a magical or spiritual capacity to transform people.

One of the magical or transformative properties of gift-giving is that it inculcates specific virtues in the givers, such as sympathetic understanding, empathy, and charity (Fischer 2000, 6). To give out of love and not interest, it would seem, makes people better, morally developing them in ways that market exchanges cannot. The gift relationship, as an alternative to the commodified activity of the marketplace, encourages behavior not found elsewhere, thereby forging social as opposed to economic bonds among people, including even strangers (Titmuss 1971). The gift economy encourages people to act from altruistic motives, and not simply economic self-interest.

The values of sympathy, virtue, compassion, and voluntarism define the domain of the nonprofit sector. The critical difference between the profit and non-profit sectors is that the former seeks to fulfill the mission of making a profit, whereas the latter makes a profit or engages in revenue generation in order to fulfill a mission. Although the public sector is premised upon constitutional or legal limits to respect the rights of individuals, it respects rights in the Kantian moral sense of treating people as ends and not means. Moreover, although openness and transparency are constitutional mandates of the public sector, Carver (1997) and others have argued that a board-driven nonprofit organization must be accountable to all of its stakeholders, including donors and clients. Its demand for accountability comes from the requirement to maintain a sense of connectedness to all interested parties and strive to redefine social relations along a noncommodified set of social relations.

The private, public, and nonprofit sectors emerged to address different social functions. The three sectors have developed unique vocabularies for use in describing their ethical imperatives. Together they refer to a series of practices and behaviors that take on meanings specific to each of the sectors, conveying specific ethical norms and judgments regarding what is expected of individuals in the sector. Concepts derive their meaning from use, and their usage reflects a specific form of life or social activity (Wittgenstein [1953] 1968). In short, as Jane Jacobs (1992) suggests in her contrast of the worlds of politics and commerce, different idioms and social positions dictate different ethical rules and standards.

COMPARING ETHICS ACROSS SECTORS

The ethical values and nouns of the public, private, and nonprofit sectors are different. What effect does this have when judgments of specific conduct are examined across the three economic sectors? One way to understand the implications of the different ethical mandates is to compare similar fact patterns or situations and see whether they merit different judgments contingent upon the sectors in which they are located.

Sales, fund-raising, and the payment of bonuses for meeting or exceeding targeted goals constitutes an area that demonstrates a difference in ethical values across economic sectors. For example, a portion of the income of a salesperson who works in the private sector may be based on a commission for each product sold. Such commissioned sales use self-interest to reward results and thus motivate effort. Commissions clearly reward merit or effort. Doing so is consistent with the notions of distributive justice common in the era when Aristotle wrote Book V of the *Ethics,* which deems allocations of social goods to be just if awarded in proportion to an accepted criterion that individuals possess.

Similarly, in the private sector, managers are paid bonuses or given part of the savings that yield from cutting costs in their department. In fact, giving bonuses or rewards for cost-cutting measures or innovative ideas is a staple of many companies. IBM, for example, has long encouraged employees to suggest ideas and, if implemented successfully, gives them a portion of the first year's savings. Using economic incentives and self-interest as tools to encourage private sector activity is not only good business but ethical.

Similar rewards would not always be viewed as ethical in the public and nonprofit sectors. In the public sector, for example, it would be unethical to provide financial incentives to police officers to encourage them to issue more traffic citations (admittedly, this does occur in some jurisdictions). Such a system would be a recipe encouraging police harassment or violations of the law and individual civil rights. Giving tax collectors a portion of the proceeds they raise by doing their job or giving clerks a portion of their compensation based upon the number of licenses or permits issued is also wrong in the public sector. In all these instances, the use of self-interest to motivate behavior is improper. Giving money to individuals based upon sales or upon savings traditionally would either constitute an impermissible use of public money- a gift to a private individual—or would be a conflict of interest. It would be giving a public sector manager a personal financial stake in a matter instead of acting for the best interests of the public. At the very least, it would rise to the level of an apparent conflict of interest, leading the public to question the motives for the action.

In the nonprofit sector, the issue of commissioned fund-raising has long been considered unethical. For example, the *Code of Ethical Principles of the Association of Fundraising Professionals* lists three relevant rules in its Standards of Professional Practice:

16. Members shall not accept compensation that is based on a percentage
    of charitable contributions; nor shall they accept finder's fees.

17. Members may accept performance-based compensation, such as bonuses, provided such bonuses are in accord with prevailing practices within the members' own organizations, and are not based on a percentage of charitable contributions.

18. Members shall not pay finder's fees, commissions or percentage compensation based on charitable contributions and shall take care to discourage their organization: from making such payments.

Similarly, the Maryland Association of Nonprofit Organizations states, in its *Standards for Excellence: An Ethics and Accountability Code for the Nonprofit Sector:* "Fundraising personnel, including both employees and independent consultants, should not be compensated based on a percentage of the amount raised or other commission formula." Why is such behavior considered unethical? Two reasons are offered. First, the principle of donor intent is paramount in the world of nonprofit charity (Fischer 2000, 169–72). Both the law and the principles of philanthropy are based upon the idea that groups that receive money from contributors should honor their intentions.

The American Red Cross was criticized for transferring extra donations received as a result of soliciting for the 9/11 fund. Donors thought they were giving to help the victims of the terrorist attacks, and not to set up a trust fund for future disasters, no matter how worthy or prudent the project was. Similarly, a person who gives money to a nonprofit believes that it is going to that organization and not toward a commission for the fund-raiser. Granted, a fund-raiser hired on the basis of a straight salary would also be compensated from the money raised, but in the latter case, fund-raisers can legitimately claim to be soliciting money for the organization first and not solely for themselves.

A second argument against the use of commissioned nonprofit fund raising is that it undermines the trust between the donor and the nonprofit or charity (Fischer 2000, 169–72). Donors give because they believe that the money is going to the charity, not to a commission, and any lack of honesty regarding the solicitation and the destination of the money will undermine the trust relationship between the donor and the charity. Moreover, with commissioned fund-raising, the donor does not know whether the solicitation is motivated by self-interest or the charity's mission. Fischer believes that doubts about the real purpose of the solicitation undermine both the trust relationship and the basic principles and virtues inculcated by the gift economy.

The activity of commissioned sales or bonuses can be emulated in all three economic sectors. Nonetheless, the ethical principles found in the public and nonprofit sectors would decry such a practice as unethical. In the private sector, however, such behavior would be permissible because self-interest would be seen as a legitimate motivating tool and mechanism to reward individuals.

Attitudes about giving gifts further illustrate the difference in ethical principles across economic sectors. In the private sector, giving gifts to those with whom one does business is a standard practice. Gift-giving may serve as a way to thank people for giving you their business. For example, a real estate agent may give a gift to clients after helping them to buy or sell a house. Similarly, gifts may be given as a token of appreciation for good work, for doing business with someone, or to encourage friendship or perhaps cultivate a relationship that will stimulate business in the future. Private sector gift-giving is generally seen as a routine cost of doing business, raising few questions or concerns.

In contrast, gift-giving is generally frowned upon in the public sector. The giving of gifts to public officials, especially by lobbyists, is viewed as an effort to influence decisions. In some cases, giving a gift with the intent to influence an official act may constitute criminal bribery. The federal government, via the Ethics in Government Act, as well as by House and Senate rules, places significant restrictions on the ability of lobbyists and other individuals to give gifts, limiting their value to less than $50. Minnesota and Wisconsin have enacted broad bans on gifts to public officials as part of an effort to prevent quid pro quo corruption.

In the nonprofit sector, gift-giving occupies an ambiguous status. As Fischer (2000) points out, the hallmark of the nonprofit sector is the promotion of specific virtues as a result of the giving of gifts. She sees donor gift-giving as different from giving gifts out of appreciation, such as when service recipients give gifts to staff. In the latter case, the gifts are tokens of appreciation and probably are not impermissible so long as they are not meant to influence or otherwise affect the delivery of services. However, if the staff accepts gifts when these donations are really meant to go to the charity, this may lead to questions regarding whether the staff person is acting selfishly or in the organization's best interest.

Overall, gift-giving raises a variety of moral concerns across all three economic sectors, but the nature of the concerns is unquestionably different in each sector.

REFERENCES

Carver, John. 1997. *Boards That Make a Difference: A New Design for Leadership in Nonprofit and Public Organizations.* San Francisco: Jossey-Bass.

Fischer, Marilyn. 2000. *Ethical Decision Making in Fund Raising.* New York: John Wiley.

Jacobs, Jane. 1992. *Systems of Survival: A Dialogue on the Moral Foundations of Commerce and Politics.* New York: Random House.

Scott, Jacquelyn Thayer. 2001. "Voluntary Sector." In *The Nature of the Nonprofit Sector*, edited by J. Steven Ott, pp. 40–56. Boulder, Colo.: Westview Press.

Putnam, Robert. 2000. *Bowling Alone: The Collapse and Revival of American Community.* New York: Simon & Schuster.

Titmuss, Richard M. 1971. *The Gift Relationship: From Human Blood to Social Policy.* New York: Vintage Books.

Tocqueville, Alexis de. [1835] 1974. *Democracy in America*, 1st ed. New York: Schocken Books.

Wittgenstein, Ludwig [1953] 1968. *Philosophical Investigations.* New York: Macmillan.

EXTREMISM IN THE SEARCH FOR VIRTUE
Kathryn G. Denhardt and Stuart C. Gilman

Denhardt and Gilman take issue with advocates of "Zero Gift" policies intended to avoid conflicts of interest and encourage public trust. They argue that such policies have adverse unintended consequences and that other approaches are preferable.

Public trust in government depends on a robust perception that government employees are acting in the public interest. . . . However, trust also depends on a perception that government employees are able to make good judgments based on standards of reasonableness. Although a zero gift policy leaves no room for doubt about expectations, it also leaves no room for participating in basic social graces because situations like the following become problematic: An employee at the Social Security Administration helps an elderly woman settle her husband's death claims. The woman sends the employee flowers. An Agriculture Department staff person ensures that a farmer gets crop damage payments that are due the farmer. In the fall, the farmer sends the employee a basket of apples.

Accepting the flowers violates a zero gift policy, but how does one return them? The basket of apples might be donated to a charity or put out for all to eat, but it would still have violated a zero gift policy. In one extreme example, an official received written advice from an ethics officer suggesting that the use of tissue paper and water in a private contractor's facility might be construed as a gift.

An unintended consequence of an absolutist approach is the creation of unnecessarily awkward situations. Should employees interact with citizens with enough detachment to ensure that no expression of appreciation is ever offered? Surely this would feed the stereotype of the rigid, uncaring bureaucrat, when we know that such "uncaring" behavior is one cause of the deteriorating trust in government (Pew Research Center for the People and the Press 1999). By modifying the gift policy to permit gifts of minimal *(de minimus)* value, such unintended quandaries can be avoided. . . .

Confidence in government is eroded when there is any appearance that a public servant's actions are influenced by a gift of any sort. In *Deconstructing Distrust*, the Pew Research Center (1999) found that "discontent with political leaders and lack of faith in the political system are principal factors that stand behind public distrust of government. Much of that criticism involves the honesty and ethics of government leaders" (p. 4). Specific statements from respondents fell into categories such as "politicians are dishonest crooks" and "only out for themselves/for own personal gain." Without a doubt, distrust is fed by revelations that personal gain may have influenced an official's actions. A gift policy is essential, and as important for elected officials as for civil servants.

Source: Kathryn G. Denhardt and Stuart C. Gilman, "Extremism in the Search for Virtue: Why Zero Gift Policies Spawn Unintended Consequences," *Public Integrity* (Winter 2002), 75–80. Reprinted with permission from the American Society for Public Administration.

A "BRIGHT LINE" DE MINIMUS POLICY IS
PREFERABLE TO A ZERO GIFT POLICY

Prohibitionist policies are well intentioned and grounded in important values, but the enforcement too often results in situations that defy common standards of reasonableness and propriety. In one case, a major procurement process had to be voided after a losing bidder reported that an official had accepted a Big Mac and fries at the local McDonald's. This cost taxpayers hundreds of thousands of dollars and the procurement officer's job, even though there was general agreement that the lunch did not influence the official's decision.

Until 1993 the federal government used the model ethics code contained in Executive Order 11222 specifying that no gifts of any value could be accepted. At that time there was no *de minimus* provision allowing gifts to be accepted. In order to enforce this policy, agencies such as the Internal Revenue Service and Defense Department imposed administrative sanctions on employees for accepting anything of value from a client, vendor, or member of the public. The largest number of actions taken by the inspector general at Defense between 1985 and 1992 was for accepting free coffee and refreshments from contractors. Almost one thousand official reprimands were issued per year for such offenses, often preventing or delaying promotions of employees receiving the reprimands. The combined total of all other violations (e.g., misuse of government proper) was no more than one hundred in any year (Office of Government Ethics 1992, 15). Enforcing this policy required ethics officials to spend an inordinate amount of time on it and squander precious resources, often to the detriment of other significant ethics considerations.

The policy was intended to raise standards of all employees and to enhance trust in government. Those enforcing the policies came to believe that the opposite was occurring. Employees were offended by the notion that they "could be bought for the price of a cup of coffee" and developed a jaundiced view of ethics policies in general. Ethics training and guidelines began to be a target of ridicule instead of representing a call to a higher standard of public service. Enforcement of the policy actually undermined respect for other critical ethics rules.

The federal government's response was to publish a new set of government-wide standards of conduct in 1993, which specifically eliminated a number of things from the definition of a gift (e.g., coffee, donuts, greeting cards, plaques and certificates intended solely for presentation) (Standards of Ethical Conduct 1993). In addition, these guidelines instituted an exception for unsolicited gifts having a market value of $20 or less per source per occasion and not to exceed an aggregate value of $50 in a calendar year. Thus the federal government abandoned a zero gift policy in favor of building in enough "breathing room" to allow for common social courtesies. . . .

One indication that respect for federal rules has rebounded is found in opinion data *(Executive Branch Employee Ethics Survey* 2000) showing that "the frequency of ethics training is directly related to employees' positive perception of an ethical culture and ethical employee behavior in their agencies" (p. 8). In addition, the findings show that "significant relationships exist between program awareness (i.e., familiarity with the ethics program and the Rules of Ethical Conduct), program usefulness (i.e., in making employees more aware of issues and in guiding decisions and conduct), and ethics outcomes" (p. 10).

A *de minimus* approach is also taken in many local governments. In 1990 the City of Los Angeles enacted a policy that creates a "bright line" for gifts of minimal value. Officials may not accept a gift or combination of gifts within a calendar year from one source that exceeds the following values: $25 from registered lobbyists and lobbying firms, $100 from other "restricted sources" as defined by law, such as persons who have matters pending before the official, and $320 from any other source. Exceptions to the gift limits include gifts from family members (spouse, child, parent, grandparent, grandchild, sibling, niece, nephew, in-laws, aunt, uncle, first cousin) (Los Angeles City Ethics Commission 1990).

It is important to note that the restriction should specify (1) a maximum value for any single gift, (2) a maximum aggregate value for all gifts from a single source in a given time period, and (3) provisions that allow for personal gifts from family members. If a provision for a maximum aggregate value for all gifts is missing, for example, the spirit of the law may be circumvented by someone giving an official a set of golf clubs—one at a time—as has occurred.

PROVISIONS FOR PUBLIC DISCLOSURE OF GIFTS AND INDEPENDENT THIRD-PARTY REVIEW

Another strategy for avoiding rigidity while promoting confidence in government is to utilize the mechanisms of disclosure and/or approval by an independent third party. On some occasions employees are offered something of value that would be of significant benefit to the government while not posing a conflict of interest. For example, after Hurricane Andrew the emergency management professionals were asked to share their knowledge and experiences with other emergency managers and consultants at meetings around the country. The invitations were often accompanied by an offer to pay travel expenses. These managers were offered something of significant value (travel expenses) for sharing what they had learned. It is likely that the manager would also learn things at the meetings that would benefit the employing government. Reasonable people might agree that this would be a worthwhile exchange, but a strictly enforced zero gift policy would probably prohibit it. An alternative is to have a policy requiring the approval of an independent third party. This party would have no conflict of interest and could make a reasonable judgment in the situation. . . .

Another option is to require disclosure of all gifts as a way of detecting and dealing with any potential conflicts of interest that could erode trust. Such a provision puts the emphasis on transparency rather than rigid rules, and it allows for public dialogue about what constitutes a reasonable situation. . . .

CONCLUSION

Efforts in recent years to rebuild trust in government by encouraging civic engagement are based in part on building bonds and partnerships between communities, governments, businesses, and nonprofit organizations. If those interactions are successful, there are likely to be more, rather than fewer, opportunities for government employees to receive "something of value" (e.g., meals or trips associated with board of directors meetings on which a public official might sit because of his/her government position). A zero gift policy may discourage employees from interacting with nonprofits, businesses, and the public during a time when we are trying to encourage greater interaction and partnerships. A more reasonable and workable solution would be a *de minimus* policy allowing the acceptance of gifts of a specified minimal value, along with mechanisms for independent third party review and disclosure of all items received.

REFERENCES

Executive Branch Employee Ethics Survey 2000: Final Report 2000. Prepared by Arthur Andersen for the U.S. Office of Government Ethics. Available at www.usoge.gov/pages/forms_pubs_otherdocs/fpo_files/surveys_ques/srvyemp_rpt.pdf.

Federal Commission on Ethics Law Reform. 1989. *To Serve with Honor: Report of the Federal Commission on Ethics Law Reform.* Washington, D.C.: Commission on Ethics Law Reform, March.

International City/County Management Association. 2000. Code of Ethics. Available at www.icma.org/go.cfm?cid=1&gid=2&sid=3.

———. 2000. "Running for a Cause." *Public Management*, February, p. 4.

Los Angeles City Ethics Commission. 1990. www.lacity.org/eth/Guides.htm.

Office of Government Ethics. 1992. *Second Biennial Report to Congress.* Washington, DC: Office of Government Ethics, March.

Pew Research Center for the People and the Press. 1999. *Deconstructing Distrust: How Americans View Government.* Available at www.people-press.org/trustrpt.htm.

Standards of Ethical Conduct for Employees of the Executive Branch. 1993. Available at www.usoge.gov/pages/laws_regs_fedreg_stats/oge_regs/5cfr2635.html.

Stark, Andrew. 1997. "Beyond Quid Pro Quo: What's Wrong with Private Gain from Public Office?" *American Political Science Review.* March, pp. 108–120.

CASE 5: THE GIFT OF A CARPET

While serving as Associate Provost for International Programs of my university, I received a couple of visitors from Pakistan who were interested in establishing a relationship between their institution and ours. It was common practice for visitors to

Source: William L. Richter, Kansas State University.

bring small gifts and for our office to present them with small gifts, such as pens or letter openers. These guests presented me with a larger gift, a Pakistani carpet. I was uncomfortable accepting a gift that I estimated to be worth at least $400, so I checked with our university attorney. I was told that state law prohibited our receiving gifts worth more than $40, either personally or on behalf of our office, if the gift appeared to be given in exchange for anticipated benefit. Since the gift both appeared to be worth more than $40 and given with the intent of facilitating the intended inter-institutional agreement, I decided I needed to return it to our visitors. When I attempted to do so, they refused to take it back, saying that it would be culturally "insulting" for them to do so. How should I have dealt with this situation?

The visitors absolutely refused to take back the carpet. The way in which I finally dealt with this issue was tied to a fortunate circumstance in our city. The local Islamic community had recently constructed a new Islamic Center, primarily a small mosque with additional meeting rooms. I made arrangements to donate the carpet to the mosque and wrote the Pakistani donors that the carpet had been given to the Islamic Center in their name. For some years now, the carpet has been an integral part of Friday worship services. We did not enter into the proposed arrangement with the Pakistani institution.

Case Study Questions

1. How might this situation have been handled better? Should I have refused the gift immediately on the ground that it exceeded legal limits under which we operated? Should I have accepted it on the assumption that it was a good-will gesture, especially since no benefits ultimately came to the donors? Did passing the gift on to another recipient absolve me of having received it in the first place? What might I have done if the Islamic Center or some similar recipient had not been available?

2. Are the policies that govern the giving and receiving of gifts appropriate? A "zero-gift" policy would present some real challenges for an international office, especially in dealing with cultures where gift-giving is a normal and expected part of establishing relations. How might policies be improved?

3. What should one do when superiors receive gifts, apparently in violation of known standards?

4. What if the gifts one receives are "incentive prizes" for fundraising for a non-profit charity? Is it wrong to realize personal benefits from charitable fundraising?

CHAPTER DISCUSSION QUESTIONS

1. Have you found yourself in conflict-of-interest situations, or have you observed others in such situations? Do you think they were handled appropriately?

2. Do you think it is true that most people who run into conflict-of-interest problems do so thoughtlessly or unintentionally? Or are some people just "out to beat the system" by wrongdoing? What are the implications for ethical management?

3. Do you think that there is such a thing as "honest" graft? Do you or others you know receive "side benefits" (i.e., rewards that are not part of your formal compensation package) in your administrative role that you regard as legitimate? How do we determine which rewards are legitimate and which not?

<hr>

FOR FURTHER EXPLORATION

Bellow, Adam. *In Praise of Nepotism: A Natural History.* New York: Doubleday, 2003.

Denhardt, Kathryn G., and Stuart C. Gilman. "In Search of Virtue: Why Ethics Policies Spawn Unintended Consequences," in *Ethics in Public Management,* ed. H. George Frederickson and Richard K. Ghere (Armonk, NY: M. E. Sharpe, 2005), pp. 259–273.

Hunt, Jennifer. *Trust and Bribery: The Role of the Quid Pro Quo and the Link with Crime.* Bonn, Germany: IZA, 2004.

Johnson, Simon. *Corruption, Public Finances, and the Unofficial Economy.* Washington, DC: World Bank, 1999.

Noonan, John Thomas. *Bribes.* New York: Macmillan, 1984.

Stark, Andrew. *Conflict of Interest in American Public Life.* Cambridge, MA: Harvard University Press, 2000.

———. "Public-Sector Conflict of Interest at the Federal Level in Canada and the U.S.: Differences in Understanding and Approach," in *Ethics and Public Administration,* ed. H. George Frederickson (Armonk, NY: M. E. Sharpe, 1993), pp. 52–75.

WEBSITES

Bibliography on the Foreign Corrupt Practices Act and International Corruption, prepared by the Office of Chief Counsel, International Commerce, U.S. Department of Commerce, www.osec.doc.gov/ogc/occic/fcpabibo.htm

International Chamber of Commerce Recommendations to Governments and International Organizations on Extortion and Bribery, www.itcilo.it/english/actrav/telearn/global/ilo/guide/iccbrib.htm

OECD site on anti-bribery convention, www.oecd.org/document/32/0,2340,en_2649_34855_1841184_1_1_1_1,00.html

U.S. Department of Commerce set of linkages on transparency and anti-bribery initiatives, www.osec.doc.gov/ogc/occic/tabi.html

U.S. Foreign Corrupt Practices Act, www.usdoj.gov/criminal/fraud/fcpa.html

Watson, Geoffrey R. "The OECD Convention on Bribery," website of the American Society of International Law, www.asil.org/insights/insigh14.htm

Wikipedia entry on Bribery, http://en.wikipedia.org/wiki/Bribery

Chapter 6

LYING, CHEATING, AND DECEPTION

LIES FOR THE PUBLIC GOOD
SISSELA BOK

In her book, Lying, *Sissela Bok examines a wide range of moral issues raised by lying and other forms of deception in both public and private life. She explores here questions we have already encountered: Where does one draw the line between acceptable and unacceptable behavior? Can we justify otherwise unethical behavior, such as deceit, if it is a means to larger goals?*

THE NOBLE LIE

Three circumstances have seemed to liars to provide the strongest excuse for their behavior—a crisis where overwhelming harm can be averted only through deceit; complete harmlessness and triviality to the point where it seems absurd to quibble about whether a lie has been told; and the duty to particular individuals to protect their secrets. I have shown how lies in times of crisis can expand into vast practices where the harm to be averted is less obvious and the crisis less and less immediate; how white lies can shade into equally vast practices no longer so harmless, with immense cumulative costs; and how lies to protect individuals and to cover up their secrets can be told for increasingly dubious purposes to the detriment of all.

When these three expanding streams flow together and mingle with yet another—a desire to advance the public good—they form the most dangerous body of deceit of all. These lies may not be justified by an immediate crisis nor by complete triviality nor by duty to any one person; rather, liars tend to consider them as right and unavoidable because of the altruism that motivates them. . . .

[T]he most characteristic defense for these lies is . . . based on the benefits they may confer and the long-range harm they can avoid. The intention may be broadly

Source: Sissela Bok, *Lying: Moral Choice in Public and Private Life* (New York: Vintage Books, 1999), pp. 166–70. Used by permission of Pantheon Books, a division of Random House, Inc.

paternalistic, as when citizens are deceived "for their own good," or only a few may be lied to for the benefit of the community at large. Error and self-deception mingle with these altruistic purposes and blur them; the filters through which we must try to peer at lying are thicker and more distorting than ever in these practices. But I shall try to single out, among these lies, the elements that are consciously and purposely intended to benefit society.

A long tradition in political philosophy endorses some lies for the sake of the public. Plato . . . first used the expression "noble lie" for the fanciful story that might be told to people in order to persuade them to accept class distinctions and thereby safeguard social harmony. According to this story, God Himself mingled gold, silver, iron, and brass in fashioning rulers, auxiliaries, farmers, and craftsmen, intending these groups for separate tasks in a harmonious hierarchy.

The Greek adjective which Plato used to characterize this falsehood expresses a most important fact about lies by those in power: This adjective is "gennaion," which means "noble" in the sense of both "high-minded" and "well-bred." The same assumption of nobility, good breeding, and superiority to those deceived is also present in Disraeli's statement that a gentleman is one who knows when to tell the truth and when not to. In other words, lying is excusable when undertaken for "noble" ends by those trained to discern these purposes.

Rulers, both temporal and spiritual, have seen their deceits in the benign light of such social purposes. They have propagated and maintained myths, played on the gullibility of the ignorant, and sought stability in shared beliefs. They have seen themselves as high-minded and well-bred—whether by birth or by training—and as superior to those they deceive. Some have gone so far as to claim that those who govern have a *right* to lie. The powerful tell lies believing that they have greater than ordinary understanding of what is at stake; very often, they regard their dupes as having inadequate judgment, or as likely to respond in the wrong way to truthful information.

At times, those who govern also regard particular circumstances as too uncomfortable, too painful, for most people to be able to cope with rationally. They may believe, for instance, that their country must prepare for long-term challenges of great importance, such as a war, an epidemic, or a belt-tightening in the face of future shortages. Yet they may fear that citizens will be able to respond only to short-range dangers. Deception at such times may seem to the government leaders as the only means of attaining the necessary results.

The perspective of the liar is paramount in all such decisions to tell "noble" lies. If the liar considers the responses of the deceived at all, he assumes that they will, once the deceit comes to light and its benefits are understood be uncomplaining if not positively grateful. . . .

Some experienced public officials are impatient with any effort to question the ethics of such deceptive practices (except actions obviously taken for private ends). They argue that vital objectives in the national interest require a measure of deception to succeed in the face of powerful obstacles. Negotiations must be carried on that are best left hidden from public view; bargains must be struck that simply cannot be comprehended by a politically unsophisticated electorate. A certain amount of illusion is needed in order for public servants to be effective. Every government, therefore, has to deceive people to some extent in order to lead them. These officials view the public's concern for ethics as understandable but hardly realistic. Such "moralistic" concerns, put forth without any understanding of practical exigencies, may lead to the setting of impossible standards; these could seriously hamper work without actually changing the underlying practices. Government officials could then feel so beleaguered that some of them might quit their jobs; inefficiency and incompetence would then increasingly afflict the work of the rest.

If we assume the perspective of the deceived—those who experience the consequences of government deception—such arguments are not persuasive. We cannot take for granted either the altruism or the good judgment of those who lie to us, no matter how much they intend to benefit us. We have learned that much deceit for private gain masquerades as being in the public interest. We know how deception, even for the most unselfish motive, corrupts and spreads. And we have lived through the consequences of lies told for what were believed to be noble purposes.

Equally unpersuasive is the argument that there always has been government deception, and always will be, and that efforts to draw lines and set standards are therefore useless annoyances. It is certainly true that deception can never be completely absent from most human practices. But there are great differences among societies in the kinds of deceit that exist and the extent to which they are practiced, differences also among individuals in the same government and among successive governments within the same society. This strongly suggests that it is worthwhile trying to discover why such differences exist and to seek ways of raising the standards of truthfulness.

The argument that those who raise moral concerns are ignorant of political realities, finally, ought to lead, not to a dismissal of such inquiries, but to a more articulate description of what these realities are, so that a more careful and informed debate could begin. We have every reason to regard government as more profoundly injured by a dismissal of criticism and a failure to consider standards than by efforts to discuss them openly. If duplicity is to be allowed in exceptional cases, the criteria for these exceptions should themselves be openly debated and publicly chosen. Otherwise government leaders will have free rein to manipulate and distort the facts and thus escape accountability to the public.

The effort to question political deception cannot be ruled out so summarily. The disparagement of inquiries into such practices has to be seen as the defense of unwarranted power—power bypassing the consent of the governed.

LYING IN THE PUBLIC INTEREST
Lynn Pasquerella and Alfred G. Killilea

Lynn Pasquerella and Alfred G. Killilea consider the issue of whether governmental lies can be justified. They review the arguments of several key theorists on this subject and suggest that there can be "just lies" on the same grounds that there can be "just wars." Is their argument persuasive? If so, do the "just lie" criteria provide sufficient guidance to public managers to know when and when not to lie? Can these arguments be applied to contemporary issues of lying and deception?

There is perhaps no more controversial issue in assessing the limits of political and administrative discretion than whether it is ever ethical for an official to lie in the public interest. While citizens commonly think of politicians as by nature challenged by truth-telling, very few would want to concede that officials have, on occasion, the right to deceive. The burden of lies Americans bear from Vietnam, Watergate, Irangate, Monicagate, and, possibly, Iraqgate makes them want to erect a firewall against even the temptation for officials to think it is ever legitimate to lie.

However, there are compelling examples of special circumstances that seem to require an official to deceive if the public interest is not to be seriously jeopardized. . . .

THE CASE FOR DECEPTION

Almost all commentators on official lying trace the roots of this practice to Machiavelli. Plato is spared paternity of the great lie presumably because he thought the myths told by his Philosopher King were not really deceptions but stories that portrayed truths that simple minds could grasp only through fictitious facts. Machiavelli countenanced more outright deception. He was not a skeptic about whether humans can know the truth, but he was a profound skeptic about whether humans in power can say the truth. Machiavelli did not advise deception for reasons of mere expediency but for reasons of necessity:

> a prudent ruler cannot, and must not, honor his word when it places him at a disadvantage and when the reasons for which he made his promise no longer exist. If all men were good, this precept would not be good; but because men are wretched creatures who would not keep their word to you, you need not keep your word to them. (1981, pp. 99–100)

Source: Lynn Pasquerella and Alfred G. Killilea, "The Ethics of Lying in the Public Interest: Reflections on the 'Just Lie,'" *Public Integrity* 7, no. 5 (Summer 2005): 261–273. Reprinted with permission from the American Society for Public Administration.

Machiavelli saw politics as a deadly serious pursuit. The prince who wants to achieve something, even (indeed especially) if it is in the interest of the people, has so many forces aligned against any change that he cannot afford to abide by the rules of ethics that apply in private life. When a person of power tries to change the status quo, Machiavelli warned, the people who will be harmed, even if they are a small minority, can usually stave off the change because they are more organized, more motivated, more aware of the advantage they will be losing. Those who will gain, especially if they are poor and downtrodden, will support the change only half-heartedly, for they have not experienced the fruits of the change and are dubious that there will be any real difference. Anyone who doubts the currency of this 500-year-old argument need only consider the campaigns of the National Rifle Association against gun control and the insurance industry against universal health care. . . .

It is [Machiavelli's] lack of self-consciousness of how extreme one may become in venturing from what is moral that seems to drive the theory of "dirty hands" articulated by Michael Walzer, the main contemporary theorist who defends the necessity of official breaking of moral codes. He agrees with Machiavelli that an effective political leader must learn how not to be good: "nor do most of us believe that those who govern us are innocent. . . even the best of them" (Walzer 1973, 161). Walzer has no illusions about the virtue of democratic leaders: "the men who act for us and in our name are necessarily hustlers and liars." He is convinced that we would not want to be governed by people who consistently took the uncompromising "absolutist" position, but he worries about leaders who accept the utilitarian calculation unreflectively with no sense of guilt about the moral norms they have broken. He attempts to reject the stiff and unworkable absolutist position without denying the reality of the moral dilemma and a loss of innocence. . . .

Walzer makes a remarkable contribution in helping to straddle a mid-course between uncompromising absolutism and a political world with no moral imperatives. He encourages political actors to take the taboos against lying very seriously, but in the end he abandons the taboos in a search for criteria by which to gauge temptations and offenses. This incompleteness in Walzer's theory seems to call out for the kind of guidance provided by the just lie theory, which appears to centrally address the problem that the dirty hands theory, as he acknowledges, does not: "questions of degree." At the very least, the just lie theory may help society to identify Walzer's "greatest liars" and gauge the excesses of their lies. . . .

MAUREEN RAMSAY ON THE FLAWS OF THE JUST LIE THEORY

The most substantial recent commentary on lying by public officials is found in a chapter authored by Maureen Ramsay in *The Politics of Lying: Implications for Democracy* (Cliffe, Ramsay, and Bartlett 2000). Before we turn to Ramsay, however, Sissela Bok's earlier work on lying should be noted. Bok attempted to demonstrate that

Michael Walzer's anguish is misplaced and unnecessary, for there is virtually no basis for officials in a democracy to deceive. In her classic challenge to almost all forms of deception, *Lying: Moral Choice in Public and Private Life*, Bok rejects Machiavelli's and Walzer's realist argument that politics inevitably demands deception. She graphically describes the naive self-serving motivations of all liars and of government officials in particular. She depicts the shortsightedness of selective truth-tellers and persuasively recounts how their moral exceptions become precedents for themselves and others. While realists think that being charged with the well-being of so many people sometimes entitles the prince to lie, Bok sees the obverse: "Political lies, so often assumed to be trivial by those who tell them, rarely are. They cannot be trivial when they affect so many people and when they are so peculiarly likely to be imitated, used to retaliate, and spread from a few to many" (Bok 1989, 175).

Bok is not as absolute as Augustine or Kant in condemning every instance of mendacity. She allows for white lies that are completely harmless and acknowledges that extraordinary crises may require officials to deceive citizens. In cases such as withholding information about early signs of an epidemic in order to prevent a panic, Bok concludes that one may be justified in lying because the deception "can be acknowledged and defended as soon as the threat is over" (1989, 178). But she also asserts that "such cases are so rare that they hardly exist for practical purposes." Her summary standard for recourse to deception is that it must be agreed to in advance: "only those deceptive practices which can be openly debated and consented to in advance are *justifiable* in a democracy" (181). Bok would extend her deep skepticism about the motives of deceptive officials to the remarkable extent that she asks: "Would we not, on balance, prefer to run the risk of failing to rise to a crisis honestly explained to us, from which the government might have saved us through manipulation?" (180).

This sacrifice of security for honesty by Bok is all the more dramatic when it is considered that the crisis to which she is referring is the one that loomed before World War II. What seems to allow her to downplay the extraordinary price of honesty in an unmet crisis is the assumption that the government is usually not as pressed as it claims to be and does not need to have recourse to deception. She argues that lies on sensitive topics, such as the intention to impose wage and price restraints, can be avoided by having an established policy that officials will not comment on matters dealing with the economy, national security, and other delicate areas.

As discussed at greater length elsewhere (Pasquerella, Killilea, and Vocino 1996, 1–4), Bok's attempt to protect democracy by avoiding official lying is totally counterproductive. The only reason that lies are not told in her strategy for government communications is that nothing is told. She would have a regime avoid speculation about its refusal to comment on an issue by keeping the people regularly in the dark about all policies on all sensitive issues, the very information that a citizenry requires in order to live in a democracy. Perhaps because of Bok's conspicuous failure to accommodate the hard realities of politics and a consistent refusal to lie, Maureen Ramsay seeks to avoid lying by wishing away the hard political realities.

In *The Politics of Lying*, Ramsay takes on the task of providing a normative evaluation of the justification for lying in politics. Ramsay begins with the definition of a lie as a statement intended to deceive others and considers two types of Machiavellian arguments in support of lying in the general interest. The first is a straightforward consequentialist argument maintaining that deliberately giving false or misleading information sometimes brings about the best results. The second is based on an appeal to the Machiavellian perception of human nature. Since other politicians are deceptive, retaliatory lies are both necessary and justified for success in politics. In focusing on a consequentialist defense of lying in politics, Ramsay rejects the realist claims that politics is outside of the moral realm. For Ramsay, there is nothing special about politics that would justify applying different evaluative criteria to political actions or require a transcendence of ordinary morality. However, she argues, even if we accept consequentialism as the appropriate theory by which to judge acts of deception and secrecy in politics, these acts will be difficult to justify, especially in a democratic political order.

Still, there are many who insist that national security sometimes mandates lies and deceit. When the national interest is at stake, there is a legitimate end that might justify the use of a means that in other circumstances would not be justified. This just lie theory, Ramsay claims, is analogous to the just war theory. There are legitimate and illegitimate uses of a lie in the same way that there are legitimate and illegitimate uses of force when it comes to conflicts between nations. Ramsay reminds us that according to the theory of just war, wars are justified if they are pursued for a just cause and when they are carried out using just means. Under the just war theory, force may be used only to correct a grave public evil. The injustice suffered by one party must significantly outweigh that suffered by the other.

In addition, the just lie theory holds that only duly constituted public authorities may use deadly force or wage war, and it must be done with the right intention. That is, the force may be used only in a truly just cause and solely for that purpose. There must also be a reasonable chance of success. It is not permissible to wage war if this involves engaging in a futile cause or in a case where disproportionate measures are necessary to achieve success. There must also be no other means available to settle the conflict. Force may be used only after all peaceful alternatives have been exhausted. Finally, the overall destruction that will arise from the use of force must be outweighed by the good to be achieved.

Ramsay points out that when this is applied to lying, the justice of a lie would depend on the cause for which it is undertaken, whether there were other means available to achieve this end, whether the harm caused by the lie is outweighed by the good achieved, and whether there is a reasonable chance of success in achieving the end through these means. Moreover, the means would have to be justified, not only because politicians would be acting in our name and in our interests, but because the public would have to consent to the deception in advance in order to comply with democratic principles.

This criticism of the just lie approach hinges on the following claims: (1) There is no consensus on what constitutes a just end, (2) there is no agreement on the concepts of a national or public interest and the amount of value that attaches to these concepts, and (3) it cannot be assumed that the citizenry would consent to being deceived in order to promote the national interest, even if it could be defined. Once we move from abstract definitions, Ramsay argues, the concepts of national and public interest prove too amorphous to justify government secrecy and deception. She admits that "All would agree that vital national interests are involved when there is a direct and acute attack on the physical survival of citizens, when basic democratic institutions are fundamentally and severely threatened, when there is imminent danger of national collapse or economic ruin" (Cliffe, Ramsay, and Bartlett 2000, 31). Yet she maintains that the concept of national security has no generally acceptable meaning. Its failure to provide a clear standard by which to justify deception adds to the looseness of the concept of just cause, which in turn provides opportunities for politicians to use the concept for private gain. Ramsay's criticism extends to the concept of the public interest. Since there is no consensus on how the public interest might be defined, the concept is weakened as a justificatory tool for assessing the morality of political theory.

Nevertheless, Ramsay herself uses the concepts of national and public interest in her arguments against lying when she says that telling lies about policy or withholding information can work against both of those interests (Cliffe, Ramsay, and Bartlett 2000, 38). It should be obvious that she is not entitled to reject the concepts of national and public interest as useless on the grounds of their vagueness when used to justify lying, but then to use them as justifications for truth-telling and full disclosure. If it is their vagueness that eliminates them from proper use, then using them to justify any course of action, including the ones Ramsay wants to defend, is wrong.

Admittedly, the concepts of national and public interest are not static. However, the instability of such concepts is not a sufficient justification for jettisoning them. Concepts can be heuristic for purposes of creating and implementing policies. To use Ramsay's approach in other areas of ethical decision-making would surely undermine higher goods. . . .

The second part of Ramsay's argument focuses on her notion that "even if secrecy and deception could be justified to protect a vital interest, the costs in terms of the toll they take on democratic principles alone could be said to outweigh their benefits" (Cliffe, Ramsay, and Bartlett 2000, 35). Ramsay contends that the use of lies, concealment, and deceit contradicts the basic principles of democratic society based on accountability, participation, consent, and representation. Is universal truth-telling a necessary condition of a fully functioning democracy? Politicians cannot possibly reveal all of the information that they have at their fingertips. Yet, Ramsay argues,

"The idea that politicians can justifiably withhold information from the public, even if this is to achieve a worthwhile and agreed upon political goal renders the requirement of accountability meaningless" (36). Patently, this does not follow. Politicians who withhold information for a just cause are still accountable for using the deception as a last resort, for their judgments that the good that is brought about will outweigh the harm, and for calculating a reasonable chance of success.

Ramsay is correct in emphasizing that a consideration of the harm brought about must include the impact on the democratic principles of consent and participation, and the likelihood of undermining trust. The right to know, she suggests, is at the basis of democratic accountability and essential to both effective participation on the part of citizens and representation on the part of public administrators. Thus, deception places these values at risk. This does not mean that the conditions of a just lie cannot be met. In some cases, the ones that involve a vital national interest, the assumption can be made that the public would have consented in advance to the deception employed. But even in cases where no such assumption can be made, the acts of deception might still be justified if done to avert some graver evil and the good consequences outweigh the bad consequences of thwarting democratic principles. . . .

CONCLUSION

Machiavelli and Michael Walzer make strong cases that there are times when public officials are compelled to lie to defend the public interest. Machiavelli sees deception as an inevitable part of politics and statesmanship. He may be faulted, however for setting no conditions or limits on official lying. Walzer seeks a limit to lying in the guilt and punishment a deceiving official should endure for protecting the public by devious means. His theory for responding to the issue of "dirty hands" is attractive in recognizing both the necessity of political means that veer from the moral standards of private life and the importance of upholding those moral standards and paying a price for violating them. However, the punishment has to be self-imposed and Walzer offers no criteria that might limit extreme or unnecessary deception and connivance by public officials. Sissela Bok and Maureen Ramsay also renege on a quest for such criteria by claiming that official lying is almost never appropriate or necessary. Bok relies on an impractical avoidance of comment by officials to shun lying, and Ramsay is convinced that all the criteria in support of the just lie theory are inevitably amorphous and self-serving. She seems to miss the key point that the just lie theory attempts to set moral and not legal standards. In her criticisms of Walzer's theory and the just lie theory, Ramsay is too literal, legalistic, and one-dimensional. She misses the need to find not a resolution but a balance between the public and the private, between moral sanctity and effective, tolerable compromise.

REFERENCES

Bok, Sissela. 1989. *Lying: Moral Choices in Public and Private Life*. New York: Vintage.

Cliffe, Lionel, Maureen Ramsay, and Dave Bartlett. 2000. "The Politics of Lying." In *Implications for Democracy*. New York: St. Martin's Press.

Gortner, Harold F. 1991. *Ethics for Public Managers*. Westport, CT: Greenwood Press.

Machiavelli, Niccolo. 1981. *The Prince*. London: Penguin.

Pasquerella, Lynn, Alfred G. Killilea, and Michael Vocino, eds. 1996. *Ethical Dilemmas in Public Administration*. Westport, CT: Praeger.

Walzer, Michael. 1973. "Political Action: The Problem of Dirty Hands," *Public Affairs* 2, no. 2: 160–80.

"PLAUSIBLE DENIABILITY"
John Poindexter and David Boren

In 1987 Congressional hearings on the Iran-Contra issue, Oliver North and John Poindexter admitted that they had lied to members of Congress, and then attempted to justify their behavior. Significant in Poindexter's argument was the concept of presidential "plausible deniability," i.e., keeping information from President Reagan so that he could plausibly deny knowing anything about any wrongdoing. In this interchange Senator David Boren (D-Oklahoma) takes issue with Poindexter's position.

Mr. Boren: (Democratic member of the Senate) . . . Now, I understand—I have to say I don't agree with—the idea of protecting the president by not telling him of controversial decisions. Having been a governor and from time to time having had people call me on the phone and say, "Governor, is this something you really want done," something I had never thought about wanting to have done, and me saying, "Absolutely not, where did you ever get that idea?" and they would say, "Well, some subordinate of yours called and said you wanted that."

I had a very strong feeling that the person elected to office by the people—not some subordinate appointed—should be making controversial decisions that, under our political process and Constitution, the elected people should make. But I don't question what you said about your intent, your intent of wanting to shield the president.

I think it was a mistake under our . . . Constitution to do that, but I take . . . your word you were sincere. But by protecting the president in advance by not telling him, I wonder when the story began to come out, starting with the Beirut newspaper and otherwise, the president is in a position, by your not having told him, to deny that he knew about it.

Source: Testimony of John M. Poindexter, former National Security Advisor to President Reagan, at the Joint Hearings of the Senate and House of Representatives committees investigating the Iran-Contra activities, July 1987.

Did you ever go to the president after this story all started to come out and say, Mr. President, you didn't know about it at the time, but this thing looks like it is really going to be controversial, and I think you should know, you should hear it from me, you should know exactly what went on because you are going to be asked so many questions?

Did you ever go to the president after the fact [i.e., after diverting funds to the Contras] at any time? . . .

Mr. Poindexter: No. I did not. Because, as I have testified earlier, up until the very last minute that month, I did not think that the transfer of residuals would come out. In fact, I specifically had directed Colonel North to leave that out of the chronologies. I was treating that as a separate issue. . . .

Mr. Boren: Again, with this press conference on the 19th, you felt the president didn't need to know?

Mr. Poindexter: That is correct.

Mr. Boren: Again, I have to say that really troubles me. Going back to my experience on a very small scale as an executive, I used to say to my staff, if you made a mistake, you've done something to inject me into controversy, I want to be the first person who knows about the mistake. Especially when trouble hits, I want to know all the facts.

Mr. Poindexter: Senator, I obviously didn't think it was a mistake. If I had discussed that in the White House before I left, I think it would have made it much more difficult for the president to distance himself from the decision. It would have raised a lot of questions as to when he knew it. This way he didn't know.

Mr. Boren: I suppose the president could have said, though, I didn't know it at the time, and I found out later. He could have said exactly when he found out?

Mr. Poindexter: I know. But I think it would have been in my opinion more difficult to believe that and decided to do it the way I did it.

Mr: Boren: I understand it. I guess I can—well, as I say, in all honesty, and I say this not unkindly because I certainly have made mistakes in my career as a public servant. Anyone who tries to do anything makes mistakes. . . . We are trying to learn from what has happened here so we can avoid this kind of situation, so we will never have John Poindexters on the witness stand; we will never have to have committees like this in the future; we can build the kind of partnership that we need in the future.

And it really did surprise me when you said I have no regrets, because it seems to me that well-intentioned as you might have been at the time, that now it is very clear that this decision was a highly—about the diversion of the residuals or use of the residuals, as you have called them—was a highly controversial decision.

It has been the flash point of this whole inquiry. The whole question has boiled down in the minds of the public as to whether or not the president knew about that because it seems to be the one area of which there is greatest potential legal question. Had the president himself ordered it? . . .

Now, I would ask you again as we try to learn from this, does it not trouble you at all in retrospect—and I am not asking you to be perfect. I am not here to condemn you. I am not here to try you.

I am here to learn for the future. That as we are thinking about our constitutional system and the heart and soul of it wouldn't you say that the President of the United States so that he, as the elected—person elected by the American people, can make those decisions for himself?

Mr. Poindexter: It certainly would make it easier on the people involved to do that. I don't know. The future is obviously going to be very complex.

Mr. Boren: Admiral Poindexter, it isn't a matter of making it easier for the people involved. It's a question that in this republic with the democratic principles we have, the Constitution says the president is the Commander in Chief. It doesn't say the National Security Advisor. It doesn't say any bureaucrat appointed by the President. It says the president, and it is because he is elected by the people.

So doesn't it trouble you, as we are talking about—we are talking about not even whether people, whether it is inconvenient, we are talking about the preservation of constitutional government.

Mr. Poindexter: Senator, the difference between the way you think about it and the way I think about it, I frankly don't think, in the whole scheme of things, it is that important a decision. It obviously is a controversial one. The thing that's made it important in your eyes, in my mind, is the overreaction of the media to it and Members of Congress have to react to the media. I think that is what happened.

DISTORTING SCIENTIFIC RESEARCH
UNION OF CONCERNED SCIENTISTS

This selection criticizes the American government for distorting scientific research findings and recommendations to fit administrative policies. Are such distortions a form of deception, or should government have the right to modify scientific statements to fit policy priorities? If you as an administrator were asked to make such modifications, should your loyalties be to the scientists or to your superiors?

Tinkering with scientific information, either striking it from reports or altering it, is becoming a pattern of behavior. It represents the politicizing of a scientific process, which at once manifests a disdain for professional

Source: "Scientific Integrity in Policymaking: The Bush Administration's Misuse of Science," Union of Concerned Scientists website, http://webexhibits.org/bush/4.html.

scientists working for our government and a willingness to be less than candid with the American people.

> —Roger G. Kennedy, a former director of
> the National Park Service, responding to the doctoring
> of findings on Yellowstone National Park[1]

Since taking office, the Bush administration has consistently sought to undermine the public's understanding of the view held by the vast majority of climate scientists that human-caused emissions of carbon dioxide and other heat-trapping gases are making a discernible contribution to global warming.

After coming to office, the administration asked the National Academy of Sciences (NAS) to review the findings of the Intergovernmental Panel on Climate Change (IPCC) and provide further assessment of what climate science could say about this issue.[2] The NAS panel rendered a strong opinion, which, in essence, confirmed that of the IPCC. The American Geophysical Union, the world's largest organization of earth scientists, has also released a strong statement describing human-caused disruptions of Earth's climate.[3] Yet Bush administration spokespersons continue to contend that the uncertainties in climate projections and fossil fuel emissions are too great to warrant mandatory action to slow emissions.[4]

In May 2002, President Bush expressed disdain for a State Department report[5] to the United Nations that pointed to a clear human role in the accumulation of heat-trapping gases and detailed the likely negative consequences of climate change; the president called it "a report put out by the bureaucracy."[6] In September 2002, the administration removed a section on climate change from the Environmental Protection Agency's (EPA) annual air pollution report,[7] even though the climate issue had been discussed in the report for the preceding five years.

Then, in one well-documented case, the Bush administration blatantly tampered with the integrity of scientific analysis at a federal agency when, in June 2003, the White House tried to make a series of changes to the EPA's draft Report on the Environment.[8]

A front-page article in the *New York Times* broke the news that White House officials tried to force the EPA to substantially alter the report's section on climate change. The EPA report, which referenced the NAS review and other studies, stated that human activity is contributing significantly to climate change.[9]

Interviews with current and former EPA staff, as well as an internal EPA memo reviewed for this report . . . reveal that the White House Council on Environmental Quality and the Office of Management and Budget demanded major amendments including:

1. The deletion of a temperature record covering 1,000 years in order to, according to the EPA memo, emphasize "a recent, limited analysis [which] supports the administration's favored message."[10]
2. The removal of any reference to the NAS review—requested by the White House itself—that confirmed human activity is contributing to climate change.[11]

3. The insertion of a reference to a discredited study of temperature records funded in part by the American Petroleum Institute.[12]
4. The elimination of the summary statement—noncontroversial within the science community that studies climate change—that "climate change has global consequences for human health and the environment."[13]

According to the internal EPA memo, White House officials demanded so many qualifying words such as "potentially" and "may" that the result would have been to insert "uncertainty . . . where there is essentially none."[14]

In a process now-departed EPA Administrator Christine Todd Whitman has since described as "brutal,"[15] the entire section on climate change was ultimately deleted from the version released for public comment.[16] According to internal EPA documents and interviews with EPA researchers, the agency staff chose this path rather than compromising their credibility by misrepresenting the scientific consensus.[17] Doing otherwise, as one current high-ranking EPA official puts it, would "poorly represent the science and ultimately undermine the credibility of the EPA and the White House."[18]

The EPA's decision to delete any mention of global warming from its report drew widespread criticism. Many scientists and public officials—Republicans and Democrats alike—were moved to decry the administration's political manipulation in this case. Notably, the incident drew the ire of Russell Train, who served as EPA administrator under Presidents Nixon and Ford. In a letter to the *New York Times*, Train stated that the Bush administration's actions undermined the independence of the EPA and were virtually unprecedented for the degree of their political manipulation of the agency's research. As Train put it, the "interest of the American people lies in having full disclosure of the facts."[19] Train also noted that, "In all my time at the EPA, I don't recall any regulatory decision that was driven by political considerations. More to the present point, never once, to my best recollection, did either the Nixon or Ford White House ever try to tell me how to make a decision."[20]

Were the case an isolated incident, it could perhaps be dismissed as an anomaly. On the contrary, the Bush administration has repeatedly intervened to distort or suppress climate change research findings despite promises by the president that, "my administration's climate change policy will be science-based."[21]

Despite the widespread agreement in the scientific community that human activity is contributing to global climate change, as demonstrated by the consensus of international experts on the IPCC, the Bush administration has sought to exaggerate uncertainty by relying on disreputable and fringe science reports and preventing informed discussion on the issue. As one current EPA scientist puts it, the Bush administration often "does not even invite the EPA into the discussion" on climate change issues. "This administration seems to want to make environmental policy at the White House," the government scientist explains. "I suppose that is their right. But one has to ask: On the basis of what information is this policy being promulgated? What views are being represented? Who is involved in the decision-making? What kind of credible expertise is being brought to bear?"[22]

Dr. Rosina Bierbaum, a Clinton administration appointee to the Office of Science and Technology Policy (OSTP) who also served during the first year of the Bush administration, offers a disturbing window on the process. From the start, Bierbaum contends, "The scientists [who] knew the most about climate change at OSTP were not allowed to participate in deliberations on the issue within the White House inner circle."[23]

Through such consistent tactics, the Bush administration has not only distorted scientific and technical analysis on global climate change and suppressed the dissemination of research results, but has avoided fashioning any policies that would significantly reduce the threat implied by those findings.

In the course of this investigation, UCS learned of the extent to which these policies seem to extend. In one case that has yet to surface in the press, the Natural Resources Conservation Service (NRCS) of the U.S. Department of Agriculture (USDA) sought in September 2003 to reprint a popular informational brochure about carbon sequestration in the soil and what farmers could do to reduce greenhouse gas emissions. According to one current government official familiar with the incident, the brochure was widely viewed as one of the agency's successful efforts in the climate change field. The NRCS had already distributed some 325,000 of the brochures and sought a modest update, as well as proposing a Spanish edition.[24]

Notably, even this relatively routine proposal was passed to the White House Council on Environmental Quality (CEQ) for review. William Hohenstein, director of the Global Change Program Exchange in the office of the chief economist at the USDA, acknowledged that he passed the request on to the CEQ, as he says he would "for any documents relating to climate change policy."[25] While Hohenstein denies that he has been explicitly ordered to do so, he says he knows the White House is concerned "that things regarding climate change be put out by the government in a neutral way."[26] As a result of CEQ's objections about the brochure, staff at the NRCS dropped their proposal for a reprint.[27] "It is not just a case of micromanagement, but really of censorship of government information," a current government official familiar with the case noted. "In nearly 15 years of government service, I can't remember ever needing clearance from the White House for such a thing."[28]

NOTES

1. As quoted in E. Shogren, "Administration, Yellowstone Staff at Odds on Park Threats," *Los Angeles Times*, June 26, 2003.

2. National Academy of Sciences, Commission on Geosciences, Environment and Resources, *Climate Change Science: An Analysis of Some Key Questions*, 2001.

3. See AGU. [American Geophysical Union website: www.agu.org]

4. P. Dobriansky, "Only New Technology Can Halt Climate Change," *Financial Times*, December 1, 2003.

5. U.S. Climate Action Report, Department of State, May 2002.

6. K. Q. Seelye, "President Distances Himself from Global Warming Report," *New York Times*, June 5, 2002.

7. See www.epa.gov/airtrends.

8. "Report on the Environment," U.S. Environmental Protection Agency, June 23, 2003.

9. A. C. Revkin and K. Q. Seelye, "Report by EPA Leaves Out Data on Climate Change," *New York Times*, June 19, 2003.

10. EPA internal memo, April 29, 2003.

11. EPA internal memo, April 29, 2003. Deleted reference: National Academy of Sciences, Commission on Geosciences, *Environment and Resources, Climate Change Science: An Analysis of Some Key Questions*, 2001.

12. Revkin and Seelye, *New York Times*. Discredited study: W. Soon and S. Baliunas, 2003. "Proxy climatic and environmental changes of the past 1,000 years," *Climate Research* 23(2): 89–110. Study discrediting it: Michael Mann et al., 2003. "On past temperatures and anomalous late 20th century warmth," *Research* 23(2): 89–110. Study discrediting it: Michael Mann et al. 2003. "On past temperatures and anomalous late 20th century warmth," *Eos* 84(27): 256–57.

13. EPA internal memo.

14. EPA internal memo.

15. *NOW with Bill Moyers* transcript, September 19, 2003.

16. Revkin and Seelye, *New York Times*.

17. Author interviews with current EPA staff members. Names withheld on request. See also "option paper" in EPA internal memo, Appendix A.

18. Author interview with EPA staff member, name withheld on request, January 2004. EPA internal memo.

19. Russell E. Train, "When Politics Trumps Science" (letter to the editor), *New York Times*, June 21, 2003.

20. Russell E. Train, "The Environmental Protection Agency Just Isn't Like It Was in the Good Old (Nixon) Days," www.gristmagazine.com, September 22, 2003.

21. White House, President's Statement on Climate Change (July 13, 2001).

22. Author interview with EPA scientist, name withheld on request, January 2004.

23. As quoted in N. Thompson, "Science Friction: The Growing—and Dangerous—Divide Between Scientists and the GOP," *Washington Monthly*, July/August 2003.

24. Author interview with USDA official, name withheld on request, January 2004.

25. Author interview with William Hohenstein, USDA, January 2004.

26. Author interview with Hohenstein.

27. Author interview with Hohenstein.

28. Author interview with USDA official, name withheld on request, January 2004.

CASE 6: GREATER GOOD VERSUS FALSIFICATION

I was working for the Dept. of Defense in the contracting department in a Middle Eastern country. More than $250,000 worth of equipment ordered by U.S. Air Force agencies was held up in customs on the other side of the country port. The politics of the time were such that the United States did not want to rock the boat.

Source: Donald Menzel, "Ethics Moment: Greater Good Versus Falsification," *PA Times*, July 2004, based on submission from an unnamed reader. Reprinted with permission from the American Society for Public Administration.

As contracting officer, I thought I'd figure out how to get the equipment released. One requirement had to do with a release document from a high-level U.S. official that was notarized. The document was time sensitive. One of the finance offices fell through on their end, and had to delay by one day. Of course, the document would now be null and void, and guess what? The U.S. official was no longer available.

I had no authority to do this but I called the legal office on the West end and said "redo the whole document, whatever you have to do, and change that date for the next day." He asked me a bunch of questions; he was an attorney after all. So, I instructed him on how to cut, paste and copy, and redo the official seal. In essence, we falsified the document.

I felt I had no choice. This process of negotiations to even get to the point of getting the equipment out of customs was over several months. Lining up and coordinating all of these agencies took a very long time, and I wasn't about to blow it on a stupid legal document.

You may ask all the what-ifs. But there are only two of us that know that the document was falsified—myself and the attorney. I received an award for my work in getting the equipment released. I did not pay for those goods, the U.S. taxpayers did. And if it were my money, I'd have done the same. If I had not been able to secure the release of the equipment, it was going to go into the Middle Eastern country's local market. They were not going to return it to the vendor.

Questions: Do you think it is ever ethical to falsify a document? Or rather, could it be possible that falsifying a document could lead to a greater good?

CHAPTER DISCUSSION QUESTIONS

1. How valid is Poindexter's defense of his actions to protect plausible deniability? Under what circumstances is it appropriate for subordinates not to inform elected representatives of their actions, in order to protect the executives from damage to their powers or reputation? What are the implications of plausible deniability for the accountability of public officials?

2. Under what conditions would you, as an administrator, be most tempted to lie, knowingly deceive, or withhold information?

3. Do you have responsibility for the ethical behavior of others as well as yourself? For instance, if you are aware of a peer's lying or cheating, what are your responsibilities to do something about it, and what should you do?

FOR FURTHER EXPLORATION

Alterman, Eric. *When Presidents Lie: A History of Official Deception and Its Consequences.* New York: Viking, 2004.

Bailey, F. G. *The Prevalence of Deceit.* Ithaca, NY: Cornell University Press, 1991.

Baker, Roland. *Liar's Manual.* Chicago: Nelson-Hall, 1983.

Bowyer, J. Barton. *Cheating: Deception in War & Magic, Games & Sports, Sex & Religion, Business & Con Games, Politics & Espionage, Art & Science.* New York: St. Martin's Press. 1982.

Haines, David W. "Fatal Choices: The Routinization of Deceit, Incompetence, and Corruption," *Public Integrity* 6:1 (Winter 2003–2004), pp. 5–23.

Pasquerella, Lynn, and Alfred G. Killilea. "The Ethics of Lying in the Public Interest: Reflections on the 'Just Lie,'" *Public Integrity* 7:3 (Summer 2005), pp. 261–73.

Pfiffner, James P. *The Character Factor: How We Judge America's Presidents.* College Station: Texas A&M University Press, 2004.

Rynard, Paul, and David P. Shugarman, eds. *Cruelty and Deception: The Controversy over Dirty Hands in Politics.* Orchard Park, NY: Broadview, 2000.

Serban, George. *Lying: Man's Second Nature.* Westport, CT: Praeger, 2001.

Tim C. Mazur, "Lying," *Issues in Ethics*, 6:1 (Fall 1993).

WEBSITES

Information on the U.S. False Claims Act, with links, www.consumerlaw.com/false.html

Markkula Center for Applied Ethics site, www.scu.edu/ethics/publications/iie/v6n1/lying.html

Wikipedia entry on deception, http://en.wikipedia.org/wiki/Deception

Wikipedia entry on plausible deniability, http://en.wikipedia.org/wiki/Plausible_deniability

Chapter 7

PRIVACY, SECRECY, AND CONFIDENTIALITY

SECRECY IN THE BUSH ADMINISTRATION
U.S. HOUSE COMMITTEE MINORITY STAFF

The George W. Bush administration has been criticized for sharply increasing governmental secrecy. Among administration arguments for such enhanced secrecy is the need for greater security following September 11, 2001. This selection is part of a 2004 minority staff report of the U.S. House of Representatives Committee on Government Reform. Regardless of whether you believe additional secrecy is warranted, what are the implications for public-sector management?

Open and accountable government is one of the bedrock principles of our democracy. Yet virtually since inauguration day, questions have been raised about the Bush administration's commitment to this principle. News articles and reports by independent groups over the last four years have identified a growing series of instances where the administration has sought to operate without public or congressional scrutiny.

At the request of Rep. Henry A. Waxman, this report is a comprehensive examination of secrecy in the Bush administration. It analyzes how the administration has implemented each of our nation's major open government laws. The report finds that there has been a consistent pattern in the administration's actions: Laws that are designed to promote public access to information have been undermined, while laws that authorize the government to withhold information or to operate in secret have repeatedly been expanded. The cumulative result is an unprecedented assault on the principle of open government.

The administration has supported amendments to open government laws to create new categories of protected information that can be withheld from the public.

Source: United States House of Representatives Committee on Government Reform—Minority Staff Special Investigations Division, "Secrecy in the Bush Administration," prepared for Rep. Henry A. Waxman, September 14, 2004.

President Bush has issued an executive order sharply restricting the public release of the papers of past presidents. The administration has expanded the authority to classify documents and dramatically increased the number of documents classified. It has used the USA Patriot Act and novel legal theories to justify secret investigations, detentions, and trials. And the administration has engaged in litigation to contest Congress's right to information.

The records at issue have covered a vast array of topics, ranging from simple census data and routine agency correspondence to presidential and vice presidential records. Among the documents that the administration has refused to release to the public and members of Congress are (1) the contacts between energy companies and the vice president's energy task force, (2) the communications between the Defense Department and the vice president's office regarding contracts awarded to Halliburton, (3) documents describing the prison abuses at Abu Ghraib, (4) memoranda revealing what the White House knew about Iraq's weapons of mass destruction, and (5) the cost estimates of the Medicare prescription drug legislation withheld from Congress.

There are three main categories of federal open government laws: (1) laws that provide public access to federal records; (2) laws that allow the government to restrict public access to federal information; and (3) laws that provide for congressional access to federal records. In each area, the Bush administration has acted to restrict the amount of government information that is available.

LAWS THAT PROVIDE PUBLIC ACCESS TO FEDERAL RECORDS

Beginning in the 1960s, Congress enacted a series of landmark laws that promote "government in the sunshine." These include the Freedom of Information Act, the Presidential Records Act, and the Federal Advisory Committee Act. Each of these laws enables the public to view the internal workings of the executive branch. And each has been narrowed in scope and application under the Bush Administration.

Freedom of Information Act

The Freedom of Information Act is the primary law providing access to information held by the executive branch. Adopted in 1966, FOIA established the principle that the public should have broad access to government records. Under the Bush administration, however, the statute's reach has been narrowed and agencies have resisted FOIA requests through procedural tactics and delay. The administration has:

- Issued guidance reversing the presumption in favor of disclosure and instructing agencies to withhold a broad and undefined category of "sensitive" information;

- Supported statutory and regulatory changes that preclude disclosure of a wide range of information, including information relating to the economic, health, and security infrastructure of the nation; and
- Placed administrative obstacles in the way of organizations seeking to use FOIA to obtain federal records, such as denials of fee waivers and delays in agency responses.

Independent academic experts consulted for this report decried these trends. They stated that the administration has "radically reduced the public right to know," that its policies "are not only sucking the spirit out of the FOIA, but shriveling its very heart," and that no administration in modern times has "done more to conceal the workings of government from the people."

The Presidential Records Act

The Presidential Records Act, which was enacted in 1978 in the wake of Watergate, establishes the important principle that the records of a president relating to his official duties belong to the American people. Early in his term, President Bush issued an executive order that undermined the Presidential Records Act by giving former presidents and vice presidents new authority to block the release of their records. As one prominent historian wrote, the order "severely crippled our ability to study the inner workings of a presidency."

The Federal Advisory Committee Act

The Federal Advisory Committee Act prevents secret advisory groups from exercising hidden influence on government policy, requiring openness and a balance of viewpoints for all government advisory bodies. The Bush administration, however, has supported legislation that creates new statutory exemptions from FACA. It has also sought to avoid the application of FACA through various mechanisms, such as manipulating appointments to advisory bodies, conducting key advisory functions through "subcommittees," and invoking unusual statutory exemptions. As a result, such key bodies as the vice president's energy task force and the presidential commission investigating the failure of intelligence in Iraq have operated without complying with FACA.

LAWS THAT RESTRICT PUBLIC ACCESS TO FEDERAL RECORDS

In the 1990s, the Clinton administration increased public access to government information by restricting the ability of officials to classify information and establishing an improved system for the declassification of information. These steps have been reversed under the Bush administration, which has expanded the capacity of the government to classify documents and to operate in secret.

The Classification and Declassification of Records

The classification and declassification of national security information is largely governed by executive order. President Bush has used this authority to:

- Reverse the presumption against classification, allowing classification even in cases of significant doubt;
- Expand authority to classify information for longer periods of time;
- Delay the automatic declassification of records;
- Expand the authority of the executive branch to reclassify information that has been declassified; and
- Increase the number of federal agencies that can classify information to include the Secretary of Health and Human Services, the Secretary of Agriculture, and the Administrator of the Environmental Protection Agency.

Statistics on classification and declassification of records under the Bush Administration demonstrate the impact of these new policies. Original decisions to classify information—those in which an authorized classifier first determines that disclosure could harm national security—have soared during the Bush administration. In fiscal years 2001 to 2003, the average number of original decisions to classify information increased 50 percent over the average for the previous five fiscal years. Derivative classification decisions, which involve classifying documents that incorporate, restate, or paraphrase information that has previously been classified, have increased even more dramatically. Between FY 1996 and FY 2000, the number of derivative classifications averaged 9.96 million per year. Between FY 2001 and FY 2003, the average increased to 19.37 million per year, a 95 percent increase. In the last year alone, the total number of classification decisions increased 25 percent.

Sensitive Security Information

The Bush administration has sought and obtained a significant expansion of authority to make designations of Sensitive Security Information (SSI), a category of sensitive but unclassified information originally established to protect the security of civil aviation. Under legislation signed by President Bush, the Department of Homeland Security now has authority to apply this designation to information related to any type of transportation.

The Patriot Act

The passage of the Patriot Act after the September 11, 2001, attacks gave the Bush administration new authority to conduct government investigations in secret. One provision of the Act expanded the authority of the Justice Department to conduct secret electronic wiretaps. Another provision authorized the Justice Department to obtain secret orders requiring the production of "books, records, papers, documents, and other items," and it prohibited the recipient of these orders (such as a telephone company or library) from disclosing their existence. And a third provision expanded the use of "sneak and peak" search warrants, which allow the Justice Department to search homes and other premises secretly without giving notice to the occupants.

Secret Detentions, Trials, and Deportations

In addition to expanding secrecy in government by executive order and statute, the Bush administration has used novel legal interpretations to expand its authority to detain, try, and deport individuals in secret. The administration asserted the authority to:

- Hold persons designated as "enemy combatants" in secret without a hearing, access to a lawyer, or judicial review;
- Conduct secret military trials of persons held as enemy combatants when deemed necessary by the government; and
- Conduct secret deportation proceedings of aliens deemed "special interest cases" without any notice to the public, the press, or even family members.

CONGRESSIONAL ACCESS TO FEDERAL RECORDS

Our system of checks and balances depends on Congress being able to obtain information about the activities of the executive branch. When government operates behind closed doors without adequate congressional oversight, mismanagement and corruption can flourish. Yet despite Congress' constitutional oversight role, the Bush administration has sharply limited congressional access to federal records.

GAO Access to Federal Records

A federal statute passed in 1921 gives the congressional Government Accountability Office the authority to review federal records in the course of audits and investigations of federal programs. Notwithstanding this statutory language and a long history of accommodation between GAO and the executive branch, the Bush administration challenged the authority of GAO on constitutional grounds, arguing that the Comptroller General, who is the head of GAO, had no "standing" to enforce GAO's right to federal records. The Bush administration prevailed at the district court level and GAO decided not to appeal, significantly weakening the authority of GAO.

The Seven-Member Rule

The Bush administration also challenged the authority of members of the House Government Reform Committee to obtain records under the "Seven Member Rule," a federal statute that requires an executive agency to provide information on matters within the jurisdiction of the Committee upon the request of any seven of its members. Although a district court ruled in favor of the members in a case involving access to adjusted census records, the Bush administration has continued to resist requests for information under the Seven Member Rule, forcing the members to initiate new litigation.

Withholding Information Requested by Congress

On numerous occasions, the Bush administration has withheld information requested by members of Congress. During consideration of the Medicare legislation in 2003, the administration withheld estimates showing that the bill would cost over $100 billion more than the administration claimed. In this instance, administration officials threatened to fire the HHS Actuary, Richard Foster, if he provided the information to Congress. In another case, the administration's refusal to provide information relating to air pollution led Senator Jeffords, the ranking member of the Senate Committee on Environment and Public Works, to place holds on the nominations of several federal officials.

On over 100 separate occasions, the administration has refused to answer the inquiries of, or provide the information requested by, Rep. Waxman, the ranking member of the House Committee on Government Reform. The information that the administration has refused to provide includes:

- Documents requested by the ranking members of eight House Committees relating to the prison abuses at Abu Ghraib and elsewhere;
- Information on contacts between Vice President Cheney's office and the Department of Defense regarding the award to Halliburton of a sole-source contract worth up to $7 billion for work in Iraq; and
- Information about presidential advisor Karl Rove's meetings and phone conversations with executives of companies in which he owned stock.

The 9-11 Commission

On November 27, 2002, Congress passed legislation creating the National Commission on Terrorist Attacks upon the United States (commonly known as the 9-11 Commission) as a congressional commission to investigate the September 11 attacks. Throughout its investigation, however, the Bush administration resisted or delayed providing the Commission with important information. For example, the administration's refusal to turn over documents forced the Commission to issue subpoenas to the Defense Department and the Federal Aviation Administration. The administration also refused for months to allow Commissioners to review key presidential intelligence briefing documents.

THE COLLECTIVE IMPACT

Taken together, the actions of the Bush administration have resulted in an extraordinary expansion of government secrecy. External watchdogs, including Congress, the media, and nongovernmental organizations, have consistently been hindered in their ability to monitor government activities. These actions have serious implications for the nature of our government. When government operates in secret, the ability of the public to hold the government accountable is imperiled.

PRIVACY IN THE UNITED STATES AND THE EUROPEAN UNION
U.S. DEPARTMENT OF COMMERCE

Rapid development of information technology in recent decades has made privacy an important concern in global business, government, and other dimensions of social life. Businesses are required to have privacy policies and to communicate them to their customers and clients. Interestingly, the United States and the European Union approach privacy issues from different angles. Is one better than the other, or are both equally appropriate policies in this sensitive area?

The United States, the EU [European Union] and its member states are committed to making privacy protections available to their citizens without unnecessarily impeding the free flow of information. The United States has largely adopted a self-regulatory approach to the development of privacy protections in the private sector, addressing specific privacy concerns in the law as needed. The concern is that privacy issues differ across industry sectors, and that "a one size fits all" legislative approach would lack the necessary precision to avoid interfering with the benefits that result from the free flow of information. Nonetheless, the United States does address specific privacy concerns in the law as needed, particularly where sensitive information is involved or there have been cases of abuses. In Europe, however, privacy laws tend to be comprehensive, applying to every industry and closely regulating what data is collected and how it is used.

Source: U.S. Department of Commerce, "Privacy in the United States and the European Union," online at www.export.gov/safeharbor/shprinciplesfinal.htm.

U.S. APPROACH TO PRIVACY

In the United States, the importance of protecting the privacy of individuals' personal information is a priority for the federal government and consumers. Consumers repeatedly cite fears that their personal information will be misused as a reason for not doing business online. In this way, moves to bolster online privacy protect consumer interests and fuel the broader growth of online communications, innovation, and business. Self-regulatory initiatives are an effective approach to putting meaningful privacy protections in place. In certain highly sensitive areas, however, legislative solutions are appropriate. These sensitive areas include financial and medical records, genetic information, Social Security numbers, and information involving children. A self-regulatory initiative could involve a number of companies in the same line of business deciding that they will follow certain rules in handling information about their customers. These companies might also decide to display a seal that shows that they follow the rules. If one of the members of this "self-regulatory regime" breaks the rules, the company's membership and permission to display the seal will be revoked. Companies across industries—and especially Internet-related fields—are increasingly hiring privacy experts and making the protection of consumer information a priority. . . .

The United States has consistently supported legislative solutions in certain sensitive areas. In 1999, Congress passed and the president signed into law the Financial Modernization Act which included significant new privacy protections for financial information. In 1998, the administration worked with Congress to pass the Children's Online Privacy Protection Act (COPPA). COPPA requires commercial websites that target children under the age of thirteen to obtain verifiable parental consent before they gather information from children under age thirteen.

THE EUROPEAN APPROACH

While the United States and EU generally agree on the underlying fair information principles, they employ different means to achieve this goal. The EU's approach to privacy grows out of Europe's history and legal traditions. In Europe, protection of information privacy is viewed as a fundamental human right. Europe also has a tradition of prospective comprehensive lawmaking that seeks to guard against future harms, particularly where social issues are concerned.

The EU began examining the impact of technology on society over fifteen years ago; the inquiry culminated in the adoption of a directive in July 1995 specifically addressing privacy issues. The European Community's Directive on Data Protection took effect in October 1998. Member States were required to bring into force laws, regulations, and administrative provisions to comply with the Directive by its effective date. . . .

HIPAA COMPLIANCE
CHRISTINA TORODE

An important field in which privacy is an important and evolving issue is health care, which spans the private, public, and not-for-profit sectors. New regulations, in the form of the Health Information Portability and Accountability Act (HIPAA) have challenged administrators to develop systems and practices in compliance with the law.

Health care organizations and those that serve this industry are alarmingly behind on the road to meeting the Health Information Portability and Accountability Act (HIPAA) compliance deadline [in 2005]. A recent report by nonprofit health care accreditation organization URAC found that none of the 300 organizations that applied for the accreditation process for HIPAA compliance were ready to do so. . . .

The main stumbling block for health care organizations is incomplete risk analysis efforts. Most did not understand the risks they were exposed to or how to mitigate the risk and did not have people in place to enforce policies and procedures to address the risks. . . .

While many health care organizations may not be taking actions to mitigate risks, individuals who feel their rights have been violated certainly are. In the 16 months between [when] HIPAA was enacted and August of [2004], the Office of Civil Rights for the U.S. Department of Health and Human Services received 8,000 HIPAA privacy complaints, according to Scott Edmiston, privacy specialist for the Office of Civil Rights out of Boston. The complaints were largely filed against private physician practices and hospitals. If found at fault the organization or individual could be fined $100 per violation and a capped charge of $25,000 for each violation, per calendar year.

To avoid such risks, providers such as Summa Health Systems in Akron, Ohio, are in the process of developing risk analyses and risk management procedures and encountered several stumbling blocks of their own.

Buy-in by top management . . . was a challenge. "I had to do a lot of research on HIPAA and the privacy rule before I even went to the IT administrators," said Anne Chance, the information security officer for Summa. "Once I explained the requirements, risk and the fact that we would be held accountable by law, they realized why I kept harping about it."

Chance's first step in the risk assessment process was a survey of the organization's systems and applications to determine which were the most critical systems. A security team of ten systems administrators and data owners in charge of the top 25 percent of

Source: Christina Torode, "HIPAA Compliance Has a Way to Go, Experts Say," *Mass High Tech*, October 10, 2004, p. 6, www.masshightech.com. Reprinted with permission of *Mass High Tech*.

what was determined to be critical systems . . . such as payroll and telecommunications, but largely systems geared towards clinical information, was put in place.

The team was asked to list threats and vulnerabilities, then determine the likelihood of threat occurring, the cost to the organization if the threat or vulnerability occurred, and how to mitigate threats. Common threats and vulnerabilities taken into consideration were employee sabotage, loss of physical and infrastructure support, malicious hackers, and industrial sabotage.

When Betty Cook, IT systems analyst with Summa, took over the HIPAA risk assessment and management program from Chance, she compared it to pulling teeth. "I asked them to fill out the forms and they all came back filled out saying none of the systems they were in charge of had any risks," said Cook. "It took several sitdowns and a lot of education to get them to finally get the forms filled out right down to how they would address a threat, and I made them prove to me how they would address that threat."

Even with risk management processes in place, Cook found that system administrators were still not reporting or addressing an incident. Finding resources to support HIPAA-related risk assessments and ongoing risk management is a hefty burden on health care organizations, said many of the attendees.

USA PATRIOT ACT: PRIVACY V. SECURITY
Maura King Scully

The importance of privacy as an ethical issue has been magnified after 9/11, as security measures have raised concerns about governmental infringement of personal privacy. Scully describes the current situation as a "balancing act" between privacy and security. Do individual administrators or even individual organizations have the discretion to do the "balancing" of these two sets of considerations?

Picture Uncle Sam as a tightrope walker, clutching the Constitution as he teeters on a high wire called the USA PATRIOT Act. He's carefully balancing on the divide between two sides: On one side stand those whose top priority is preventing future terrorist attacks against U.S. citizens; on the other are those clamoring against what they view as actions that threaten to erode the fundamental rights at the foundation of the American Way.

Welcome to the War on Terrorism, a struggle as broad in scope as the constitutional issues at stake. Like the decades-long Cold War that preceded it, the War on Terrorism is a comprehensive effort—involving state and federal agencies, law enforcement, intelligence, and the military—and encompassing a vast array of domestic and

Source: Maura King Scully, "Balancing Act: Privacy v. Security," *Suffolk University Law*, Fall 2003, pp. 16–20. Reprinted with the permission of Suffolk University Law School.

international issues. Within U.S. borders, the controversy surrounding the war has centered on the USA PATRIOT Act, the handy acronym for "Uniting and Strengthening America by Providing Appropriate Tools Required to Intercept and Obstruct Terrorism." Passed by Congress within weeks following September 11, 2001, the act grants broad powers to wiretap phones, track Internet traffic and examine private financial and educational records in robust pursuit of terrorists. It also breaks down the government-constructed barriers between various law enforcement agencies and the intelligence community, allowing them to share information and leads for mutual benefit.

Proponents argue that the USA PATRIOT Act brings law enforcement up to speed with technological advances made since the first wiretap laws were passed in the late 1960s and early 1970s. "The Act retrospectively satisfies the preexisting needs of law enforcement in areas where criminals have taken advantage of technological advances and where the law has lagged behind and levels the playing field between law enforcement and criminals," says First Assistant U.S. Attorney in Boston Gerry Leone. . . .

"It's somewhat tame," adds Robert Roughsedge, director of the nonprofit Citizens for the Preservation of Constitutional Rights and a trial attorney at Lawson and Weitzen in Boston. Pointing out that today's criminals use the Internet, Palm Pilots, pagers, and disposable cell phones, "strengthening existing laws makes a lot of sense," he says.

Others, however, fear the act goes too far. "The War on Terrorism is a loaded phrase used to justify some very troubling government policies," says Visiting Assistant Clinical Professor Tamar Birckhead, a former member of the defense team for convicted "shoe-bomber" Richard Reid. With the act, she notes, "the FBI has broadened powers to wiretap suspects without having evidence of criminal activities; they're able to monitor conversations of incarcerated federal inmates and lawyers and secure national search warrants, rather than those for just a specific jurisdiction." All of which, she points out, threaten civil and privacy rights. "In times of crisis, we have a tendency to overestimate the need for greater law enforcement and to underestimate the cost in terms of our basic political freedoms and civil rights," says Birckhead.

FEAR FACTOR

There's a story Associate Professor Jeff Pokorak, director of clinical programs, tells from his days as a public defender in Florida. In the mid-1980s, as he recalls, one particular county had a big problem involving illegal drugs. "There was one detective who used to say, 'Give me six police units and throw out the Constitution, and I could clean up the county in a week,'" recalls Pokorak.

That's exactly what Pokorak and others worry about with the USA PATRIOT Act—that law enforcement will overstep its bounds and citizens will tolerate the excesses because they're afraid. "The country is in the grips of the politics of fear," explains Associate Professor Michael Avery, president of the National Lawyers Guild.

"Today is an orange alert, tomorrow a yellow alert. We hear, 'we have credible information that this weekend there may be terrorist activities,' so guards are posted at the Golden Gate Bridge. . . .'"

Take, for example, defining what a terrorist is. According to Leone, with the PATRIOT Act, the United States Code was altered so that domestic and international terrorism were defined as virtually the same. According to the Code, Title 18, Section 2331: "'international terrorism' means activities that involve acts dangerous to human life that are a violation of the criminal laws of the United States or of any State; appear to be intended to intimidate or coerce a civilian population; to influence the policy of a government by intimidation or coercion; or to affect the conduct of a government by mass destruction, assassination or kidnapping."

"By making the definitions of domestic and international terrorism virtually synonymous, some people are concerned about probes that implicate arguable First Amendment rights and civil liberties," says Leone.

A well-founded fear, say critics. With the PATRIOT Act, "The government is saying: 'Trust us, trust us,'" asserts Pokorak. "But history has proven that's not a good idea—look at the Cold War excesses against communism, like McCarthyism."

To those who think such wide-reaching government fishing expeditions couldn't happen in this day and age, Birckhead points to a contemporary case. "Recently the FBI grew concerned that terrorists might attack using SCUBA gear," she explains, and began serving federal grand jury subpoenas on SCUBA organizations across the country to learn who'd recently taken diving lessons. "One store in Beverly Hills refused to turn over the information because there were many celebrity names on list. Then the government dropped the subpoena request. They knew they were over-reaching and couldn't defend it."

"My biggest complaint with the Act is the enforcement method being employed. It's arrogant; it's contrary to how we live," says Pokorak. "The fact is, the U.S. has always had enemies. The question remains: Do we want to change the nature of our societal compact potentially and forever because of one act of terrorism?"

HITTING HOME

That one act of international terrorism was huge, however. With the events of 9/11, "Terrorism struck the heart of small-town America," says Michael Sullivan, . . . U.S. attorney for the District of Massachusetts. "It was no longer an evening news story about some far place. It made us recognize there is vulnerability within our own borders."

The USA PATRIOT Act was passed to address that vulnerability, and, according to Leone, "Once the act is understood and the myths dispelled, the debate should then be framed around whether there is the potential for abusing the powers through law enforcement's execution and exercise of the powers, and not the powers themselves the act allows."

Sullivan notes, "The constant challenge we hear is that the USA PATRIOT Act has the potential to erode our basic constitutional rights and liberties." But following 9/11, say Sullivan and others, the country did not draft a new constitution—it strengthened some law enforcement tools to combat a heightened risk of terrorism. "Protecting our basic constitutional rights is the highest responsibility of the Department of Justice. I like to engage those people who are critical to reinforce that message," Sullivan says. . . .

Another often overlooked factor is that there are checks and balances written into the law, adds Roughsedge, a former U.S. Army counter-terrorism specialist.

NOT JUST A DRIVER'S LICENSE
AMITAI ETZIONI

Privacy and security are often seen in tension with one another, especially in the period following September 11, 2001. Sociologist Amatai Etzioni argues against absolutist defenders of privacy in his advocacy of reliable national identity cards.

It's Not Just a Driver's License Anymore. It's a De Facto National ID. We Should Make It Secure.

Every time a Transportation Security Administration (TSA) agent closely examines my driver's license, I have a hard time not making one of those wisecracks that gets you into trouble. The reason? I know that drivers' licenses as a means of identification are a joke. Fake ones can still be ordered on the Internet or purchased for about $60 in many cities, and real ones can be obtained fraudulently.

The joke becomes a lot less funny when one recalls that several of the 9/11 hijackers used phony documents to acquire driver's licenses, which they used to obtain credit cards, enroll in flight school, and purchase airplane tickets. Yet little has been done since then to make driver's licenses more reliable, despite the fact that they are by far the most commonly used means of identification in the United States—not just for travel, but also for entering most public buildings and numerous private ones. As a result, the "no fly" and "selectee" watch lists (used by the TSA to identify passengers who pose threats to airline safety), as well as other security-related databases, are at least partially blinded.

I am hardly a smart-card expert (or even a dull-witted one). But as a sociologist and social philosopher, I have studied circumstances under which concern for the common good might trump the right to privacy—for instance, the question of whether convicted pedophiles should be required to notify the communities in which they settle of their predilections. As a result, the New York-based Markle

---

Source: Amitai Etzioni, "It's Not Just a Driver's License Anymore," *Washington Post*, May 16, 2004, p. B03.

Foundation, which focuses on technology policy, invited me to join a task force composed of privacy advocates and former officials from the Pentagon, National Security Administration and CIA to study national security and information technology. I chaired a subgroup on reliable identification.

Our deliberations opened with a bombshell. Robert J. Cramer of the General Accounting Office described a test in which GAO agents had been able to enter the United States using counterfeit driver's licenses without being stopped—25 out of 25 times in late 2002 and early 2003. They entered through seaports from Canada, walked through border crossings from Mexico and arrived at airports from Jamaica. Shocked by these findings, our subgroup issued a report in 2003 with a long list of remedies. In March and April this year, Jared Bloom, my research assistant, and I queried officials in the 50 states and the District of Columbia about measures taken on these matters. The findings reveal how useless driver's licenses are as a means of identification:

- It is still impossible for any state to find out whether a person applying for a driver's license has already been issued one by another state (unless the applicant has had a license revoked or suspended). Thus, anyone with a clean driver's record can get a handful of licenses and hand over the extras to terrorists or other criminals.
- Sixteen states still do not check online to see if an applicant presents a valid Social Security number. Instead, they submit hard copies of Social Security numbers for confirmation. While waiting for replies, several of these states let applicants, who can be very hard to locate later, walk away with possibly false temporary, or sometimes even permanent, licenses.
- Each state follows its own procedures in deciding which so-called breeder documents (those used to obtain other cards or forms of identification) will be used to determine applicants' identities.
- Seventeen states do not require proof that applicants are legally in the United States.
- Only nine states collect biometric information (facial features, iris patterns, or fingerprints), which is the most reliable means of identification. (In Texas, for example, fingerprints are taken and put on file, but not on the licenses themselves.)

Driver's licenses—like other state-issued ID cards—are relics of the past. They were never meant to be used for national security purposes, or even national identification purposes. Hence, a relatively low level of reliability sufficed for the original purpose of confirming that a person had passed a driving test, met the physical requirements and was old enough to operate a vehicle.

The rub is that since 9/11, these state-issued pieces of plastic have been used increasingly as *de facto* national security cards, because a driver's license issued in one state is honored by all others and because federal authorities, especially TSA, treat them as the equivalent of national passports. However, the federal government has not taken over the issuance of these cards the way it controls the issuance of Social Security or green cards. It has not even required states to improve their own issuance practices. It has merely treated the licenses as though they were high-grade certificates.

Why has America been so slow to take remedial actions? It is not an accident, or a matter of plain neglect, that the states largely act as if 9/11 did not happen. One reason is that because of a strong U.S. tradition of states' rights, the country is reluctant to move from an archaic state system to a twenty-first-century form of government in which more tasks—especially those concerning national security—are federalized. And no state wants the folks in Washington to tell it how to issue licenses.

If the federal government did ask the states to meet standards suitable for what amounts to a domestic passport—needed to travel within the United States by air, by road and by rail—it would have to provide the states with the resources needed, otherwise it would be just another unfunded mandate.

Another major reason elected officials dare not touch ID cards is that backing for privacy with respect to this issue is particularly strong, with support spanning the ideological spectrum from conservative activist Phyllis Schlafly to the American Civil Liberties Union (ACLU). In a 2002 letter to President Bush, a group of privacy advocates led by the ACLU and the Free Congress Foundation wrote, "The administration should not take any steps to implement such a system or fund any proposals that would result in a national ID, including the study or development of standardized state drivers' licenses." And in a letter to the *New York Times* published on May 2, 2002, Schlafly and ACLU president Nadine Strossen, stirred by one U.S. senator's proposal for standardizing driver's licenses as an effort to implement national ID cards, wrote: "A national identity card would diminish privacy in America and do nothing to prevent further acts of terrorism on our soil."

The privacy lobby disregards the fact that such cards are commonly used in many other democracies. I prefer to call them national security cards because they differ from national ID cards in two profound ways: A person is required to carry a national ID card at all times and to produce it on demand from police without any reason. . . .

I am not arguing that ID cards are harmless. In a civil libertarian utopia, they would not exist. However, our world changed on 9/11. Moreover, this issue is governed by the Fourth Amendment, which is much less absolute than the First. It does not state that Congress shall make no law allowing search and seizure, only that there should be no *unreasonable* search and seizure—which, on the face of it, implies that there is a whole category of searches that are reasonable and fully compatible with the Constitution. No one has the right to a false ID. And if, after 9/11, we are going to identify people entering secure areas, then such identification should be reliable.

CASE 7: "OUTING" AGENTS AND PROTECTING SOURCES

One of the arguments made by U.S. President George W. Bush for the invasion of Iraq and the "regime change" removal of Saddam Hussein was the claim that Saddam was actively involved in seeking to acquire "yellow cake" uranium from the African country of Niger. Former U.S. Ambassador Joseph Wilson, who had been sent earlier to investigate the yellow cake rumors, had reported back that they were just that: fabricated rumors. When he heard the president use these fabrications as a ground for going to war, he wrote an op-ed piece in the *New York Times* that revealed his role in the matter and took issue with what he saw as the administration's misrepresentation of the facts.

Shortly thereafter, in July 2003, columnist Robert Novak revealed in a column that Wilson's wife, Valerie Plame, was a CIA agent who had been influential in the decision to send Wilson to Niger. Novak claimed to have received this information from unnamed sources at the White House. Wilson, angered by this revelation of his wife's undercover identity, charged that the White House was using the leak to Novak as retaliation for his op-ed piece. Since there was a law prohibiting publicly revealing the names of secret CIA agents, special counsel Patrick Fitzgerald was appointed to look into the matter, in December 2003. President Bush denied that anyone in the White House had done anything wrong and vowed to fire anyone if it turned out there had been any wrongdoing.

Nearly two years later, in mid-2005, the issue resurfaced, this time because two other reporters who had investigated the issue were threatened with imprisonment if they would not reveal their sources. *New York Times* reporter Judith Miller held firm to her claim of confidentiality and was sent to jail. Matthew Cooper of *Time* was let off the hook at the last minute by his editor's agreement to release emails relevant to the controversy, on the ground that the White House source had waived the claim to anonymity.

It then became known that the president's chief political advisor, Karl Rove, and Vice Presidential Assistant "Scooter" Libby had told at least some of the reporters that "Wilson's wife" was a CIA agent. Democrats called for Rove to resign. Republicans argued that Rove had not mentioned Plame by name, or had only confirmed information reporters already had, and had therefore not actually broken any law. Libby was later convicted of lying to the Grand Jury. Prosecutor Fitzgerald decided not to bring charges against Karl Rove.

Case Study Questions:

1. What are the ethical issues involved here? Which are most important?

Source: William L. Richter, Kansas State University.

2. Was it unethical for Bush to have used the "yellow cake" argument (as well as other WMD arguments) to go to war in Iraq? What if other reasons for the war (e.g., getting rid of a ruthless dictator) would ultimately be used to justify it?

3. Was Plame wrong to have suggested her husband for the Niger fact-finding mission?

4. Was Wilson wrong to have made a public statement (in the form of the op-ed piece) disagreeing with the administration?

5. Were officials wrong to have divulged information concerning Plame? Even if the law did not exist, would this have been an unethical use of classified information?

6. Were the reporters wrong to have kept their sources confidential, even in response to a Grand Jury inquiry into a case of law-breaking? Is it fair that Miller should go to jail?

CHAPTER DISCUSSION QUESTIONS

1. What guidelines do you follow in determining which information to share with others? Are your guidelines different for your personal life and for administrative roles?

2. By and large, do you think government is too secretive, too open, or just about right?

3. Are secrecy and confidentiality merely matters of "information management"? Is there anything wrong with "leaking" confidential information if it serves public policy interests to do so?

4. Besides the obvious legal and technological compliance issues, what might be the *administrative* challenges of dealing with Health Information Portability and Accountability Act (HIPAA) issues?

FOR FURTHER EXPLORATION

Bok, Sissela. *Secrets: On the Ethics of Concealment and Revelation.* New York: Pantheon, 1982.

Dean, John W. *Worse Than Watergate: The Secret Presidency of George W. Bush.* New York: Little, Brown and Company, 2004.

Etzioni, Amitai. *How Patriotic is the Patriot Act? Freedom Versus Security in the Age of Terrorism.* New York: Routledge, 2004.

Leo, Ross, ed. *The HIPAA Program Reference Handbook.* Boca Raton, FL: Auerbach Publications, 2005.

Lapham, Lewis H. *Gag Rule: On the Suppression of Dissent and the Stifling of Democracy.* New York: Penguin Press, 2004.

Laurent, Eric. *Bush's Secret World.* Cambridge, UK: Polity Press, 2004.

Westby, Jody, ed. *International Guide to Privacy.* Chicago: American Bar Association, 2004.

WEBSITES

Federation of American Scientists Project on Government Secrecy, http://fas.org/sgp

Fox News report on opinion poll showing Americans to be concerned about secrecy in government, March 13, 2005, www.foxnews.com/story/0,2933,150266,00.html

Item on issue of secrecy in Canadian government, http://canadaonline.about.com/library/weekly/aa062101a.htm

Project on Government Oversight site on secrecy in government, including links, www.pogo.org/p/x/2004governmentsecrecy.html

U.S. Department of Health and Human Services site on health information and privacy (HIPAA), www.hhs.gov/ocr/hipaa

Chapter 8

ABUSE OF AUTHORITY AND "ADMINISTRATIVE EVIL"

THE MALEK MANUAL
FREDERICK MALEK

Personnel suggestions in Malek's manual were carried out with varying degrees of enthusiasm and success by President Nixon's agency heads. These patterns of political manipulation of the public service illustrate continuing tensions and dangers, which are found at all levels of government around the world.

The best politics is still good government. But you cannot achieve management policy or program control unless you have established political control. The record is quite replete with instances of the failures of program, policy, and management goals because of sabotage by employees of the executive branch who engage in the frustration of those efforts because of their political persuasion and their loyalty to the majority party of Congress rather than the executive that supervises them. And yet, in their own eyes, they are sincere and loyal to their government. . . .

ORGANIZATION

The ideal organization to plan, implement and operate the political personnel program necessary is headed by a special assistant to the head of the department, or agency, or to the assistant head of the department, or agency, for administration.

. . . The overriding goal to be achieved is to insure placement in all key positions of substantively qualified and politically reliable officials with a minimum burden on line managers in achieving that goal. The objective of that goal is firm political control of the department, or agency, while at the same time effecting good management and good programs.

Source: White House Personnel Office, *The Malek Manual* (1970). Reprinted in U.S. Senate, Select Committee on Presidential Campaign Activities of 1972, *Executive Session Hearings*, 93d Cong. 2d Sess (1974), pp. 8903–9041.

Another function is to insure that personnel, which is a resource of the government, is utilized in a manner which creates maximum political benefit for the president and the party. . . . [The] office must then study and know the suitability of whatever incumbents occupy those positions. Where an unsuitable incumbent does occupy one of those positions, that office must effect his removal or devise a plan to organize the critical responsibilities he administers from without his control. . . .

TECHNIQUES FOR REMOVAL THROUGH ORGANIZATIONAL OR MANAGEMENT PROCEDURES

The civil service system creates many hardships in trying to remove undesirable employees from their positions. Because of the rape of the career service by the Kennedy and Johnson administrations, . . . this administration has been left a legacy of finding disloyalty and obstruction at high levels while those incumbents rest comfortably on career civil service status. Political disloyalty and insimpatico relationships with the administration, unfortunately, are not grounds for the removal or suspension of an employee. Career employees . . . can only be dismissed or otherwise punished for direct disobedience of lawful orders, actions which are tantamount to the commission of a crime, and well-documented and provable incompetence (see FPM Section 752). Even if you follow the time-consuming process of documenting a case to proceed with an adverse action, the administrative and legal process is slow and lengthy and great damage can accrue to the department prior to your successful conclusion of your case. However, there are several techniques that can be designed, carefully, to skirt around the adverse action proceedings. One must always bear in mind the following rules. The reduction of a person to a position of lower status and/or grade is considered an adverse action, which necessitates formal proceedings. Secondly, any administrative or management decision cannot be based on the political background or persuasion of an individual, his race, sex, religion, or national origin.

INDIVIDUAL TECHNIQUES

Frontal Assault

You simply call an individual in and tell him he is no longer wanted, that you'll assist him in finding another job and will keep him around until such time as he finds other employment. But you do expect him to immediately relinquish his duties, accept reassignment to a make-shift position at his current grade and then quietly resign for the good of the service. Of course, you promise him that he will leave with honor and with the finest recommendations, a farewell luncheon, and perhaps even a departmental award. You, naturally, point out that should he not accept such an offer, and he later is forced to resign or retire through regular process or his own volition, that his employment references from the department and his permanent personnel record may not look the same as if he accepted your offer. There should be no witnesses in the room at the time. Caution: this technique should only be used for the timid at heart with a giant ego. This is an extremely dangerous technique and the very fact of your conversation can be used against the department in any subsequent adverse action proceedings. It should never be used with that fervent, zealous employee committed to Democratic policies and programs or to the bureaucracy, who might relish the opportunity to be martyred on the cross of his cause.

Transfer Technique

By carefully researching the background of the proposed employee-victim, one can always establish that geographical part of the country and/or organizational unit to which the employee would rather resign than obey and accept transfer orders. For example, if you have an employee in your Boston regional office, and his record shows reluctance to move far from that location (he may have family and financial commitments not easily severed), a transfer accompanied by a promotion to an existing or newly created position in Dallas, Texas, might just fill the bill. It is always suggested that a transfer be accompanied by a promotion, if possible. Since a promotion is, per se, beneficial to the employee, it immediately forecloses any claim that the transfer is an adverse action. It also reduces the possibility of a claim that the transfer was motivated for prohibited purposes since, again, the transfer resulted in a beneficial action for the employee and the word discrimination implies some adversity to have been suffered. . . . The technical assistance of your personnel office is indispensable in prosecuting such transfers. . . .

Special Assistant Technique (The Traveling Salesman)

This technique is especially useful for the family man and those who do not enjoy traveling. What you do is to suddenly recognize the outstanding abilities of your employee-victim and immediately seize upon his competence and talent to assign him to a special research and evaluation project. This is best explained by way of example. Let us assume that our employee is a program analyst with the Department of Transportation. You immediately discover the high-level interest and policy requirements for creating a program to meet the transportation needs of all U.S. cities and towns with a population of 20,000 and under. Nothing is more revealing than first-hand inspections and consultation with town officials. . . .

NEW ACTIVITY TECHNIQUE

[One] organizational technique for the wholesale isolation and disposition of undesirable employee-victims is the creation of an apparently meaningful, but essentially meaningless, new activity to which they are all transferred. This technique, unlike the shifting responsibilities and isolation technique designed to immobilize a group of people in a single organizational entity, is designed to provide a single barrel into which you can dump a large number of widely located bad apples. Again let us use an example to illustrate this technique. Let us apply this to the Department of Health, Education, and Welfare. A startling new thrust to HEW's participation in the Model Cities Program might be a new research and development Model Cities Laboratory. With the concurrence of the governor of Alabama, one might choose Alabama, or a region thereof, to be a "model state" or "model region." . . .

CONCLUSION

There is no substitute in the beginning of any administration for a very active political personnel operation. Whatever investment is made in positions, salaries, systems, training, and intelligent work in this area will yield a return tenfold. Conversely, the failure to invest what is necessary to a political personnel program, will cost the administration and the department or agency fifty-fold what they might otherwise have invested. These estimates are borne out by experience. Where departments and agencies, and administrations, have failed to invest the manpower and other necessary aforementioned items into an effective political personnel program—blindly paying lip service to such a function and proceeding immediately to invest heavily in the management and program functions—they have only been plagued by such folly. The time consumed of high level administration appointees, and the manpower and expenses involved in the creation of firefighting forces caused by acts in an attempt to frustrate the administration's policies, program objectives, and management objectives, as well as to embarrass the administration, engaged in by unloyal employees of the executive branch has far exceeded investment a political personnel operation would have required. . . . In short, it is far better and healthier to swallow a large bitter pill in the beginning, and then run rigorously toward your objectives, than to run toward your objectives stopping so frequently for small bitter pills that you become drained of the endurance, the will, and the ability to ever reach your objectives. . . .

THE BANALITY OF EVIL
Hannah Arendt

The concept of "evil" in political affairs was given widespread exposure in Hannah Arendt's discussion of the trial of Nazi official Adolf Eichmann in Jerusalem in 1961. More specifically, Arendt coined the phrase "banality of evil" to underline the

Source: Hannah Arendt, *Eichmann in Jerusalem: A Report on the Banality of Evil*, revised and enlarged edition (New York: Penguin, 1965), pp. 135–37, 287–88. Copyright: 1963, 1964 by Hannah Arendt. Used by permission of Viking Penguin, a division of Penguin Group (USA) Inc.

thoughtlessness of Eichmann's evil actions. Was Eichmann a "good" administrator, as
he felt himself to be? Is it possible that public officials today are committing evil in
the ordinary execution of their duties?

So Eichmann's opportunities for feeling like Pontius Pilate were many, and as the
months and the years went by, he lost the need to feel anything at all. This was the
way things were, this was the new law of the land, based on the Fuhrer's order; whatever he did he did, as far as he could see, as a law-abiding citizen. He did his *duty*, as
he told the police and the court over and over again; he not only obeyed *orders*, he
also obeyed the *law*. Eichmann had a muddled inkling that this could be an important distinction, but neither the defense nor the judges ever took him up on it. The
well-worn coins of "superior orders" versus "acts of state" were handed back and
forth; they had governed the whole discussion of these matters during the Nurem-
berg Trials, for no other reason than that they gave the illusion that the altogether
unprecedented could be judged according to precedents and the standards that went
with them. Eichmann, with his rather modest mental gifts, was certainly the last man
in the courtroom to be expected to challenge these notions and to strike out on his
own. Since, in addition to performing what he conceived to be the duties of a law-
abiding citizen, he had also acted upon orders—always so careful to be "covered"—
he became completely muddled, and ended by stressing alternately the virtues and
the vices of blind obedience, or the "obedience of corpses," *Kadavergehorsam,* as he
himself called it.

The first indication of Eichmann's vague notion that there was more involved
in this whole business than the question of one soldier's carrying out orders that
are clearly criminal in nature and intent appeared during the police examination,
when he suddenly declared with great emphasis that he had lived his whole life according to Kant's moral precepts, and especially according to a Kantian definition
of duty. This was outrageous, on the face of it, and also incomprehensible, since
Kant's moral philosophy is so closely bound up with man's faculty of judgment,
which rules out blind obedience. The examining officer did not press the point,
but Judge Raveh, either out of curiosity or out of indignation at Eichmann's having dared to invoke Kant's name in connection with his crimes, decided to question the accused. And, to the surprise of everybody, Eichmann came up with an
approximately correct definition of the categorical imperative: "I meant by my remark about Kant that the principle of my will must always be such that it can become the principle of general laws" (which is not the case with theft or murder,
for instance, because the thief or the murderer cannot conceivably wish to live under a legal system that would give others the right to rob or murder him). Upon
further questioning, he added that he had read Kant's *Critique of Practical Reason.*
He then proceeded to explain that from the moment he was charged with carrying out the Final Solution he had ceased to live according to Kantian principles,
that he had known it, and that he had consoled himself with the thought that he

no longer "was master of his own deeds," that he was unable "to change anything." What he failed to point out in court was that in this "period of crimes legalized by the state," as he himself now called it, he had not simply dismissed the Kantian formula as no longer applicable, he had distorted it to read: Act as if the principle of your actions were the same as that of the legislator or of the law of the land—or, in Hans Frank's formulation of "the categorical imperative in the Third Reich," which Eichmann might have known: "Act in such a way that the Führer, if he knew your action, would approve it" *(Die Technik des Staates,* 1942, pp. 15–16). Kant, to be sure, had never intended to say anything of the sort; on the contrary, to him every man was a legislator the moment he started to act: By using his "practical reason" man found the principles that could and should be the principles of law. But it is true that Eichmann's unconscious distortion agrees with what he himself called the version of Kant "for the household use of the little man." In this household use, all that is left of Kant's spirit is the demand that a man do more than obey the law, that he go beyond the mere call of obedience and identify his own will with the principle behind the law—the source from which the law sprang. In Kant's philosophy, that source was practical reason; in Eichmann's household use of him, it was the will of the Führer. Much of the horribly painstaking thoroughness in the execution of the Final Solution—a thoroughness that usually strikes the observer as typically German, or else as characteristic of the perfect bureaucrat—can be traced to the odd notion, indeed very common in Germany, that to be law-abiding means not merely to obey the laws but to act as though one were the legislator of the laws that one obeys. Hence the conviction that nothing less than going beyond the call of duty will do. . . .

[W]hen I speak of the banality of evil, I do so only on the strictly factual level, pointing to a phenomenon which stared one in the face at the trial. Eichmann was not Iago and not Macbeth, and nothing would have been farther from his mind than to determine with Richard III "to prove a villain." Except for an extraordinary diligence in looking out for his personal advancement, he had no motives at all. And this diligence in itself was in no way criminal; he certainly would never have murdered his superior in order to inherit his post. He *merely,* to put the matter colloquially, *never realized what he was doing.* It was precisely this lack of imagination which enabled him to sit for months on end facing a German Jew who was conducting the police interrogation, pouring out his heart to the man and explaining again and again how it was that he reached only the rank of lieutenant colonel in the S.S. and that it had not been his fault that he was not promoted. In principle he knew quite well what it was all about, and in his final statement to the court he spoke of the "revaluation of values prescribed by the [Nazi] government." He was not stupid. It was sheer thoughtlessness—something by no means identical with stupidity—that predisposed him to become one of the greatest criminals of that period.

REFERENCE

Frank, Hans. *Die Technik des Staates*. Munich, 1942.

TORTURE AS PUBLIC POLICY
James Pfiffner

James Pfiffner seeks explanations for the inhumane behavior of Americans toward prisoners at Abu Ghraib. He summarizes two classic experiments and one more recent case that demonstrate the tendency of ordinary people to commit evil acts in certain roles. What are the implications and the prospects for ethical behavior in such circumstances?

Many citizens asked themselves, "How could these violent acts have been committed by U.S. soldiers?" Part of the answer is that most human beings can be heavily influenced by their immediate social settings.

The essence of professional military forces is the channeling of violence in effective and controlled manner, Military training must first overcome the socialized inhibitions against killing other humans, and it must then limit that killing to the designated enemy. The dynamics of violence are so volatile that strict discipline is essential in any military force. Discipline is of course necessary in order to get humans to risk their lives in the face of extreme danger and to coordinate forces in battle. But discipline is also necessary to limit the violence to mission accomplishment and not allow it to spill over to noncombatants. Thus discipline and honor have been the hallmarks of the best professional military organizations throughout history. In addition to the protection of noncombatant persons from violence, the system of limits extends to enemy forces that are captured. Despite the failure of many military organizations to live up to these ideals, the ideals are important to limit the destructiveness of warfare and the need to control the most violent tendencies of humans under pressure.

Thus U.S. military training includes familiarity with the general limits of violence and specifically the provisions of the Geneva Accords with regard to prisoners. What then, went wrong at Abu Ghraib? How could U.S. soldiers commit the terrible acts that have been recorded in the photographs that have been spread throughout the world? . . .

Source: James Pfiffner, "Torture as Public Policy," unpublished manuscript, 2005. Other portions of this manuscript were published as James P. Pfiffner, "Torture and Public Policy," *Public Integrity*, 7:4 (Fall 2005), pp. 313–29.

In trying to understand how the Holocaust could have occurred in Germany in the 1930s and 1940s, scholars have posited a number of explanations. But it has become clear that the actions necessary to exterminate Jews in large numbers were carried out in part by ordinary people (military and civilian) and not merely by Nazi party members or S.S. forces. One of the insights of Hannah Arendt, in what she describes as "the banality of evil," was that ordinary people doing what they saw as their jobs and duties, were capable of contributing to heinous acts.[1] In *Unmasking Administrative Evil*, Guy Adams and Danny Balfour explore how public administrators can contribute to evil acts as they conscientiously perform their expected duties. Their argument is that large scale evil is often masked; that is, the perpetrators are merely doing their assigned tasks conscientiously and do not believe they are doing anything wrong. But their acts cumulatively result in evil outcomes, as in the Holocaust.[2]

In the 1960s psychologist Stanley Milgram of Yale designed an experiment intended to show how Americans would not be as compliant as were Germans when asked to inflict pain on other human beings. In the experiment the subject was told that it was about the connection between electrical shock and memory. The subject was supposed to deliver a shock to a person (in reality, an actor) in the next room every time an incorrect response was given. The shocks were calibrated from 15 volts to 450 volts, and as the supposed voltage of the shocks was increased the actor expressed increased pain. If the subject hesitated to administer the next level of shock, the experimenter, with the help of a white lab coat and the voice of scientific authority, prompted the subject to apply the shock despite the screams of pain from the actor in the next room. Ninety-nine percent of the subjects were willing to administer the "strong" shock of 135 volts, and 62 percent were willing to go to the "XXX" category of 435 and 450 volts.[3]

This classic experiment (which would not be allowed in any universities now) demonstrated that regular Americans with their individualistic cultural values were not as different from what Germans were thought (by Americans) to be with their supposedly more authoritarian and conformist culture. One of the lessons of this experiment is that Americans would go much further than was predicted (by Milgram) along a path of inflicting pain on others if it were seemingly sanctioned by science and authority.

The other classic experiment on the malleability of Americans' behavior was conducted at Stanford University in the 1970s. The purpose of the experiment was to examine the nature of adopted roles in organizational behavior. The experimenters in the psychology department selected what they determined to be 22 normal undergraduate men and randomly assigned them to be either jailors or prisoners in a simulated prison set up in the basement of the psychology building. The "ground rules" were that the prisoners would be treated as prisoners but would not be subject to any inhumane treatment. The experiment had to be terminated after six days rather than running the planned two weeks because of the brutality that the "guards" developed and their brutality toward and mistreatment of the "prisoners."

Again, this experimental evidence illustrates how seemingly ordinary and normal people can exhibit extraordinarily inhuman behavior under the right conditions. In this case the conditions were only the "prison" environment. The guards knew the prisoners were guilty of nothing but being part of the experiment that assigned them the role of prisoner. The experimenters concluded: "In less than a week, the experience of imprisonment undid (temporarily) a lifetime of learning; human values were suspended, self-concepts were challenged and the ugliest, most base, pathological side of human nature surfaced. We were horrified because we saw some boys ('guards') treat other boys as if they were despicable animals, taking pleasure in cruelty. . . ."[4]

The power of role playing was also illustrated during Army training exercises at Guantanamo Bay in 2003. Specialist Sean Baker, 37, of the 438th Military Police Company was playing the role of an uncooperative detainee. Baker was beaten so harshly by four soldiers that he suffered traumatic brain injury. Finally when the soldiers realized that he could be an American, they stopped beating him.[5]

Given the two classic experiments, it should not surprise us that good, normal American young men and women would be capable of inhumane behavior when guarding prisoners who were of a different racial/cultural background and who very well might have been guilty of attacks on U.S. forces. This is why rules, procedures, and strict adherence to standard operating procedures are so important in military prisons.

NOTES

1. Hannah Arendt, *Eichmann in Jerusalem: A Report on the Banality of Evil* (NY: Viking Press, 1963).

2. Guy B. Adams and Danny L. Balfour, *Unmasking Administrative Evil*, revised edition (Armonk, NY: M.E. Sharp, 2004).

3. Stanley Milgram, *Obedience to Authority* (NY: Harper and Row, 1974). See the detailed description of the experiment and its implications in Guy B. Adams and Danny L. Balfour, *Unmasking Administrative Evil* (NY: M. E. Sharp, 2004), pp. 36–39, from which this description is taken.

4. C. Hanley, C. Banks, and P. Zimbardo, "Interpersonal Dynamics in a Simulated Prisons," *International Journal of Criminology and Penology*, vol. 1 (1974), pp. 69–97. See the detailed description of the experiment and its implications in Guy B. Adams and Danny L. Balfour, *Unmasking Administrative Evil* (NY: M. E. Sharp, 2004), pp. 27–29, from which this description is taken.

5. Associated Press, *New York Times* (9 June 2004), p. A10.

WHAT ABOUT EVIL?
H. GEORGE FREDERICKSON

Among the many reactions to Unmasking Administrative Evil *was this essay by H. George Frederickson. Drawing upon M. K. Gandhi, Frederickson questions whether social inequalities, such as plenty in the midst of poverty, might be ipso facto evil.*

Evil is certainly among the most powerful and evocative words in contemporary public discourse. There was once an empire of evil and now there is an axis of evil. Evil regimes and leaders are abroad in the world, dangerous, threatening, dark and mysterious. There is evil among us and some of it, we are told, is administrative, administrative evil needing to be unmasked. Evil and its opposite, good, are, it is said, dichotomous categories into which individuals and their actions, groups and their actions, ideologies and even cultures can be reliably placed.

Among the more useful considerations of evil is the description of it by Gandhi. He too used dichotomous categories to describe good and evil but rather than characterizing particular leaders, their regimes or their policies as evil, he found evil to be well within each individual's capacity to both understand and act on. He had good reason to characterize the particular leaders, regimes and actions of his time as evil, but he chose instead to set out an understanding of evil that is abstract and therefore particularly useful and enduring. In his description Gandhi did not include those evils so obvious and fundamental to human understanding that they did not require elaboration, such as involuntary servitude or the taking of innocent life. An abstract and even philosophical approach to evil on the part of a political leader was unusual in Gandhi's time and would be even more unusual today, when the word evil is so frequently and casually used.

Here, in summary form and [paraphrased] is Gandhi's description of the forms of evil.

Poverty amid plenty is evil and those policies and actions that consciously favor the interests of those with plenty at the expense of those in poverty are likewise evil. Virtually all forms of theology teach us that those with resources have responsibilities toward those without resources. Persons and groups of persons who have plenty have responsibilities toward those who do not and well-off nations have responsibilities toward less well-off nations. Nothing, not race, not gender, not ideology, not geography, can mitigate the evil of those with plenty ignoring the needs of those

---

Source: H. George Frederickson, "What About Evil?" *PA Times*, September 2004. Reprinted with permission from the American Society for Public Administration.

with little. The reason the concept of social equity has such resonance as a core ethic in American public administration is that we instinctively recognize the evil of poverty amid plenty.

Wealth without work is evil. Because the poor in our uneven world usually work tirelessly just to survive, it is evil for those with plenty to be idle. Remember the little rhyme by Sarah Gleghorn (1915) that so profoundly captured the evil of wealth without work that it influenced the development of much stronger British and American child labor laws:

> The golf links lie so near the mill
> That almost any day
> The laboring children can look out
> And see the men at play.

Although there has been progress in many parts of the world, the challenges of child labor and human exploitation are no less now than they were in Gandhi's time. Our wealth is easily seen by others, but it is not easy for us to see their privation.

Commerce without morality can be evil. In most respects the modern corporation and its operation in the capitalist marketplace is a positive force for good in the world, forming the base of gainful work for millions while improving products and providing services. But the exploitation of both humankind and our environment for commercial gain is far too evident in the world and is a great evil.

Science and technology without humanity can be evil. Science gives us better food, better health and longer lives. Technology can reduce human toil and greatly enhance human communication and knowledge. Science and technology can be instruments for a more humane world. But when the benefits of science and technology are so unevenly distributed around the world or when science and technology are used for inhumane purposes they are evil. The moral implications of nuclear wars on the one hand and suicide bombers on the other are clear. Modern science and technology both bless us and cause us to face potential evils never before faced by humankind.

The practices of politics and administration without principles can be evil. In his time Gandhi was probably most concerned with the evils associated with European policies of empire and their implementation in India. In our time we face the challenges of political and administrative evil in Iraq, for example the evil of Saddam Hussain on one hand and prisoner abuse on the other. We should never tire of asking these questions: what exactly are our political and administrative principles and do we believe them to be good? For whom are our principles good? Do current policies or proposed policies further those principles? How can policies thought to be favorably associated with our principles be implemented without doing evil?

Knowledge without character can be evil. Although we live, it is said, in a knowledge society, knowledge never has been synonymous with either wisdom or character. One way to ensure greater character in the application of knowledge to human affairs is to do all that can be done to make knowledge widely available and to demand transparency. Knowledge comes in many forms and in the hierarchies of knowledge, local knowledge tends to be discounted. This is nonsense because all knowledge when applied must be applied locally. It is at the local level where policy is carried out that character is most likely to meet knowledge and ideas passing for knowledge. Consider, for example, local school districts. It would seem that local school officials do not know as much about schooling as do expert policy makers and politicians at the state and national level. It requires little character to push knowledge-based arguments that one is not asked to carry out. The denial of local knowledge reduces the prospects of bringing real character to policy implementation at the level where it matters most.

Knowledge based on technical expertise is vital but so too is local knowledge based on culture, tradition, and context. Effective politics and administration very often involve carefully built patterns of accommodation between technical expertise and local knowledge. Promiscuous use of the word evil in contemporary political discourse drains it of meaning and does little to advance a generalized good.

Without doubt there is evil in the world. Gandhi teaches us that the evil that matters most and the evil we are likely to be able to influence is near at hand. It is the evil of poverty amid plenty, wealth without work, commerce without morality, politics and administration without principles, science and technology without morality, and knowledge without character. If we individually and collectively face down these evils the world would be a better place.

HISTORY AS CAUSE: *COLUMBIA* AND *CHALLENGER*
Columbia Accident Investigation Board

Adams and Balfour, in Unmasking Administrative Evil, *drew connections between Hitler's German Nazi rocketry program and postwar American aerospace programs. The special board appointed to investigate the space shuttle* Columbia *tragedy draws remarkable parallels between the* Columbia *and* Challenger *accidents.*

Source: Columbia Accident Investigation Board, *Report,* vol. 1 (August 2003). Washington, D.C.: U.S. Government Printing Office (2003), ch. 8, Sections 8.4, 8.6. The report is available online at www .caib.us/news/report/default.html.

ORGANIZATION, CULTURE,
AND UNINTENDED CONSEQUENCES

How could the lessons of *Challenger* have been forgotten so quickly? . . . [H]istory was a factor. First, if success is measured by launches and landings,[1] the machine appeared to be working successfully prior to both accidents. *Challenger* was the 25th launch. Seventeen years and 87 missions passed without major incident. Second, previous policy decisions again had an impact. NASA's Apollo-era research and development culture and its prized deference to the technical expertise of its working engineers was overridden in the Space Shuttle era by "bureaucratic accountability"—an allegiance to hierarchy, procedure, and following the chain of command.[2] Prior to *Challenger*, the can-do culture was a result not just of years of apparently successful launches, but of the cultural belief that the Shuttle Program's many structures, rigorous procedures, and detailed system of rules were responsible for those successes.[3] . . . The fact that many changes had been made supported a belief in the safety of the system, the invincibility of organizational and technical systems, and ultimately, a sense that the foam problem was understood. . . .

CHANGING NASA'S ORGANIZATIONAL SYSTEM

The echoes of *Challenger* in *Columbia* . . . have serious implications. These repeating patterns mean that flawed practices embedded in NASA's organizational system continued for 20 years and made substantial contributions to both accidents. . . .

During the *Columbia* investigation, the Board consistently searched for causal principles that would explain both the technical and organizational system failures. These principles were needed to explain *Columbia* and its echoes of *Challenger*. They were also necessary to provide guidance for NASA. . . .

Leaders create culture. It is their responsibility to change it. Top administrators must take responsibility for risk, failure, and safety by remaining alert to the effects their decisions have on the system. Leaders are responsible for establishing the conditions that lead to their subordinates' successes or failures. The past decisions of national leaders—the White House, Congress, and NASA Headquarters—set the *Columbia* accident in motion by creating resource and schedule strains that compromised the principles of a high-risk technology organization. The measure of NASA's success became how much costs were reduced and how efficiently the schedule was met. . . .

Changes in organizational structure should be made only with careful consideration of their effect on the system and their possible unintended consequences. Changes that make the organization more complex may create new ways that it can fail.[4] When changes are put in place, the risk of error initially increases, as old ways of doing things compete with new. Institutional memory is lost as personnel and records are moved and replaced. Changing the structure of organizations is complicated by external political and budgetary constraints, the inability of leaders to conceive of the full ramifications of their actions, the vested interests of insiders, and the failure to learn from the past.[5] Nonetheless, changes must be made. . . .

Strategies must increase the clarity, strength, and presence of signals that challenge assumptions about risk. Twice in NASA history, the agency embarked on a slippery slope that resulted in catastrophe. Each decision, taken by itself, seemed correct, routine, and indeed, insignificant and unremarkable. Yet in retrospect, the cumulative effect was stunning.

NOTES

1. Richard J. Feynman, "Personal Observations on Reliability of the Shuttle," *Report of the Presidential Commission,* Appendix F:1.

2. Howard E. McCurdy, "The Decay of NASA's Technical Culture," *Space Policy* (November 1989), pp. 301–10; See also Howard E. McCurdy, *Inside NASA* (Baltimore: Johns Hopkins University Press, 1993).

3. Diane Vaughan, "The Trickle-Down Effect: Policy Decisions, Risky Work, and the *Challenger* Tragedy," *California Management Review* 39, no. 2 (Winter 1997).

4. Lee Clarke, *Mission Improbable: Using Fantasy Documents to Tame Disaster* (Chicago: University of Chicago Press, 1999); Charles Perrow, *Normal Accidents,* op. cit.; Scott Sagan, *The Limits of Safety,* op. cit.; Diane Vaughan, "The Dark Side of Organizations," *Annual Review of Sociology,* vol. 25 (1999), pp. 271–305.

5. Typically, after a public failure, the responsible organization makes safety the priority. They sink resources into discovering what went wrong and lessons learned are on everyone's minds. A boost in resources goes to safety to build on those lessons in order to prevent another failure. But concentrating on rebuilding, repair, and safety takes energy and resources from other goals. As the crisis ebbs and normal functioning returns, institutional memory grows short. The tendency is then to backslide, as external pressures force a return to operating goals. William R. Freudenberg, "Nothing Recedes Like Success? Risk Analysis and the Organizational Amplification of Risks," *Risk: Issues in Health and Safety* 3, 1 (1992), pp. 1–35; Richard H. Hall, *Organizations: Structures, Processes, and Outcomes,* (Englewood Cliffs, NJ: Prentice-Hall, 1998), pp. 184–204; James G. March, Lee S. Sproull, and Michal Tamuz, "Learning from Samples of One or Fewer," *Organization Science* 2, no. 1 (February 1991), pp. 1–13.

CASE 8: WHEN THE COUNTY KNOWS BEST?

West Nile virus, an illness transmitted from wildlife to humans by mosquitoes, has made its second appearance in two years in Phoenix, Arizona, resulting in a number

Source: Thomas Babcock, "Ethics Moment: When the County Knows Best—or Does It?" *PA Times,* December 2004. Reprinted with permission from the American Society for Public Administration.

of confirmed fatal cases among birds and a growing number of positive cases in humans, reported by hospitals and doctors to the Maricopa County health department's vector control program.

In response, the county has tracked the locations of most intense activity, has ramped up its public education program to ask people to be vigilant in draining any stagnant water sources where mosquitoes breed, and advised the public to wear repellent, particularly in the evenings, at night, and early morning when the insects are most active.

After plotting the outbreaks, the county identified a large "hot zone" of cases and determined that this area—mostly residential neighborhoods—should be fogged with insecticide to reduce the mosquito population. The insecticide of choice is a synthetic pyrethroid called Anvil. According to the EPA "pyrethroids can be used . . . without posing unreasonable risks to human health when applied according to the label. Pyrethroids are considered to pose slight risks of acute toxicity to humans, but at high doses, pyrethroids can affect the nervous system." [www.epa.gov/pesticides/factsheets/pyrethroids4mosquitos.htm]

Maricopa county proceeded with a program to fog an area of about eight square miles in the early morning hours of a Friday; a time when mosquitoes are active, winds are calm, and most people are in their homes asleep. Maricopa County also made the decision to not notify residents in the affected area in advance that their neighborhood would be fogged.

Many of those homes, however, use evaporative cooling, a process that draws outdoor air into the home. The pesticide fog was also drawn into the homes, and the residents exposed while they slept. Some symptoms of pyrethroid exposure include rash and breathing difficulties. Persons with lung ailments and small children are susceptible at a lower dosage than the "average" person. Persistent exposure or exposure to large concentrations can cause other health problems. Pyrethroids are a carcinogen.

While it is unknown how many residents of Phoenix were affected by the insecticide, none knew they may have been exposed. Therefore none knew whether, if they did show symptoms, they should seek medical treatment. I am one who came down with a rash after sleeping with an evaporative cooler running on a night when the county fogged my neighborhood. Evaporative coolers bring in outside air, cooling the air with water. In this case, the water was off, so it was ambient outdoor air being drawn in. I woke up to the smell of it, but had no idea as to the source. I learned a few days later that one of my neighbors saw the trucks on our street at 3 A.M. the day I came down with the rash

The ethics question—aside from any legal exposure notification or informed consent requirements—is: "Why did the county health department proceed with this application of pesticides without notifying the residents in the target area that they could be exposed, what the pesticide was, and what actions they should take if they wished to limit their exposure?" Is it possible that county officials believed they knew what was in the best interest of the citizens? Or was this just an act of insensitivity or incompetence?

— · · —

CHAPTER DISCUSSION QUESTIONS

1. What do you see as the benefits, and conversely the problems, of the use of "administrative evil" as an explanation for certain types of organizational practices?

2. War has often been used as a rationale to engage in activities that would not be considered ethical or legal in peacetime. Should the twenty-first–century "global war on terror" justify the use of torture to secure needed information, rendition of suspected terrorists to other countries for questioning (and probable torture), or indefinite imprisonment of "enemy combatants" without either criminal charges or Geneva Accords protection?

3. The administrative flaws that led to the *Challenger* disaster, the Board's report argues, were still present years later in the *Columbia* accident. Are these flaws characteristic of all organizations? If not, what are the factors that might help to avoid similar disasters in the future?

— · · —

FOR FURTHER EXPLORATION

Adams, Guy B. "Administrative Ethics and the Chimera of Professionalism," in *Handbook of Administrative Ethics*, second ed., ed. Terry Cooper (New York and Basel: Marcel Dekker, 2001), pp. 291–308.

Adams, Guy B., and Danny L. Balfour, "Public Service Ethics and Administrative Evil: Prospects and Problems," in *Ethics in Public Management*, ed. H. George Frederickson and Richard K. Ghere (Armonk, NY: M.E. Sharpe, 2005), pp. 114–138.

Adams, Guy, and Danny Balfour, *Unmasking Administrative Evil*, rev. ed. (Armonk, NY: M.E. Sharpe, 2004).

Balfour, Danny L. "Understanding Abu Ghraib," *PA Times* 37, no. 9 (September 2004), pp. 10.

Griffin, Ricky W., and Anne M. O'Leary-Kelly, eds. *The Dark Side of Organizational Behavior* (San Francisco: Jossey-Bass, 2004).

Ignatieff, Michael. *The Lesser Evil: Political Ethics in an Age of Terror* (Edinburgh: Edinburgh University Press, 2004). [8]

Strasser, Steven, ed. *The Abu Ghraib Investigations* (New York: Public Affairs, 2004).

Waller, James. *Becoming Evil: How Ordinary People Commit Genocide and Mass Killing*. (Oxford: Oxford University Press, 2002).

WEBSITES

American Civil Liberties Union (ACLU) fact sheet on extraordinary rendition, www.aclu .org/safefree/extraordinaryrendition/22203res20051206.html

CBS News report on Abu Ghraib scandal, www.cbsnews.com/stories/2004/05/12/iraq/main 616921.shtml

Jane Mayer, "Outsourcing Torture: The Secret History of America's 'Extraordinary Rendition' Program," *New Yorker*, February 14, 2005, www.newyorker.com/fact/content?050214fa_fact6

Wikipedia entry on practice of extraordinary rendition, with links, http://en.wikipedia.org/ wiki/Extraordinary_rendition

PART III

STRATEGIES: WHAT TO DO WHEN THE ANGELS ARE MISSING

In Part I of *Combating Corruption, Encouraging Ethics*, we examined the strong foundations, current condition, and fermenting future of management ethics. Part II highlighted the ambiguity of ethics and ethical decision-making and the need to identify the many and diverse problems of this field. In this final section, we offer a wide range of management tools and strategies that can be applied to combat unethical practices and to encourage ethical behavior. This part raises questions of trust, deterrence, and appropriate behavior "when the angels are missing."

One obvious starting point in attacking problems of corruption and other abuses is to identify the kinds of policies (or lack thereof), programs and positions which are most likely to be vulnerable to fraud, waste, abuse, and corrupt practices. As the President's Council on Integrity and Efficiency noted in 1981, procurement contracts, loans and grants programs, and computer operations (especially those concerned with contracts and with personnel files) were, and still are, prime areas for potential corruption and mismanagement. Employees responsible for fire safety inspection, for monitoring restaurants in relation to sanitary codes, and for processing licenses and permits in a wide range of areas may also be unusually vulnerable to bribery and extortion. These current vulnerable areas and those of the future (including megaprojects, cyberspace, and other global overlapping jurisdictional operations) are subject to unethical actions and corruption.

To target policies, programs, and positions is only a starting point. Any area that is allowed to drift—without clear leadership and without an active, continuous effort to monitor the infrastructure operations where discretion is possible—will in time fall prey to forms of abuse and corruption. Some of these abuses will be initiated by officials within the governmental agency. Others arise within global organizations via business agents and clients of government agencies, who are glad to provide large speaking fees, free vacations, and other benefits to an individual public official in return for special opportunities to drain off the taxpayers' dollars.

When we frame the ethics problem in this broad way, we may seem to imply that unethical behavior is rampant throughout the public service, and in the many connections and interactions between the government and the private sector. In fact, our own strong view is that most public employees demonstrate high levels of personal and professional integrity and responsibility. We think it likely that most business officials and others in the private domain also behave, and prefer to behave, ethically and responsibly. But that is not the end of wisdom. As James Madison observed sagely more than 200 years ago in *Federalist No. 51:*

> If men were angels, no government would be necessary.
> If angels were to govern men, neither external nor internal controls on government would be necessary.

Since the power of government in this world is held only by mere women and men, a thoughtful approach to providing the tools of deterrence, including both external and internal controls, seems essential. Such controls will increase the difficulties and risks for those who are hungry for greater power and prestige. Moreover, a range of vigorous controls will protect the greater number of employees, who are honest and responsible, from the pressures and blandishments of their less savory compatriots and friends.

The various management tools, approaches, and strategies discussed in this Section are divided into four major areas:

1. Strengthening trust through establishing guidelines, incorporating accountability and measured expectations;
2. Providing for dissent and the application of transparency and whistleblowing;
3. Adding management tools to institutionalize modes of compliance, oversight, and sanctions; and,
4. Examining the responsibility of leaders and others in bringing about an ethical culture.

STRENGTHENING TRUST

Checks and balances, the rule of law, a strong middle class, and an informed electorate are cited as many of the elements contributing to a democratic country. Further, participatory democracy rests on a bed of trust, and, as we know, a high level of trust contributes to citizens' confidence in government.

The highly developed ethics infrastructure throughout the U.S. Office of Government Ethics (OGE), according to Amy Comstock, is the key to faith in government. The trust engendered by the Designated Agency Ethics Officer (DAEO) positioned in each federal agency "ensures that public officials are held accountable and that government operations are open to public scrutiny." Moreover, there are three organizations featured herein which provide oversight and regulation of the U.S. security markets (Securities and Exchange Commission), management measures of integrity, core values, and transparency (Organization for Economic Cooperation and Development), and the methodology to measure corruption and governance (World Bank). Each of these organizations, institutions, or commissions was designed to bar and inhibit wrongdoing, or to apply the tools and techniques to minimize the opportunity for fraud, waste, abuse, or corrupt practices.

Yet, it is these very tools and techniques developed to measure, to provide barriers to wrongdoing, and to set high expectations for integrity that have been questioned as to their effectiveness. In a news story in the June 27, 2003, *Financial Times*, Stephen Overell wrote about the possibility of unintended consequences:

> The way society seeks to encourage responsibility at work—regulation, targets, mission statement, performance indicators, and penalty clauses—in some ways seem to be achieving the opposite end: they foster mutual distrust and suspicion of being cheated. The prevalence of tools designed to ensure trust indicates its absence.

The Miami-Dade County survey of cities with populations greater than 50,000 people found that 80 percent have rules or regulations in place to support management ethics. The concern exhibited, however, was that many of these cities evoked a lack of public trust.

Contrary to these cautions about building trust through measurement, tools, and techniques of the time, many world organizations are focused on engendering transparency, eliminating bribery by laws and regulations, and featuring the use of anticorruption approaches. Finally, we offer ten everyday ethical dilemmas for all of us to ask ourselves: "Are you an ethical public official?"

ETHICAL IMPERATIVES AND ETHICAL REASONING

As professional associations, governmental units, and other entities have grappled with the challenges of encouraging ethics in their respective spheres of activity, they have developed various codes and guidelines for ethical administrative behavior. Some codes carry the force of law, others may entail organizational sanctions, while others may simply declare principles, priorities, or appropriate behavior. Some codes are broad and general, others narrow and specific, some long, others short. The codes of ethics of two leading professional associations for public managers—the American Society for Public Administration (ASPA) and the International City/County Management Association (ICMA)—illustrate some of these differences.

The ICMA Code, developed in the 1920s, is much more specific and carries sanctions. The ASPA code, developed in the 1980s and 1990s, is more general and does not entail sanctions. Both codes, as well as those of other professional associations, are generally consistent, however, with respect to their *content*. That is, the imperatives articulated, the concerns addressed, and the professional attitudes encouraged are largely in agreement, regardless of the professional association or governmental entity that has formulated them. Collectively, they provide a fairly clear picture of what it means to be an ethical administrator.

TRANSPARENCY, WHISTLE-BLOWING, AND DISSENT

If a staff member believes that violations of law, ethics, or approved policy have occurred, and that senior officials are reluctant to take remedial action, the individual faces an important ethical issue. If one "blows the whistle" collegial relationships may be broken beyond repair, and the risk of losing one's position may be very real. Yet to permit the pattern of corruption or abuse to continue will—for many people—be an uncomfortable and often an unacceptable choice. A number of professional organizations have, in recent years, begun to encourage their members to recognize the tensions involved in deciding whether to release information regarding illegal and other abusive activities within their agencies, and to "go public" when they believe doing so is the appropriate ethical action. Early on, ASPA developed a position statement on whistle-blowing which noted the division in public opinion.

> To some, whistle-blowing is considered to be an ultimate expression of accountability. To others, whistle-blowing is the spiteful behavior of disgruntled employees and an act of organizational disloyalty.

The ASPA statement went further, however, both in encouraging government officials to "blow the whistle" and in encouraging ASPA Chapters around the country to provide counsel and support to their members when the issue of whistle-blowing arises.

The selection by Roberta Ann Johnson reviews the development of whistle-blower protection legislation over the last few decades. A major change was the inclusion of whistle-blowing provisions into the Civil Service Reform Act of 1978. The Act created two new national units: the Office of the Special Counsel and the Merit Systems Protection Board, each designed to prevent reprisals against open dissenters and to combat serious economic losses suffered by whistle-blowers.

During this time efforts to increase transparency in government and citizen participation in its operations encouraged the development of sunshine laws, ombudsmen offices, access channels, hot lines, and similar mechanisms. This push led to laws, rules, and procedures governing open meetings, open documents, and open records, as well as openly posted information about public sector operations. The principle espoused is that the public, the media, and interest groups will more actively monitor the actions of government if those actions are open for all to see; moreover, visible program decisions are less likely to be abusive or otherwise unethical.

An example of the effective opening of management channels through the practice of listening is provided in Richard Loverd's essay describing the "Shriver Prescription." Patrick Dobel explores the ethics of resignation from office. An abbreviated discussion of Transparency International's (TI) anti-bribery programs, the United Nations Global Compacts, Accessibility Guides and Global Report Initiatives (GRI) as well as the TI Integrity Pact (IP) is provided by Brooks. The IP is an agreement between the procuring agent and all contractual bidders to comply with transparency and non-corrupt practices. These open documents give transparency to actions and decisions and, it is hoped, will provide those employees who have detailed inside knowledge the evidence to "blow the whistle"; and also provide to contractors and others the encouragement to become more diligent in policing themselves.

APPLIED ACCOUNTABILITY

What are the strategies by which governmental responsibility and accountability might be ensured, or at least encouraged? Deterrence through organizational units was targeted by the U.S. Office of the Attorney General (OAG) beginning in 1978, by the Office of Governmental Ethics (OGE) that same year, and via the President's Council on Integrity and Efficiency established by Executive Order in 1981. The national system of Inspectors General (IG) was created to improve efficiency and effectiveness of government programs, and was strengthened when reauthorized in 1988.

The first State Inspector General was created in 1978 in the Commonwealth of Massachusetts in order to anticipate and confront fraud, waste, abuse, and corrupt practices. At this time also many state governmental units focusing on accountability were set up with independent oversight mechanisms covering several sensitive functions such as personnel, capital planning, and electoral reporting. Twenty-five years later in July 2005, Acting Governor Richard J. Codey signed Inspector General legislation for New Jersey, announcing that "today accountability, integrity, and confidence will become the standard." The IG, whether federal, state, or local (such as NYC), is mandated to root out waste, mismanagement, and fraud in government spending. Inspectors General have the authority to review procurements and public contracts, receive complaints (many through hot lines) and perform investigations into programs, conduct performance reviews to determine whether programs could be run more efficiently, and look into technology and better management practices that would save taxpayers dollars.

The business and financial scandals of the past decade or so resulted in major changes to the accounting industry. As William Voorhees informs us there was widespread concern about the Governmental Accounting Standards Board (GASB) and the Financial Accounting Standards Board (FASB), each of which set accounting and financial rules for the private sector. Voorhees notes that "since accounting standards are the unseen foundation of public confidence in government," the Boards and their parent Board, Financial Accounting Foundation, must be clear of concerns and whistle clean. The Sarbanes-Oxley Act (SOX) was passed by Congress in response to these concerns and to evidence of serious wrongdoing in corporate America. The new Public Company Accounting Oversight Board (PCAOB) was mandated to restore integrity to the auditing and accounting reportage.

The role of the U.S. Securities and Exchange Commission (SEC) in compliance, oversight, and sanctions—the heart of applied accountability—is identified in the selection from William H. Donaldson, then SEC Chair. SOX required the SEC to review and renew all the extensive rulemaking in auditing and accounting operations as well as establish rulemaking for the new governmental unit—PCAOB. The SEC is enforcer and regulator as well as standard setter for the market system including the equity and mutual funds market.

The need for public oversight of nonprofit management has become increasingly evident, as scandals have arisen over abuses of tax-exempt status, excessive executive compensation, inappropriate use of charitable funds, and other problems. These issues have been addressed by Congressional committee hearings, several state legislatures, and a special panel appointed by Independent Sector, the leading association of nonprofit organizations. The panel's 2005 report, partially reproduced here, recommended numerous actions by Congress and by nonprofits.

CHANGING CULTURE THROUGH ETHICAL LEADERSHIP

Throughout the readings in this volume, references are made to the vital importance of guidance from "the top" on questions of public trust. Ethics is no exception to the general role of management that the success of any strategy, technique, or process depends on the strength of the signals—plus the active support—from leaders. Daily ethical problems are more easily resolved with reinforcement from one's supervisor that one is "doing right."

Kenneth Ashworth's ethical advice to a new public administrator draws upon his own experience as a public administrator in Texas. The selection included in this volume includes the phrase engraved on the old Philadelphia Customhouse:

Our country, right or wrong. When right, to be kept right,
When wrong, to be set right.

The Debra Stewart piece examines integrity in her query as to what extent should the "individual be cast as a 'moral actor' in a work setting?" Answering firmly that the public administrator *is*—and must be—an ethical agent, Stewart provides guidance for identifying where responsibility resides and why ignorance of the ethical path is not acceptable at any level of the organization.

William Eimicke, in his discussion of Eliot Spitzer, provides what may be the ultimate case study to test the leadership qualities of Stewart's "responsible leader as ethical agent." The basic question raised repeatedly about Spitzer's time in public office: Is "Eliot Spitzer . . . a moral exemplar or merely a political opportunist?" The case highlights the two themes that characterize Spitzer's years in office—legal activism and aggressive pursuit of press coverage. When the "angels are missing," calling upon an ethical public manager to be the angelic and ethical exemplar may provide an important factor in changing the culture; another may be evidenced in the Spitzer case where he provides in-depth understanding of one's legal and ethical enemies.

Our last selection, the City on the Hill speech by John F. Kennedy, provides a comprehensive list of his four characteristics of visionary leadership: courage, judgment, integrity, and dedication. Integrity constantly stands out as one of the strongest qualities of public servants whom "neither financial gain nor political ambition could ever divert from the fulfillment of our sacred trust."

We have learned throughout that doing right and overcoming wrong in our fast-moving twenty-first century requires checks for constant oversight, constant care, and constant accountability. Assistance provided globally by Transparency International in their annual *Global Corruption Report*, The World Bank through its formula for anti-corruption and its yearly *Country Reports*—as well as from professional organizations such as ICMA, ASPA, and the European Group for Public Administration (EGPA)—help shape the ethical character of the world we live in. We must pay constant attention to the new ethical challenges. We must gain insight and sensitivity to the changing world with ethical dimensions unheard of a decade ago. Sometimes world events, megaprojects, and the pace of change in today's world outrun our ethical reasoning. As R. D. Laing's words remind us:

> We live in a moment of history where change is so speeded up that we begin to see the present only when it is already disappearing.

Being ever alert to crucial change is required by those who wish to live in a world where ethical choices provide the pathway to strengthening our vision and direction.

Chapter 9

ESTABLISHING EXPECTATIONS, PROVIDING GUIDELINES, AND BUILDING TRUST

MAINTAINING GOVERNMENT INTEGRITY
Amy Comstock

Amy Comstock, as Director of the United States Office of Government Ethics (OGE) explains here the role that the OGE plays in encouraging ethical behavior by U.S. federal employees. She also examines some of the structure of the federal ethics program, including the role of Designated Agency Ethics Officials (DAEOs). Could this ethics infrastructure be of use at the state level?

In the American experience, accountability of public officials is deeply ingrained within the constitutional framework of the country. The political and civic culture of the United States is based on the notion that public officials should always perform their duties in the public interest. For example, the constitution begins with the words "We the People." These words signify that all government authority, whether exercised by elected or appointed officials, is ultimately derived from, and accountable to, the American people. Given this conception of public service, misconduct on the part of public officials presents one of the greatest threats to citizen confidence in the government . . .

When we look at the executive branch of the U.S. federal government today, we find a highly developed ethics infrastructure. This infrastructure includes a variety of specialized agencies that carry out preventive, investigative, prosecutorial, and oversight functions. These agencies implement a comprehensive framework of laws and administrative rules that are intended to preserve the integrity and impartiality of government operations and decision-making, and maintain public confidence in democratic governance. Much of the infrastructure that supports the current ethics program was created in the wake of the Watergate crisis of the 1970s. The Watergate crisis vividly illustrated the dangers of when those in power become

Source: Amy Comstock, "Maintaining Government Integrity: The Perspective of the U.S. Office of Government Ethics." Remarks to the Global Forum II Law Enforcement Workshop, The Hague, Netherlands May 29, 2001 (www.state.gov/g/inl/rls/rm/2001/may/3403pfhtrn, retrieved June 11, 2004).

too self-absorbed and far removed from the people they are meant to serve. . . . The perceived abuses of the Nixon administration threatened to put a wall of distrust and fear between the U.S. government and its citizens. This threat spurred the government to launch a series of ongoing initiatives to promote ethics and financial integrity in government programs and operations and prevent the sort of abuse exposed during Watergate from occurring again.

As part of this reform effort, Congress also passed the Ethics in Government Act of 1978 which, among other things, established the U.S. Office of Government Ethics (OGE). . . . In partnership with other executive branch agencies and departments, OGE's mission is to foster high ethical standards within the public service and to strengthen the public's confidence that the government's business is conducted with impartiality and integrity.

. . . OGE is a policy-making body responsible for issuing and interpreting the rules that govern the standards of conduct and conflict of interest policies. In this capacity, OGE establishes the ethics program requirements which agency ethics offices are required to fulfill. In order to implement these requirements, agency ethics offices are responsible for carrying out the daily administration of the ethics program within each of the 125 agencies and departments that comprise the executive branch. Through cooperation with one another, OGE and agency ethics offices strive to protect the integrity of the government and the federal workforce by administering systems designed to identify and resolve conflicts, and to provide counseling and advice to those who educate public officials about the rules that govern their conduct. . . .

Each arm of the integrity infrastructure—prevention, investigation, and prosecution—in the federal government has its own contribution to make. Effective enforcement is absolutely necessary to maintain the credibility of ethics laws and regulations. However, in one sense a prosecution for public corruption is an admission of systemic failure. Large numbers of arrests and prosecutions do nothing to reinforce the public's belief in the fairness and legitimacy of government institutions. While enforcement is vital, it is largely reactive. Preventive measures, on the other hand, are proactive. Each has an important role with the overall integrity infrastructure, and when performed effectively they can even have the added benefit of reinforcing one another. Credible law enforcement actions have the potential to encourage further compliance to the policies and systems that have been established to prevent misconduct. Likewise, preventive measures raise awareness among public officials of the rules governing their conduct and help them avoid unintentional wrongdoing that might result in enforcement actions against them. . . .

Having a DAEO [Designated Agency Ethics Official] and an adequately staffed ethics office in every agency is critical because the DAEO is most likely to know the issues particular to their agency and how best to address ethics matters as they relate to agency initiatives with senior officials. For this reason, no matter how detailed a policy OGE issues, it is the DAEO who "breathes life" into the ethics program on a daily basis. Agency DAEOs are the primary intermediaries between the policies OGE issues and public officials. DAEOs accomplish this role by coordinating policy implementation with OGE; reviewing financial disclosure reports; conducting ethics education and training; providing advice and counsel to employees on ethics matters; and monitoring administrative actions and sanctions related to ethics policies. In order to fully understand the interaction between OGE and agency ethics offices, it is useful to examine the broad scope of OGE's programmatic responsibilities. For example:

- OGE issues executive branch-wide regulations dealing with standards of conduct, financial disclosure, conflict of interest waivers, post-employment restrictions, and ethics training;
- OGE provides guidance and interpretation to agencies, including providing informal advisory opinions and publishing annually versions of selected opinions (without personal identifying information);
- OGE oversees systems of both the public and confidential financial disclosure systems and plays a key role in reviewing the financial disclosure reports of presidential nominees in the confirmation process;
- OGE provides leadership in ethics training to executive branch agencies; and
- OGE regularly reviews agency ethics programs to ensure that they maintain effectiveness.

As this list indicates, the relationship between OGE and agency ethics offices determines the successful implementation of the ethics program. Each side has to work with the other to ensure the program is accomplishing its objectives and is operating in the most effective manner possible. However, the final measure of the ethics program is whether it succeeds in strengthening the public's confidence in government institutions and processes while at the same time giving appropriate and practical guidelines to employees. This is the ultimate challenge that OGE and agency ethics offices face. . . .

THE INVESTORS' ADVOCATE
Securities and Exchange Commission (SEC)

The United States Securities and Exchange Commission (SEC) is one of many government agencies that oversee and regulate important aspects of the private economy. In this case, the SEC moniters "stock exchanges, broker-dealers, investment advisors, mutual funds and public utility holding companies." How far does public responsibility for the effective operation of private-sector institutions extend?

Source: Securities and Exchange Commission website, www.sec.gov.

INTRODUCTION—THE SEC: WHO WE ARE, WHAT WE DO

The primary mission of the U.S. Securities and Exchange Commission (SEC) is to protect investors and maintain the integrity of the securities markets. As more and more first-time investors turn to the markets to help secure their futures, pay for homes, and send children to college, these goals are more compelling than ever.

The world of investing is fascinating, complex, and can be very fruitful. But unlike the banking world, where deposits are guaranteed by the federal government, stocks, bonds, and other securities can lose value. There are no guarantees. That's why investing should not be a spectator sport; indeed, the principal way for investors to protect the money they put into the securities markets is to do research and ask questions.

The laws and rules that govern the securities industry in the United States derive from a simple and straightforward concept: All investors, whether large institutions or private individuals, should have access to certain basic facts about an investment prior to buying it. To achieve this, the SEC requires public companies to disclose meaningful financial and other information to the public, which provides a common pool of knowledge for all investors to use to judge for themselves if a company's securities are a good investment. Only through the steady flow of timely, comprehensive, and accurate information can people make sound investment decisions.

The SEC also oversees other key participants in the securities world, including stock exchanges, broker-dealers, investment advisors, mutual funds, and public utility holding companies. Here again, the SEC is concerned primarily with promoting disclosure of important information, enforcing the securities laws, and protecting investors who interact with these various organizations and individuals.

Crucial to the SEC's effectiveness is its enforcement authority. Each year the SEC brings between 400–500 civil enforcement actions against individuals and companies that break the securities laws. Typical infractions include insider trading, accounting fraud, and providing false or misleading information about securities and the companies that issue them.

Fighting securities fraud, however, requires teamwork. At the heart of effective investor protection is an educated and careful investor. The SEC offers the public a wealth of educational information on its Internet website at www.sec.gov. The website also includes the EDGAR database of disclosure documents that public companies are required to file with the Commission.

Though it is the primary overseer and regulator of the U.S. securities markets, the SEC works closely with many other institutions, including Congress, other federal departments and agencies, the self-regulatory organizations (e.g., the stock exchanges), state securities regulators, and various private sector organizations. . . .

Securities Act of 1933

Often referred to as the "truth in securities" law, the Securities Act of 1933 has two basic objectives:

- Require that investors receive financial and other significant information concerning securities being offered for public sale; and
- Prohibit deceit, misrepresentations, and other fraud in the sale of securities.

TRUST IN GOVERNMENT: ETHICS MEASURES IN OECD COUNTRIES OECD

The Organization for Economic Cooperation and Development (OECD) has been a major positive force for encouraging ethical reform in member countries. In its 2000 survey of ethical practices, titled Trust in Government, the close connection between ethics and the public trust is highlighted. OECD membership includes thirty European, Asian, and North American countries.

Integrity has become the fundamental condition for governments to provide a trustworthy and effective framework for the economic and social life of their citizens. The institutions and mechanisms for promoting integrity are more and more considered basic components of good governance. This report provides—for the first time—a comprehensive database of integrity measures used in . . . OECD member countries and it also takes stock of common trends and good practices.

Ensuring integrity means that:

- Public servants' behavior is in line with the public purposes of the organization in which they work.
- Daily public service operations for businesses are reliable.
- Citizens receive impartial treatment on the basis of legality and justice.
- Public resources are effectively, efficiently, and properly used.
- Decision-making procedures are transparent to the public, and measures are in place to permit public scrutiny and redress.

Countries are under constant pressure to bring their integrity measures into line with today's rapidly changing realities—including globalization, European integration, citizens' demands for performance and accountability. Governments of member countries have reformed their public sectors to allow for more flexibility in achieving

Source: *Trust in Government: Ethics Measures in OECD Countries* (OECD, 2000), pp. 11–16.

desired public goals. Decentralization and devolved public service management have reduced controls and given greater flexibility for discretion by officials. While the increased use of private sector methods enhanced public sector efficiency and effectiveness, it also had led to a fragmentation of "traditional" public service values, standards, and ways of operating.

This situation requires enhanced mechanisms to improve public servants' accountability for their new discretionary powers and to ensure that . . . they adhere to the updated values as well as to citizens' expectations. The right balance between devolution and accountability is of central importance in achieving a well-performing, professional public service. As traditional central regulations and controls are reduced, the role of values—and the public interest concepts that they embrace—becomes increasingly significant, both as a guide for behavior and as the common reference point and unifying thread for the whole public service. . . .

Building a supportive working environment begins with general management measures. The report shows that the vast majority of OECD countries employ the following key management measures for ensuring transparency:

- Setting standards of timeliness.
- Requiring reasons for decisions.
- Providing redress against decisions.

These management measures are seen as the primary instruments to build a supportive working environment.

In particular, human resources management plays an essential role in promoting an ethical environment by developing professionalism and enforcing transparency in daily practice. The survey showed that OECD countries are aware of the importance of sound human resources management and almost unanimously base recruitment and promotion on merit in their public service. The vast majority of countries secure the openness of their selection processes by publishing both the recruitment rules and vacant positions. Over half of the countries also take ethical considerations into account in recruitment and performance appraisal. . . .

Two-thirds of Member countries either oblige their public servants to report misconduct and/or provide procedures to facilitate its reporting. Among those countries with whistle-blowing schemes, two-thirds define the rules and procedures to be followed in their legal framework, whereas other countries define them in their internal organizational rules. Moreover, managers as well as designated organizations are in charge of both providing assistance and investigating the individual cases. Nowadays, the Internet provides a new device for the public to report misconduct.

A growing need to provide protection for whistle-blowers in the public service is visible across OECD countries. Almost half of the Member countries offer general protection mainly in their public service framework. The most commonly provided safeguards are legal protection and anonymity. . . .

DATA REGULATION: MEASURING GOVERNANCE AND CORRUPTION
The World Bank

One of the challenges of dealing with corruption is the need to base judgments, poli-cies, and programs on factual data rather than opinion. The World Bank explains here why it seeks a firm data foundation for its anticorruption programs. What sorts of data would be appropriate for ethics programs in public agencies or not-for-profit organi-zations with which you are familiar?

Until not long ago, measuring corruption and governance was regarded as nearly im-possible. It was not considered possible to estimate the extent of corrupt annual transactions worldwide.

But there has been an "explosion" in measurement techniques in recent years, stemming the tide of skepticism, says World Bank Institute Governance Director Daniel Kaufmann. These new approaches focus on constructing indicators based on surveys of experts as well as measuring, in surveys of enterprises and users of public services, the extent of misgovernance and bribery.

The increasing availability of surveys and polls by many institutions, containing data on different dimensions of governance, has permitted the construction of a worldwide governance databank. Utilizing scores of different sources and variables, as well as a novel aggregation technique, this databank now covers about 200 coun-tries worldwide, and contains key aggregate indicators in areas such as rule of law, corruption, regulatory quality, government effectiveness, voice and accountability, and political instability.

This new governance data, coupled with the information technology revolution, and the will by many reformists in governments, civil society, and international or-ganizations to generate data and transparently disseminate it, has resulted in such widespread use of governance data that the notion of *data power* has been coined.

Why is data regarded as so important in this field? Kaufmann points to five key dimensions:

- It debunks long held popular notions and outright myths. For example the myth that a country needs first to be rich to have good governance and low corrup-tion; or that anti-corruption commissions and legal drafting are the solutions.
- It permits management and decision-making based on performance-based measurement—such as identifying and monitoring the most vulnerable deter-minants and institutions of governance in a country.
- It empowers reformists, civil society, and the media with a powerful tool to af-fect change.

Source: The World Bank Group, "The Data Revolution: Measuring Governance and Corruption New Techniques Have Revolutionized the Fight Against Corruption," April 8, 2004. http://www.worldbank.org.

- Data demystifies, "de-emotionalizes," and "de-sensationalizes" the field of governance, corruption, and institutional change, enabling more rigor and level-headed dialogue.
- It permits the quantitative research of the lessons provided by the evidence, helping the field move forward.

Data from enterprise surveys has also helped in codifying the *extent* to which governance and corruption matters. For instance, in recent research, it was found that on average corruption is [a] top (and often 'the top') constraint to a firm in emerging markets. It was also found that the business sector could grow on average 3 percent a year faster where corruption is lower, and property rights and the rule of law are improved. . . .

In sum, the data shows that good governance and addressing corruption ought to be central elements of an improved investment climate and business environment. But because of the particular interface between the private and public sectors, the corporate sector also has a key responsibility in an improved investment climate. . . .

MAXIMIZING TRUST, MINIMIZING CONFLICTS
Robert Meyers and Christina Prkic

Meyers and Prkic look at the state of ethics policies and practices at the U.S. local government level by means of a survey, which explores what cities of 50,000+ populations are doing to promote accountable and ethical governance. In addition, the authors noted that 80 percent of the jurisdictions provide ethics assistance. How would your community respond to these questions? If you were conducting the survey, what other questions might you ask?

Ethics and accountability in government, and more specifically the public's perception of their absence in the administration of government, are subjects of continued analysis and debate. What are the ethical issues and concerns that underlie public administration? What are effective mechanisms to restore the public's trust in government? What is government, at all levels, doing to promote ethics, integrity, and accountability in government?

At the federal level, the Ethics in Government Act of 1978, created the Office of Government Ethics, an executive branch ethics agency. Today . . . , the agency works with executive branch agencies and departments to prevent conflicts of interest through education and advice giving.

Source: Robert Meyers and Christina Prkic, "Maximizing Trust, Minimizing Conflicts: What Are Cities and Counties Doing to Promote Ethical Governance," unpublished working paper, (n.d.), Miami-Dade County Commission on Ethics and Public Trust.

States have done their part as well. Presently, each state has some form of ethics oversight of its officials and state government personnel, either by way of an external ethics commission or an ethics committee within the state legislature. Although the functions and authorities of such commissions and committees vary, state efforts to promote ethical governance and accountability customarily include adoption of ethics codes for state officers and personnel, lobbyist regulations, and disclosure laws.

On the local front, the efforts are less known. What is known, however, is that the local government landscape is not immune from the stories of unethical behavior and the conflicts of interest, which have similarly plagued the federal and state governments. Yet how have local governments responded? Several of the larger U.S. cities established local ethics boards or commissions. New York City was the first, in 1963. These agencies, through education, enforcement, and advice-giving, are specifically focused on local governmental decision-making entities and officials. Outside these formal and more well-established agencies, little else is recognized, or easily ascertainable for that matter, in the way of local ethics efforts across the country. Consequently, the Miami-Dade County Commission on Ethics and Public Trust prepared this "ethics survey." We were interested to know what cities were doing to promote accountable and ethical governance. Furthermore, we wanted to know among other things, what mechanisms, both formal and informal, were in place to promote ethics and accountability in local governmental decision-making entities. Understanding that this would not gauge the ethical climate of local government in the United States in any exact or scientific manner, at a minimum though, it could foster new dialogue and study of the subject. The sixteen-question survey was mailed to five hundred and forty-seven [547] cities and counties with populations of 50,000 or more. . . .

WHAT WAS DISCOVERED

Nearly one-quarter of all respondents indicated they had some formal ethics board or commission. Interestingly, of those governments that have no formal ethics panel or board, 93 percent stated there was no real interest in creating one. The lack of interest in creating a formal ethics panel may be attributed to two factors: (1) the perceived lack of need—that ethical lapses are uncommon in their jurisdiction, and (2) the redundancy of having a second ethics tribunal with overlapping jurisdiction with the state ethics commission. Incidentally, each state has adopted a code of ethics, but in fifteen states the codes are not applicable to local government.

More than 80 percent of the responding governments have their own set of formal policies/laws/rules that establish minimum standards of ethical conduct for their personnel, separate from those obligations the respective states impose. This finding suggests that some local government personnel must adhere to at least two codes of conduct—those mandated by the state and those imposed by their municipalities. In cases where the county government promulgates ethics policies which are binding on the municipalities, these local public officials and employees would be required to comply with a third set of standards. When multiple, possibly conflicting, standards exist, training is essential to ensure that local government personnel are adequately prepared to act within the constraints of the law. . . .

More than 40 percent of all local governments surveyed offer some form of regular ethics training or education to employees. This figure drops to 30 percent for those in management positions and only 17 percent of all elected officials are mandated to participate in ethics training. These findings indicate that local governments do not wholeheartedly embrace ethics training. In an era of belt-tightening and reduced budgets, the perceived luxuries, such as training, may be the first items cut. Thus, the lack of ethics training may be on account of economic hardships. On the other hand, governments simply may not be willing to sacrifice other forms of training in favor of ethics training. . . .

Exposure to ethics comes in another form as well. Ethics is included in the new employee orientation program in more than one-half of the jurisdictions. It is encouraging that a majority of local governments deem that ethics is worth addressing in employee orientation sessions, but there were no related questions about the time allocated to ethical issues as a percentage of the entire training curricula. Most local governments, more than 80 percent, have resources available for officials and employees who request or seek ethical advice. . . .

These findings support national polling that the general public does not rate campaign finance reform as the greatest impediment to ethical governing. It is difficult to interpret why there was such an overwhelming number of respondents who cited general conflict of interest questions as the most pressing concern. One can speculate that local government personnel are regularly faced with predicaments that require them to reaffirm their commitment to public service at the expense of personal gain. Another explanation could be that local public servants all too frequently witness their colleagues engaging in questionable conduct. . . .

BATHO PELE PRINCIPLES AND SERVICE DELIVERY
KISHORE RAGA AND JOHN DEREK TAYLOR

Raga and Taylor identify a set of principles rooted in South African culture, which can serve as guidelines for accountability in the delivery of public services. Do these principles of "The People First" complement or negate Bailey's set of ethical qualities?

Source: Kishore Raga and John Derek Taylor, "Impact of Accountability and Ethics on Public Service Delivery: A South African Perspective," paper delivered at the 66th National Conference of the American Society for Public Administration, Milwaukee, WI, April 2–5, 2005.

The thrust of the Batho Pele Principles is the improvement of service delivery in the public service. Implicit in the eight Batho Pele Principles . . . is an attempt to adapt the norms of service delivery in the private sector, such as a focus on customer/client satisfaction, into the public service (Khoza, 2002:33). While this attempt is a welcome innovation, it is of paramount importance not to lose sight of the fact that (1) Batho Pele is a means to an end in itself and (2) that there are certain indelible features of the public service which make it distinct from the private sector.

The concept Batho Pele was devised by a former Minister for Public Service and Administration in South Africa and is a Sesotho saying meaning: "The people first." It can be argued that all attempts at serving communities should be checked against the principles of Batho Pele, which are:

1. Consultation. Citizens should be consulted about the quality of the services they receive.
2. Service standards. Communities should be informed what level and quality of service they will receive so that they know what to expect.
3. Access. All citizens should have equal access to the services they are entitled to.
4. Courtesy. All members of the community should be treated with courtesy and consideration.
5. Information. Communities should be given full and accurate information about the public services they are entitled to.
6. Openness and transparency. Citizens should be informed on how local authorities function and the information they are entitled to.
7. Redress and handling of complaints. If community members do not receive promised services they should be entitled to a full explanation and also to a speedy remedy.
8. Value for money. Services should be provided economically and efficiently in order to provide citizens with the principle of best value for money. . . .

The success of Batho Pele will be determined by the progress made in efforts to transform the public service as well as transformation occurring in society in general. While there is scope for success, the limitations are more likely to be in the form of inherent qualities of the public service such as the bureaucracy and extensive legal regulations (Khoza, 2002:34).

THE ASPA CODE OF ETHICS
AMERICAN SOCIETY FOR PUBLIC ADMINISTRATION

The ethical expectations of businesses, professional associations, governmental agencies, and larger organizational entities are often spelled out in a set of principles, standards

Source: American Society for Public Administration www.aspanet.org/scriptcontent/index_code ofethics.cfm Reprinted with permission from the American Society for Public Administration.

of integrity, or formal Codes of Ethics. These may vary in length, in specificity, and in the extent to which sanctions are involved. The American Society for Public Administration (ASPA) Code of Ethics was developed in 1984 and evolved to its present structure of five broad themes and 32 specific prescriptive statements. How well does a Code of Ethics contribute to public confidence in public sector operations? What role should this and other codes play in public life? Are there points from Weber, Bailey, and Ingraham evidenced in the ASPA Code?

I. SERVE THE PUBLIC INTEREST

Serve the public, beyond serving oneself. ASPA members are committed to:

1. Exercise discretionary authority to promote the public interest.
2. Oppose all forms of discrimination and harassment, and promote affirmative action.
3. Recognize and support the public's right to know the public's business.
4. Involve citizens in policy decision-making.
5. Exercise compassion, benevolence, fairness, and optimism.
6. Respond to the public in ways that are complete, clear, and easy to understand.
7. Assist citizens in their dealings with government.
8. Be prepared to make decisions that may not be popular.

II. RESPECT THE CONSTITUTION AND THE LAW

Respect, support, and study government constitutions and laws that define responsibilities of public agencies, employees, and all citizens. ASPA members are committed to:

1. Understand and apply legislation and regulations relevant to their professional role.
2. Work to improve and change laws and policies that are counterproductive or obsolete.
3. Eliminate unlawful discrimination.
4. Prevent all forms of mismanagement of public funds by establishing and maintaining strong fiscal and management controls, and by supporting audits and investigative activities.
5. Respect and protect privileged information.
6. Encourage and facilitate legitimate dissent activities in government and protect the whistle-blowing rights of public employees.
7. Promote constitutional principles of equality, fairness, representativeness, responsiveness, and due process in protecting citizens' rights.

III. DEMONSTRATE PERSONAL INTEGRITY

Demonstrate the highest standards in all activities to inspire public confidence and trust in public service. ASPA members are committed to:

1. Maintain truthfulness and honesty and to not compromise them for advancement, honor, or personal gain.
2. Ensure that others receive credit for their work and contributions.
3. Zealously guard against conflict of interest or its appearance: e.g., nepotism, improper outside employment, misuse of public resources, or the acceptance of gifts.
4. Respect superiors, subordinates, colleagues, and the public.
5. Take responsibility for their own errors.
6. Conduct official acts without partisanship.

IV. PROMOTE ETHICAL ORGANIZATIONS

Strengthen organizational capabilities to apply ethics, efficiency and effectiveness in serving the public. ASPA members are committed to:

1. Enhance organizational capacity for open communication, creativity, and dedication.
2. Subordinate institutional loyalties to the public good.
3. Establish procedures that promote ethical behavior and hold individuals and organizations accountable for their conduct.
4. Provide organization members with an administrative means for dissent, assurance of due process, and safeguards against reprisal.
5. Promote merit principles that protect against arbitrary and capricious actions.
6. Promote organizational accountability through appropriate controls and procedures.
7. Encourage organizations to adopt, distribute, and periodically review a code of ethics as a living document.

V. STRIVE FOR PROFESSIONAL EXCELLENCE

Strengthen individual capabilities and encourage the professional development of others. ASPA members are committed to:

1. Provide support and encouragement to upgrade competence.
2. Accept as a personal duty the responsibility to keep up to date on emerging issues and potential problems.

3. Encourage others, throughout their careers, to participate in professional activities and associations.

4. Allocate time to meet with students and provide a bridge between classroom studies and the realities of public service.

—— ——

ARE YOU AN ETHICAL PUBLIC OFFICIAL?
ICMA

The ethics vignettes that follow offer an opportunity to test our own ethical standards. Readers should take the test without looking at the answers. The test is based on the International City/County Management Association (ICMA) Code of Ethics.

Every day, you, as a city official, face situations in which your personal and professional integrity and ethics are tested. . . .

Each of the ten ethical dilemmas described below can be answered with a "yes" or "no." After you have completed your answers, you can score and interpret your responses in accordance with the instructions provided.

1. The board of directors of the chamber of commerce has an annual weekend outing at a resort some miles from your city. During the weekend there is golf, tennis, swimming, card games, dinner dances with entertainment and numerous cocktail parties. During the day, there are sessions at which the chamber board reviews progress for the past year and discusses plans for the coming year. For several years, the city has contributed $100,000 annually for the support of the chamber. You are a council member or the city administrator, and have been invited to the weekend outing with all expenses paid by the chamber.

Do you accept the invitation and go for the weekend? Yes ☐ No ☐

2. You have been asked to speak to a Sunday brunch meeting of the city council of another city some miles away. They want you to tell them about your city's cost-reduction program, in anticipation of a Proposition 13-type measure that is being proposed by the citizens of their community. At the conclusion of your appearance, the chairman hands you an envelope containing an honorarium check for $250

Source: "Are You an Ethical Public Official?" *Town and Country* (Arkansas Municipal League), September 1984, pp. 14–15. Reprinted with permission from the May 1982 issue of *Public Management (PM)* magazine, published by the International City/County Management Association (ICMA), Washington, D.C. University Research Corporation originally developed the test for workshops sponsored by the National Institute of Justice.

and explains that "This is in appreciation of you giving up your Sunday morning."

Would you accept the honorarium? Yes ☐ No ☐

3. For many years, you and Frank Jordan have been close friends. You went to high school together and were college classmates. You were best man at each other's weddings. Your wives are good friends. For the past ten years, Frank and his wife have taken you and your wife to dinner on your birthday. It is just something he insists upon doing and it has become something of a tradition. He can well afford it—Frank owns the largest plumbing supply business in the state and does more than $500,000 in business each year with the city. You are a council member and you chair the council committee that oversees procurement contracts, including plumbing supplies. Your birthday is coming up in a couple of weeks. Frank has called to remind you that he and Mrs. Jordan have a special treat for your birthday dinner this year. He had made reservations at a fancy new restaurant that everyone is talking about.

Do you accept? Yes ☐ No ☐

4. For some time, police officers on three adjacent beats have met each day for a coffee break at a restaurant near a point where the three beats intersect. They usually have coffee and a donut, and occasionally a piece of pie. You are a police officer and were just assigned to one of the beats. When you go for the coffee break the first day, and you walk up to pay the check, the proprietor says, "No charge. I am glad to have you officers around." The other officers leave without paying.

Do you pay your check? Yes ☐ No ☐

5. Henry Settles has worked in your department for a long time. He is conscientious and in fact, may be too conscientious, in the view of many of his fellow workers. He is always at work on time, always puts in all his hours, and works hard. But he expects others to do the same and frequently complains about others who are tardy or who take long lunch hours or call in sick when almost everyone knows they are not. You are head of the department that employs Henry. Recently, Henry reported to you that some employees of the department were using city automobiles to drive to pro football games in a city about 100 miles away. You put a stop to that, but Henry has been *persona non grata* with many of the employees of the department since he "snitched" on them. Henry is a leading candidate for a new position in the department—one that would mean a promotion for him.

Do you promote Henry? Yes ☐ No ☐

6. A new civic plaza is included in the plans to restore the downtown area of your city. The bond issue *for* developing the plaza, which was passed three years ago, is already too little to assure completion of the project, because of inflation. A developer

who wants to erect a high-rise building near the plaza offers to buy a large tract of undeveloped land in the plaza area and donate it to the city, as a trade-off for permission to construct his proposed building higher than the present zoning restrictions will permit. He has privately made this offer to you, the city administrator, and it is up to you to decide whether to communicate the offer to the city council.

Do you pass on the offer to the council? Yes ☐ No ☐

7. You are the city administrator. A few days before Christmas, a package arrives at your office. Inside is a card from the vice president of a large corporation in your city. The company has never done any business with the city. The card says, "You are doing a great job for our city and we just wanted you to know that we appreciate it. We hope you will accept this token of our gratitude." You open the package and find a beautiful crystal vase, which you estimate to be worth $75 to $100.

Do you accept the vase? Yes ☐ No ☐

8. Your favorite brand of scotch is Chivas Regal, but you don't buy it too often because it is so expensive. You have told this to the liquor dealer from whom you buy your booze. It's a kind of joke. "Think rich and drink cheap," you sometimes remark when you buy a less expensive brand. The liquor dealer gets in trouble for bookmaking and his license is in jeopardy. You, as city administrator, have nothing to do with the hearing on suspension of his license, but the next time you go to buy liquor, you discover when you get home that the sack containing your liquor includes a fifth of Chivas Regal, which you didn't order or pay for.

Do you keep the scotch? Yes ☐ No ☐

9. A physician friend of yours asks if you would be interested in investing in a doctors' building, which a group of physicians plan to erect in the city of which you are the administrator. No decisions involving your job are expected as part of the investment; the doctors are simply selling shares in their venture. It will be next to a shopping center in a rapidly growing part of town. You stand to more than quadruple the $25,000 cost of your investment in a short time; maybe make even more than that. You have the money.

Would you invest in the doctors' building? Yes ☐ No ☐

10. You are a department head and Hazel Stevens is one of your most valuable employees. She worked for you for years and is the kind of worker you can depend upon to put in extra time and effort when it is needed. She is always there during a crisis and several times she has handled situations that would have been uncomfortable for you. You really owe her a lot. Recently, Hazel came to you and admitted that for some time, she'd been "borrowing" money from the petty cash fund and writing false receipts to cover it. It was never much, usually $10 or $15, and she always repaid it. But her conscience has bothered her so much that she had to confess. Under the city's personnel policies, her action is clearly a cause for dismissal.

Do you fire her? Yes ☐ No ☐

AN EXPLANATION OF THE ANSWERS

1. No. Not if the chamber pays your expenses. Since the city's annual donation to the chamber presumably is designed to encourage business and improve the city's tax base, it may be legitimately important for one or two city officials, such as the mayor, or city manager to attend. If so, the cost of the yearly outing should be figured into the city's annual budget. Attendance under such circumstances—where the city pays your way—would be acceptable.

2. No. The only reason you were invited was because of the knowledge and experience you possess because of your association with the city. There is an expectation that you will share your professional expertise with your municipal colleagues. You may only accept expenses, i.e., mileage, parking, etc. at the customary rates.

3. Yes. Public service does not require that you give up previous acquaintances and friendships. What is required is that at any point in the future in which your friend's business is involved, i.e., contract negotiations, bids, etc., you disqualify yourself from influencing the decision in any way. If you decide not to go with Frank, you are still ethical, but probably over-zealous.

4. Yes. Police officers and other city employees provide a service for which they are paid. Why shouldn't others—such as the postman, bus driver, etc.—receive the same benefits? It has been clearly demonstrated that small acts of corruption set the stage for, and lead to, larger, more pervasive problems. In one city, a new police chief, observing a scenario similar to the above, posted an immediate order prohibiting such activity; violators to be fired. A sergeant came to him with the statement that "he hadn't realized it, but because of free coffee and donuts, he had been hesitant to report the restaurant's filthy restrooms."

5. Yes. If based on his performance, Henry should receive the promotion because: (1) he qualified for the promotion; (2) promoting Henry reinforces the fact that you expect ethical behavior on the part of your employees. And you'd better have a talk with your staff.

6. Yes. You probably have a responsibility to pass on any bona fide offer to the city council. If specific city regulations prohibit this or you feel uncomfortable in this role, you should suggest the individual make a written offer to city council.

7. No. Send it back. When a person accepts a job with the city he or she accepts the compensation that accompanies it. After all—a simple thank you letter would have accomplished the same purpose—wouldn't it?

8. No. Return the liquor immediately, for the same reasons noted above.

9. Yes. Strictly personal, private investments are fine. A prudent person would investigate the opportunity to ensure that no special considerations, zoning changes, interest rates, etc., were involved in the deal. Any special considerations: Don't invest. Remember, even the appearance of your involvement in special favors could call your integrity into question. If in doubt about the investment, ask yourself: How would this look in the newspapers?

10. Yes. Strictly speaking, Hazel has committed a felony. If you excuse her, what does that say to other employees? How has she replaced the "trust and value"

you placed in her? If the same situation occurred with an employee who was not Hazel, would you be lenient?

HOW TO SCORE YOUR ANSWERS

Points are awarded for each question on a weighted basis, as indicated below. If, for example, you answered the first question "yes," award yourself 3 points; if you answered "no," give yourself one point.

Question	Number of Points for "Yes"	"No"	Question	Number of Points for "Yes"	"No"
1	3	1	6	1	2
2	2	1	7	3	1
3	1	1	8	1	3
4	1	3	9	1	1
5	1	3	10	1	2

According to the ethical experts who devised this quiz, your score is "perfect" if you received one 1 point for each of the 10 questions. If your total score is 10 to 14, indications are that you have high standards, are clearly a dedicated public servant, and set a good example for those around you.

A score of 2 for any question means that while you may not break the law or allow or encourage others to do so, neither do you assertively pursue wrongdoing, or marginal practices. Probably you're more interested in keeping things smooth than in righting wrongs. If you scored 15–20, you need to do some serious reflection on your own vulnerability to unethical practices.

A score of 3 for any answer shows trouble and indicates tendency toward conduct that is not based on ethics or values and shows a real disregard for any perspective reflecting such commitment, or the impact of these acts on your community—and position. If you score 20–25, you probably need a good lawyer.

CASE 9: LEGAL, WRONG, OR MORALLY REQUIRED?

Articles have appeared daily in the Richmond, Virginia, press framing an ethics debate—whether to use a "loophole" in federal Medicaid regulations to collect $259

Source: Ralph Hambrick, Virginia Commonwealth University. Submitted as "Ethics Minute: Legal, Wrong . . . or Morally Required?" *PA Times*, June 2002. Reprinted with permission from the American Society for Public Administration.

million from the federal government. Through several transactions, the state of Virginia could receive matching funds for money it never actually spends. Both participating localities and the state would net large sums that could be used for health care or for any other public purpose since the money would go into the general fund.

The state official leading the effort to secure this funding has argued adamantly that it is morally required that the state seek and accept the money since not doing so would penalize fiscally stressed health programs and needy Virginia citizens. Many localities and associated nursing homes have refused to participate and are zealous in asserting that it would be morally wrong to accept the money since it would be acquired through gimmickry and subterfuge—even though legal gimmickry and subterfuge! An intermediate position is that it would be OK to accept the money if it is used only for Medicaid-related purposes.

What is the ethically correct position? Do legality and need trump honesty and forthrightness? Is this really an ethical problem? Or is it a public relations problem created when the press made it visible to the public?

CHAPTER DISCUSSION QUESTIONS

1. To what extent is trust in government a function of good and effective government and to what extent is it a function of manipulation of public opinion, "spin," and public relations?

2. Should administrations pursue ethical practices in order to build trust in government, in order to "do the right thing," or for other reasons?

3. How helpful are the establishment and clarification of expectations for encouraging ethics? What limitations, if any, do you see to this approach?

FOR FURTHER EXPLORATION

Feldman, Mary Ann, and Xizohu Wang, "Ethics and Public Trust: Results from a National Survey," *Public Integrity*, 6:1 (Winter 2003–2004), 63–75.

Roberts, Robert, "Federal Ethics Management and the Public Trust," in *Handbook of Administrative Ethics*, second ed., ed. Terry Cooper (New York and Basel: Marcel Dekker, 2001), pp. 367–85.

Shalala, Donna E. "The Buck Starts Here: Managing Large Organizations with Honesty and Integrity," *Public Integrity*, 6:4 (Fall 2004), pp. 349–56.

Thompson, Dennis F. *Restoring Responsibility: Ethics in Government, Business, and Healthcare.* Cambridge, MA: Cambridge University Press, 2005.

West, Jonathan P. and Even M. Berman, "Ethics Training in U.S. Cities: Content, Pedagogy, and Impact," *Public Integrity*, 6:3 (Summer 2004), pp. 189–206.

WEBSITES

The Council for Excellence in Government, www.excelgov.org

Council on Government Ethics Laws (COGEL; membership fee for full access), www.co-gel.org

Ethics Officer Association, www.eoa.org/home.asp

International City/County Management Association (ICMA) Code of Ethics, http://cpm.icma.org/go.cfm?cid=1&gid=2&sid=3&did=889

Partnership for Trust in Government, www.trustingov.org

Minneapolis Mayor's Trust in Government Initiative, www.ci.minneapolis.mn.us/mayor/priorities/ethics_trust_government.asp

Securities Act of 1933, full text located at www.sec.gov/about/laws/sa33.pdf

Chapter 10

TRANSPARENCY, WHISTLE-BLOWING, AND DISSENT

DEALING WITH DISSENT: LEARNING TO LISTEN
RICHARD A. LOVERD

Richard Loverd argues that managerial listening in an organization can be a valuable alternative to the painful processes of whistle-blowing. As he notes, however, listening and openness might also entail risks or difficulties. What risks? What difficulties? Should managers opt for strategies of greater openness?

> Know how to listen, and you will profit
> even from those who talk badly.
>
> —Plutarch

WHEN WHISTLES WAIL

In a recent article, a disillusioned whistle-blower recounted the following recurrent dream:

> It's a dark and nasty night; I'm at one of those roadside telephone booths, with an important call to make, but the person inside won't give up the phone. When he does, I have only one quarter; I drop it, pick it up and put it into the slot; the phone malfunctions. I press the buttons futilely, sometimes garbling the number I want, sometimes getting a wrong number—but no matter what I do, my call won't go through.
>
> Having learned, the painful way, that there are no "right" choices for a whistle-blower—only a series of choices that are all "heads they win, tails I lose"—would I, confronted with the choice again, make the same decision?

Source: Richard A Loverd, "Dealing with Dissent: Learning to Listen for an Ethical Organization," in *Combating Corruption/Encouraging Ethics*, ed. William L. Richter, Frances Burke, and Jameson W. Doig (Washington, DC: American Society for Public Administration, 1990), pp. 217–23.

I'd like to think that I would, but I'd also like to think that, this time, someone would answer the phone.[1]

Unfortunately, in all too many instances, this sort of dream is very much the reality for whistle-blowers: whistles wail, but no one listens. Moreover, by the time the
shrill blast sounds, the level of managerial conflict, concealment, and cacophony may
be so great as to limit any possible resolution of whistle-blower grievances. Instead,
high-level legalistic salvos of charges and countercharges may be exchanged by managers with few questions satisfactorily answered, careers ruined, and little long-term
positive benefit.

What can be done to deal with dissent? Because whistle-blowing constitutes a
desperation effort on the part of the dissenter and stands near the extreme end of the
conflict continuum, other more preventative questions for managers suggest themselves. For example, it might be asked whether whistles are perceived as providing the
only realistic recourse for those seeking to disagree with their organizations; and if
this is so, this view could in turn imply that managers are proving less than effective
in dealing with dissent *before* it reaches the whistle-blowing stage. Furthermore, such
ineffectiveness may tend to signal a certain lack of skill, or will, on the part of managers to listen to conflict at *any* level of intensity.

In this article, the development of the managerial skill and stomach to deal with
dissent before it reaches crisis proportions will be of central concern. Such a responsibility is no easy task. In fact, it will be stressed that *the courage of managers to listen is
every bit as important as the courage of grievants to speak out*; for only through listening
can one begin to move toward the resolution of conflicts. . . .

Consequently, in the pages that follow, an emphasis will be placed upon the need
for managers to be willing to assume the responsibility to listen to dissenters by *opening channels* so that the way is clear for grievants to raise issues; by *enhancing reception,*
through proven managerial authority and accessibility; and by *turning up the volume,*
through the encouragement of heightened differences of opinion which require
managers to work with conflict, and make conflict work, for an ethical organization.

OPENING CHANNELS

. . .[M]anagers should investigate the array of channels currently available to grievants and, where possible, make certain to provide unorthodox, as well as orthodox,
avenues for dissent. For example, besides listening through hierarchy, managers might
consider creating independent review boards, ombudsmen, or separate investigative
units. In this regard, an investigative board that has come to be known as the "Shriver
Prescription" was established by Sargent Shriver during his tenure as head of the
Peace Corps and the Office of Economic Opportunity. Through his "prescription,"

an independent reporting outfit was inaugurated, completely separate from the normal chain of command, with its mission to roam the field, find out what was going on, and report directly back to its head, Sargent Shriver. In so doing, "The chain of command could be dragged in later to argue and explain itself, but the evaluation reports wouldn't be filtered through it."[2] Thus, in a very real sense, new channels were created to gather information that might otherwise be missed or distorted through the more traditional ones.

The grapevine provides yet another useful albeit unorthodox avenue for dissent. While there are those who may wish to ignore it, they do so at their own peril; for the grapevine tends to enhance and complement some of the more formal methods of communication. Moreover, studies show it to be efficient, spreading information faster than most management communications systems,[3] and surprisingly accurate, with 75 percent of its views valid.[4] Thus, keeping an ear to the grapevine is well worth the manager's time, particularly given that some of the 25 percent of the information may require correction.

In addition to the preceding *structural* aspects of communication channels, managers should also consider their *mode* when assessing how open they intend to be. In particular, the degree of dependence placed upon written communication needs to be examined. How dependent are managers on memoranda and other more formal methods of reporting when discovering or diagnosing a problem? When one considers the golden bureaucratic dictum "Never to write if you can say it, and never say it if you can nod your head,"[5] or the similar caveat from Dean Acheson noting that "A memorandum is written not to inform the reader but to protect the writer,"[6] there tend to be gaps in this mode of written listening. . . .

ENHANCING RECEPTION

Even with channels open, there is still no guarantee that dissenters will be inclined to use them. Therefore, to enhance reception from dissenters, managers need to demonstrate *authority* and accessibility through their actions.

To prove authority, managers need to legitimize their roles[7] as individuals capable of demonstrating the capacity for positive action and following through on employee requests (after all, if they cannot, or will not "deliver," why approach them?). In so doing, they should be considered able, in the sense of being technically skillful, and they should be credible, by knowing the "rules of the game," the norms and the expectations that exist in their particular workplaces. They should have a history of being able to bring back benefits and protection/autonomy for their employees, and they should be regarded as persistent in the face of adversity.

To prove accessibility, managers need to show a personal loyalty toward those they manage and create a feeling of approval[8] among them which suggests that each is valued as an individual. Each should feel that the manager is "out to help me rather than out to get me." Only then can the manager expect loyalty, and information, to flow toward his or her office. . . .

TURNING UP THE VOLUME

The possibility remains that, despite open channels and enhanced reception, some dissenters may still be loath to speak out, and what is heard from others may present only a self-serving suboptimal part of the picture. As well, if there is cognitive dissonance between what the manager previously knows and what the employee is saying, there may be a very great temptation to "shoot the messenger" by discounting the employee's story, smoothing over the outcry and avoiding the issue entirely.

At base, what is needed is a willingness to hear and encourage differences of opinion, a task which is not always easy. Indeed, as Harlan Cleveland has noted,

> It is too easy to get people to cooperate. People are, if anything, too conformist. That is why the executive's most difficult task is almost precisely the reverse of inducing cooperation. It is to maintain an adequate degree of tension within the organization—enough fruitful friction among its members so that all possible points of view are weighed. . . .[9]

Therefore, to counteract conformity, *conflict*, the existence of "fruitful friction," should be viewed as a way to turn up the volume and help managers hear more about the dimensions of the larger picture which can help improve the quality of their actions. In so doing, conflict can serve to improve the caliber of decisions made,[10] stimulate creativity and innovation,[11] foster a climate of self-evaluation and change, allow all points, even unusual and minority views, to be considered in important decisions, and serve as an antidote for "groupthink." . . .

PROVING THE COURAGE TO LISTEN

While much of this article has tried to emphasize the benefits of using the listening skills of opening channels, enhancing reception and turning up the volume, there is, of course, a potential darker side. Listening is not without its risks. Channels can be poorly designed, authority and accessibility can be abused, and conflict can prove destructive to organizational health. Furthermore, if a manager listens to an unpopular person or position, he or she runs the risk of being perceived as an organizational pariah as much as the dissenter, with groupthink preferring smoothness over *any* form of dissent.

And the risks do not end there. *If* a manager takes the time to listen, the opportunity to plead ignorance as an excuse and escape responsibility for the issues discussed diminishes accordingly. Indeed, perhaps the *key question* asked during the Watergate cover-up crisis was the one posed by Senator Howard Baker when he asked,

"What did the president know, and when did he know it?" a question not altogether different from the one . . . broached regarding President Reagan's possible involvement in the Iran-Contra affair.[12] If a manager knows about a problem, he can be held responsible for his knowledge *and* actions and the knowledge and actions of others responsible to him. . . .

NOTES

1. Don Rosendale, "A Whistle-Blower," *New York Times Magazine*, June 7, 1987, p. 56.

2. Jack Gonzales and John Rothchild, "The Shriver Prescription: How the Government Can Find Out What It's Doing," in *The Culture of Bureaucracy*, Charles Peters and Michael Nelson (New York: Holt, Rinehart and Winston, 1979), p. 119.

3. Keith Davis, *Human Relations in Business* (New York: McGraw-Hill, 1957), p. 244.

4. Keith Davis, cited in Roy Rowan, "Where Did That Rumor Come From?" *Fortune*, August 13, 1979, p. 134.

5. Esmond Wright, "Taking the Rap for Benedict Arnold," *New York Times Book Review*, July 5, 1987, p. 10.

6. James Q. Wilson, *American Government: Institutions and Policies*, 3rd ed., (Lexington, MA: D.C. Heath, 1986), p. 382.

7. See "Legitimating the Leadership Role" in *Leadership*, Leonard R. Sayles (New York: McGraw-Hill, 1979), pp. 37–44.

8. This section is based on a discussion in Leonard R. Sayles and George Strauss's *Human Behavior in Organizations* (New York: Prentice-Hall, 1966), pp. 186–189.

9. Cited by Donald Nightingale, "Conflict and Conflict Resolution," in *Organizational Behavior: Research and Issues* by George Strauss, Raymond Miles, Charles Snow, and Arnold Tannenbaum, (Madison, WI: Industrial Relations Research Association Series, 1974) p. 151.

10. For more discussion of the following points, see Stephen Robbins's *Organizational Behavior* (Englewood Cliffs: Prentice-Hall, 1983), pp. 336–347.

11. See Victor Thompson, "Bureaucracy and Innovation," *Administrative Science Quarterly* 10 (1965), pp. 1–20.

12. Stephen Pressman, "New Chief of Staff: Former Senator Baker to Succeed Regan at the White House," *Congressional Quarterly*, February 28, 1987, p. 359.

THE ETHICAL IMPORTANCE OF RESIGNING
J. Patrick Dobel

Patrick Dobel explores here and elsewhere the ethical issues of both staying in office in the face of ethical challenges and resigning. What are the conditions under which it might be appropriate to resign from a responsible administrative position?

Source: J. Patrick Dobel, *Public Integrity* (Baltimore and London: The Johns Hopkins University Press, 1999), 110–13.

Resigning has a profound role in the moral life of a person. First, resignation supports integrity. Integrity matters because it enables persons to claim life as their own and enables society to allocate responsibility on the assumption that individuals can in fact act with consistency and discipline on behalf of promises. Our integrity involves the capacity to take a reflective stance toward roles and actions and make sense of how they cohere. Through self-reflection individuals move across roles and actions and assesses their compatibility or consistency with each other and with an individual's commitments. This reflective movement across roles, obligations, and actions spins the threads that stitch together selfhood and creates a wholeness, even a beauty, across the quilted fabric of a person's life. Personal integrity emerges when individuals sew the roles, obligations, and promises together into a life quilt that possesses durability, wholeness, and coherence.[1] Personal integrity also means that people can direct and revise actions on the basis of belief and commitment. People of integrity can keep promises and play by the rules because they have the self-discipline and character to overcome temptations, opposition, and problems.[2] They can seek greater compatibility by revising actions or roles to restore moral coherence. If all else fails and a role threatens the fabric of life, then people can sever the role and resign.

Second, resigning sustains moral responsibility. Individuals in public office possess responsibility for their actions, and resigning is a basic moral resource of responsible people. Although the level of personal responsibility may vary, individuals above the ministerial levels possess some co-responsibility for institutional actions because they materially contribute their competence to the outcomes. Too often individuals respond to moral conflict by denying responsibility with excuses such as "following orders," "no choice," or "not my job." The existence of the option to leave office prevents them from escaping responsibility and exculpating themselves with such excuses.[3] . . . The issues of maintaining personal moral capacity, competence, effectiveness, and access apply across the board. The option of resigning means that the theoretical linkage of personal responsibility and position is real.

The resignation option complicates the moral and psychological temptations to save integrity yet deny responsibility. The knowledge of this option means that a person cannot escape responsibility by pretending that he or she had no choice. Participation becomes a matter of choice, not force or inertia. It means individuals know that they contribute in a substantial way to the realization of goals. This matters because the social and psychological pressures of office push individuals to live by group norms. Everyday organizational life impels people to stay and blinds them to the resignation option. I want to make clear that I am referring to a robust notion of integrity and responsibility. This is not a call for hair-trigger resignations. In public life, no persons get all they want all the time. Most officials lose more battles than they win, and victories are always imperfect. So public officials find themselves compromising and contributing to imperfect outcomes. Moral effectiveness does not flow from innocence or scrupulosity, and a responsible public official cannot resign over every conflicted principle but has to learn to live with moral imperfection while keeping his or her moral compass and integrity intact.[4] As British Minister Aneurin Bevan said in his resignation speech, "No member ought to accept office in a government without a full consciousness that he ought not to resign it for frivolous reasons."[5]

Third, resignation can help ensure accountability to democratic institutions. As Albert Hirshman made clear in his classic study on "exit" and "voice" in organizations, exit from an institution can signal to the public the existence of a debate over deeper or more serious issues than had been exposed in public deliberations. A public resignation with "voice" adds information and credibility to dissent. Like any human action, however, resignation cuts both ways and can also harm accountability. If everyone opposed to a policy exits, the institution loses its capacity for internal reform. Exits of dissenters narrow the range of options within an inner circle, encourage groupthink, and undermine the internal trust and communication needed for honest policy discussion.[6]

The willingness to resign buttresses the moral and psychological core of integrity and responsibility. If people become so wedded to office that they will not resign under any circumstances, they risk violating their integrity, the norms of office, and effectiveness. A classic case demonstrates how facing resignation is crucial to keeping integrity. As Secretary of State for President Ronald Reagan, George Shultz fought the plans of the National Security Council and the CIA to trade weapons to Iran in exchange for the freeing of hostages. In November 1986 the administration's actions exploded in the press and the Iran-Contra scandal was born. Officials such as National Security Advisor Admiral John Poindexter and Director of the CIA William Casey pressed to continue the exchanges. Shultz believed the actions to be fundamentally wrong because they encouraged more hostage taking, undercut administration policy, and damaged President Reagan. He also feared the policy would curtail efforts to end to the Cold War with Russia.

Shultz faced considerable pressure to resign from White House staff that viewed his opposition as disloyal. At this point, Shultz made a vital moral decision. In August 1986, he had submitted a letter of resignation to the president, but Reagan had refused the resignation and encouraged Shultz to stay.[7] In November 1986, when the story broke, Shultz told President Reagan that the president could accept his resignation at any point: "My credibility with the president could only be enhanced by his knowledge that I was the easiest guy in Washington for him to get rid of." Shultz began a very rough and public effort because, "I had to stop completely any further arms-for-hostage deals. I know my job was on the line, but proud as I was to be secretary of state and conscious as I was of possible achievements of great significance, *I knew I could not want the job too much*" (emphasis added).[8] The resignation in the drawer liberated Schultz's integrity to begin the arduous and ultimately successful struggle to change policy and not conform.

Although extremely important morally, resignation remains only one moral resource for public officials facing moral conflict. For example, in October 1973 President Richard Nixon ordered Special Prosecutor Archibald Cox to cease his attempts to subpoena any more tapes from Nixon concerning the Watergate cover-up. President Nixon believed that this order would force Cox to resign. Cox did not. As he explained, "I don't think there was ever any thought in my mind or talk in the office about resigning—it was so obvious it wouldn't be the right thing to do. . . . You were rather expected to fight. . . . You had to go about doing what your job was. To resign would be to run away from it"[9] Nixon chose to fire Cox and ignited the firestorm that contributed to his downfall. Career public officials have additional obligations both to protect their institutions and to work with policies about which they have moral qualms as long as the actions are legal and accountable.[10] These officials may choose to stay in such circumstances for moral reasons and pursue a number of defensible strategies such as internal dissent, ameliorating the problems in implementation, waiting out the policy, or mobilizing external allies to oppose it. Resigning is an essential moral resource, not a panacea.

NOTES

1. Stephen L. Carter, *Integrity* (New York: Basic Books, 1996), 3–14.

2. The capacity to act despite costs to oneself is central to most definitions of integrity. For a seminal work see Lynne McFall, "Integrity," *Ethics* 98 (October 1987): 5–23; also see Carter, *Integrity*, 15–22.

3. Dennis Thompson, "Moral Responsibility in Government: The Problem of Many Hands," *American Political Science Review* 74 (1980): 905–16; J. Patrick Dobel, "Personal Responsibility and Public Integrity," *Michigan Law Review* 86, no. 6 (1988): 1450–65, expands this argument.

4. Public officials regularly make this point. For clear expositions, see George Ball, *The Past Has Another Pattern: Memoirs* (New York: W.W. Norton, 1982), 424–34; Cyrus Vance, *Hard Choices: Critical Years in America's Foreign Policy* (New York: Simon and Schuster, 1983), 398–413; George P. Shultz, *Turmoil and Triumph: My Years as Secretary of State* (New York: Charles Scribner's Sons, 1993), 783–840; Colin Powell, *My American Journey* (New York: Random House, 1995). For the classic statement of the position, see Stephen Bailey, "Ethics and the Public Service," in *Administration and Democracy*, ed. R.C. Martin (Syracuse, NY: Syracuse University Press, 1965), 283–98.

5. Edward Weisband and Thomas M. Franck, *Resignation in Protest: Political and Ethical Choices between Loyalty to Team and Loyalty to Conscience in American Life* (New York: Grossman, 1975), 112.

6. Albert Hirshman, *Exit, Voice, and Loyalty: Responses to Decline in Firms, Organizations, and States* (Cambridge, MA: Harvard University Press, 1977).

7. Shultz, *Turmoil and Triumph*, 725–26.

8. Shultz, *Turmoil and Triumph*, 792.

9. "The Saturday Night Massacre," part C, Kennedy School of Government Case C1477-543, 16 (1977).

10. See J. Patrick Dobel, *Public Integrity* (Baltimore and London: The Johns Hopkins University Press, 1999), Chapter 5; Myron Peretz Glazer and Penina Migdal Glazer, *The Whistle Blowers: Exposing Corruption in Government and Industry* (New York: Basic Books, 1989); John P. Burke, *Bureaucratic Responsibility* (Baltimore: Johns Hopkins University Press, 1986); Deena Weinstein, *Bureaucratic Opposition: Challenging Abuses in the Workplace* (New York: Pergamon Press, 1979), all discuss the ways in which individuals can come to terms with morally troubling policy as well as the legitimate methods of moral dissent within office.

PROTECTING THE WHISTLE-BLOWER
ROBERTA ANN JOHNSON

Roberta Johnson's book on whistle-blowing offers examples of whistle-blowers and their need for protection from retaliation. She also provides a summary of whistle-blower protection in the United States. Do the current laws provide sufficient protection at this time? If not, what is needed?

Robert Jackson slipped into a San Diego pay phone, nervously dialed the downtown hotel where a congressman's aide was staying and whispered, "My life is in danger!" Jackson was a whistle-blower, a young sailor who reportedly had gathered "2,000 pages of Navy documents that showed case after case of fraud, forgery, and kickbacks aboard the aircraft carrier *Kitty Hawk*." He was arranging to turn over these materials to Congress "if in return Representative Jim Bates (D-CA) could keep him off the carrier's upcoming deployment and away from enlisted men who had threatened him" (Bunting 1985: 3).

This description of Robert Jackson's experience is a dramatic example of a fact of life for most whistle-blowers, namely, that there are dire personal consequences for blowing the whistle. Reprisals are usually less severe than the bodily harm that Jackson feared, and are typically dismissal, transfer, demotion, and harassment.

The experience and impact of reprisals on the whistle-blower has been a theme for many scholars and practitioners, from Ralph Nader in 1972, to Myron and Penina Glazer in 1989, and C. Fred Alford in 2001. What they and others have found is that in most cases of whistle-blowing, instead of the problem raised by the whistle-blower becoming the focus of attention, typically the individual whistle-blower becomes the issue. The strategy has been referred to as "nuts and sluts," because, according to some whistle-blowers, "their claims are ignored by finding them to be emotionally disturbed or morally suspect" (Alford 2001: 104).

"The government does not respond to the problems raised by whistle-blowers," says Louis Clark, executive director of the Government Accountability Project.

Source: Roberta Ann Johnson, *Whistleblowing: When It Works—And Why* (Boulder and London: Lynne Rienner Publishers, 2003), pp. 91–93, 111–13.

"Instead the government makes the whistle-blower the problem" (1978: 12). There is ample evidence to support this perspective. According to Frome (1978), "when a revelation is made public, the question inside the bureaucracy is not 'Is it right or wrong?' but 'Who leaked it?'" The attention is on the "squealer," the "damaged good" who is "ostracized" (Branch 1979; Weisband and Franck 1975) and who, according to Senator Howell Heflin, is often "sent to do-nothing jobs in undesirable locations, or [is] demoted or fired" (Senate 1983: 3).

The case of the sailor Robert Jackson amply illustrates this attitude. When he became a whistle-blower, the navy imputed a range of "personal motives" to his action. Although he was portrayed as credible, having appeared on national television and in *Time, Newsweek,* and *People* magazines, the navy characterized him as a "bitter" and "vindictive" sailor, out "to get" the captain of the ship for not paying him enough for a training course he submitted through their suggestion program. Jackson, who was a "born-again Christian," was also portrayed by navy officials as an "evangelical troublemaker" (Bunting 1985: 10).

The list with names of whistle-blowers who themselves became the issue abounds. Louis Clark (1978) describes the "favored ways" the bureaucracy reserves "to get" the whistle-blower and points to nearly a dozen cases, including that of the well-known whistle-blower A. Ernest Fitzgerald.

A. Ernest Fitzgerald was an analyst for the Department of Defense who blew the whistle on cost overruns for the large C-5A cargo plane (Senate 1983: 150). Starting in 1965, he held the position of deputy for management systems in the office of the secretary of the air force.

The Lockheed Aircraft Corporation had contracted to design and build the C-5A. By 1968, they were seriously behind schedule and over budget and needed the federal government's C-5A contract to continue to be able to survive financially (Fitzgerald 1972: 212). Some members of Congress were opposed to additional funding for the plane. In October 1968, the Joint Economic Committee, chaired by Senator William Proxmire, held hearings on the subject, and Fitzgerald was invited to testify (p. 216).

Fitzgerald's superiors, knowing him as a critic of the procurement programs, "counseled" him to "stay away from the C-5A" in his testimony (p. 220). Unfortunately, Fitzgerald was specifically asked about the aircraft contract and he answered truthfully about the billions more than were estimated that it would cost (Westman 1991: 13).

Seven months later, Fitzgerald was again invited to testify in front of the Joint Economic Committee about another air force procurement. "I was strangely and uncharacteristically depressed by the array of power against me," he wrote (Fitzgerald 1972: 243). Although warned again not to be too forthcoming in his responses, once more he answered the legislators' questions truthfully and was critical of the project. By November 1969, Fitzgerald was notified that his agency position had been eliminated. It took ten years of creative litigation, including a lawsuit against President

Richard Nixon, for Fitzgerald to be reinstated to his air force position (Westman 1991: 14).

What was demonstrated here, and is repeated in a wide and varied range of cases, is that the *whistle-blowers* were consistently on trial, not the policies they had criticized and exposed. Fitzgerald complained, "We have turned the rewards and punishment system on its head. The people who make waves are discouraged, put down; their careers are destroyed, even if they win, as I have been said to have done" (Senate 1983: 150).

The pattern across countless examples, almost without exception, is that the individual whistle-blower experiences reprisals. This is one of the major reasons why people do not blow the whistle (U.S. Merit Systems Protection Board 1993: ii; General Accounting Office 1992a: 2-4). Yet even with this shadow of almost certain dire consequences, in the United States a legal tradition has helped to create an environment that encourages whistle-blowing. . . .

TYING IT ALL TOGETHER

Chief Justice Earl Warren once said that "law floats in a sea of ethics" (Cooper 1979: 78); for over one hundred years, many laws and practices protecting whistle-blowers have been floating in the United States' ethical ocean. The False Claims Act, passed during the Civil War and resurrected with great fervor during the last few decades, twentieth-century federal labor law, and the many court common-law interpretations of "public policy" across various states all offered some protection to some of the employees who came forward to report and expose wrongdoing.

In addition, starting in the 1970s, Congress passed a number of federal laws that included special whistle-blower–protection provisions. In these laws there were sections that prohibited "adverse actions by employers against employees who assist in carrying out the regulatory purpose of the legislation" (Chalk and von Hippel 1979: 51). Many of these laws were in the environmental field such as the Federal Water Pollution Control Act Amendments of 1972, the Toxic Substances Control Act of 1976, and the Clean Air Act Amendments of 12977. In the next decades, dozens more federal statutes and some state statutes followed in providing such protections.

For its sheer impact, however, the most significant protective statute was the Whistleblower Protection Act, passed in 1978 and amended in 1989 and 1994. This legislation aimed to protect all federal government employees, no matter what laws they were implementing and where they worked. Over half the states and some local governments have enacted similar legislation protecting state workers.

The federal Whistleblower Protection Act had a disappointing start. For years, the act promised more than it delivered because the Office of Special Counsel did not seem to champion the whistle-blowers who sought its help. But in its 1989 revised form, the act allowed employees to circumvent the Office of Special Counsel and take their retaliation claim directly to the Merit Systems Protection Board. Although the Merit Systems Protection Board has its critics, at least at MSPB, approximately one out of three whistle-blower claimants were getting some kind of settlement. Congress acted to revise the law in 1994, and . . . again in 2002. With the 1994 congressional changes in the MSPB, procedures improved in at least twenty areas and better safeguards and new personnel are helping strengthen whistle-blower protection.

The establishment of federal agency hotlines, in 1978, also represented a significant contribution to whistle-blowers. Critics have argued that the federal hotlines are not well-enough known and are far from user-friendly, but agencies boast large numbers of contacts and large monetary savings because of them. There are data that can be used to support both positions. No studies, as yet, have analyzed, unraveled, and evaluated the way politics, merit, and luck determine how hotline cases are handled.

Whistle-blowers represent a mixed bag of characters. There are devils and angels in the group; not every whistle-blower seeks revenge and not every well-intentioned whistle-blower is amply rewarded and protected.

REFERENCES

Alford, C. Fred. 2001. *Whistleblowers' Broken Lives and Organizational Power*. Ithaca, NY: Cornell University Press.

Branch, Taylor. 1979. "Courage Without Esteem: Profiles in Whistle-Blowing." In *Culture of Bureaucracy*, ed. Charles Peters and Michael Nelson. New York: Holt, Rinehart, and Winston.

Bunting, Glenn F. 1985. "Navy Whistle-Blower to Testify Before House Panel," *Los Angeles Times*, September 30, pp. 3, 10.

Chalk, Rosemary, and Frank von Hippel. 1979. "Due Process for Dissenting 'Whistle-Blowers,'" *Technology Review* 81 (June–July): 49–55.

Clark, Louis. 1978. "The Sound of Professional Suicide," *Barrister* 5 (summer): 10–13, 19.

Cooper, Melvin G. 1979. "Administering Ethics Laws: The Alabama Experience," *National Civic Review* 68 (February): 77–81, 110.

Fitzgerald, A. Ernest. 1972. *The High Priests of Waste*. New York: W. W. Norton.

Frome, Michael. 1978. "Blowing the Whistle on Waste," *Center Magazine* (November–December): 50–58.

General Accounting Office. 1992a. *Whistleblower Protection: Survey of Federal Employees on Misconduct and Protection from Reprisal*, Fact Sheet for the Chairman, Subcommittee on the Civil Service Committee on Post Office and Civil Service, House of Representatives, July.

Senate. 1983. Subcommittee on Administrative Practice and Procedure of the Committee on the Judiciary. *Examining the Role of Whistleblowers in the Administrative Process: Hearings Before the Subcommittee on Administrative Practice and Procedure of the Committee on the Judiciary*, 98th Cong., 1st Sess., November 14.

U.S. Merit Systems Protection Board. 1993. A Report to the President and the Congress of the United States by the U.S. Merit Systems Protection Board. *Whistleblowing in the Federal Government: An Update*. Washington, DC, October.

Weisband, Edward, and Thomas M. Franck. 1975. *Resignation in Protest.* New York: Grossman.
Westman, Daniel P. 1991. *Whistleblowing: The Law of Retaliatory Discharge.* Washington, DC: Bureau of National Affairs.

——— ———

CIRCUMSCRIBED PROTECTION: THE CEBALLOS CASE
U.S. SUPREME COURT

The case of Garcetti et al. v. Ceballos was decided by the U.S. Supreme Court in a 5–4 decision on May 30, 2006. The majority ruled that Ceballos, as a government servant, was not protected against retaliation because what he said was pursuant to his employment duties. What are the implications of this decision for the protection of government whistle-blowers?

Respondent Ceballos, a supervising deputy district attorney, was asked by defense counsel to review a case in which, counsel claimed, the affidavit police used to obtain a critical search warrant was inaccurate. Concluding after the review that the affidavit made serious misrepresentations, Ceballos relayed his findings to his supervisors, petitioners here, and followed up with a disposition memorandum recommending dismissal. Petitioners nevertheless proceeded with the prosecution. At a hearing on a defense motion to challenge the warrant, Ceballos recounted his observations about the affidavit, but the trial court rejected the challenge. Claiming that petitioners then retaliated against him for his memo in violation of the First and Fourteenth Amendments, Ceballos filed a 42 U. S. C. §1983 suit. The District Court granted petitioners summary judgment, ruling, inter alia, that the memo was not protected speech because Ceballos wrote it pursuant to his employment duties. Reversing, the Ninth Circuit held that the memo's allegations were protected under the First Amendment analysis in *Pickering v. Board of Ed. of Township High School Dist. 205, Will Cty.*, 391 U. S. 563, and *Connick v. Myers*, 461 U. S. 138.

JUSTICE KENNEDY DELIVERED THE OPINION OF THE COURT

. . . The controlling factor in Ceballos's case is that his expressions were made pursuant to his duties as a calendar deputy. See Brief for Respondent 4 ("Ceballos does not dispute that he prepared the memorandum 'pursuant to his duties as a prosecutor'"). That consideration—the fact that Ceballos spoke as a prosecutor fulfilling a responsibility to advise his supervisor about how best to proceed with a pending case—distinguishes Ceballos's case from those in which the First Amendment provides

Source: *Garcetti et al. v. Ceballos*, available online at www.supremecourtus.gov/opinions/05pdf/04-473.pdf.

protection against discipline. We hold that when public employees make statements pursuant to their official duties, the employees are not speaking as citizens for First Amendment purposes, and the Constitution does not insulate their communications from employer discipline.

Ceballos wrote his disposition memo because that is part of what he, as a calendar deputy, was employed to do. It is immaterial whether he experienced some personal gratification from writing the memo; his First Amendment rights do not depend on his job satisfaction. The significant point is that the memo was written pursuant to Ceballos's official duties. Restricting speech that owes its existence to a public employee's professional responsibilities does not infringe any liberties the employee might have enjoyed as a private citizen. It simply reflects the exercise of employer control over what the employer itself has commissioned or created. Cf. *Rosenberger v. Rector and Visitors of Univ. of Va.*, 515 U. S. 819, 833 (1995) ("[W]hen the government appropriates public funds to promote a particular policy of its own it is entitled to say what it wishes"). Contrast, for example, the expressions made by the speaker in Pickering, whose letter to the newspaper had no official significance and bore similarities to letters submitted by numerous citizens every day.

Ceballos did not act as a citizen when he went about conducting his daily professional activities, such as supervising attorneys, investigating charges, and preparing filings. In the same way he did not speak as a citizen by writing a memo that addressed the proper disposition of a pending criminal case. When he went to work and performed the tasks he was paid to perform, Ceballos acted as a government employee. The fact that his duties sometimes required him to speak or write does not mean his supervisors were prohibited from evaluating his performance.

This result is consistent with our precedents' attention to the potential societal value of employee speech. See supra, at 7–8. Refusing to recognize First Amendment claims based on government employees' work product does not prevent them from participating in public debate. The employees retain the prospect of constitutional protection for their contributions to the civic discourse. This prospect of protection, however, does not invest them with a right to perform their jobs however they see fit.

Our holding likewise is supported by the emphasis of our precedents on affording government employers sufficient discretion to manage their operations. Employers have heightened interests in controlling speech made by an employee in his or her professional capacity. Official communications have official consequences, creating a need for substantive consistency and clarity. Supervisors must ensure that their employees' official communications are accurate, demonstrate sound judgment, and promote the employer's mission. Ceballos's memo is illustrative. It demanded the attention of his supervisors and led to a heated meeting with employees from the sheriff's department. If Ceballos's superiors thought his memo was inflammatory or misguided, they had the authority to take proper corrective action.

Ceballos's proposed contrary rule, adopted by the Court of Appeals, would commit state and federal courts to a new, permanent, and intrusive role, mandating judicial oversight of communications between and among government employees and their superiors in the course of official business. This displacement of managerial discretion by judicial supervision finds no support in our precedents. When an employee speaks as a citizen addressing a matter of public concern, the First Amendment requires a delicate balancing of the competing interests surrounding the speech and its consequences. When, however, the employee is simply performing his or her job duties, there is no warrant for a similar degree of scrutiny. To hold otherwise would be to demand permanent judicial intervention in the conduct of governmental operations to a degree inconsistent with sound principles of federalism and the separation of powers. . . .

JUSTICE SOUTER, WITH WHOM JUSTICE STEVENS AND JUSTICE GINSBURG JOIN, DISSENTING

The Court holds that "when public employees make statements pursuant to their official duties, the employees are not speaking as citizens for First Amendment purposes, and the Constitution does not insulate their communications from employer discipline." Ante, at 9. I respectfully dissent. I agree with the majority that a government employer has substantial interests in effectuating its chosen policy and objectives, and in demanding competence, honesty, and judgment from employees who speak for it in doing their work. But I would hold that private and public interests in addressing official wrongdoing and threats to health and safety can outweigh the government's stake in the efficient implementation of policy, and when they do public employees who speak on these matters in the course of their duties should be eligible to claim First Amendment protection. . . .

ETHICS, TRANSPARENCY INTERNATIONAL, AND THE PRIVATE SECTOR
JERMYN BROOKS

Transparency International (TI) is a private global organization devoted to combating corruption. Its goal is to publicize and challenge bribery and other corrupt practices worldwide. Jermyn Brooks, elected to TI's Board of Directors in 2003, provides here a review of some of TI's efforts to deal with corporate corruption globally.

Source: Jermyn Brooks, "Leading by Example: Ethics, Transparency International and the Private Sector," *Transparency International Quarterly*, September 2004, p. 12. Reprinted with the permission of Transparency International.

If ever there was a time for calling upon the private sector to behave more honestly, it is surely now. Repeated corporate scandals around the world have demonstrated how business leaders frequently ignore basic business ethics. Whether manipulating results, deliberately creating complex and opaque corporate structures, paying bribes to third parties and excessive remuneration to themselves, all in disregard for the stakeholders of the corporations they are supposed to serve, corrupt practices seem to have become accepted behavior. . . .

Given the poor performance of the private sector, what has been Transparency International's response? TI recognizes that curbing corruption requires a combination of more effective laws and voluntary action by the business community. That is why we have supported anti-bribery conventions, including those of the OECD [Organization for Economic Cooperation and Development], the AU [African Union], the OAS [Organization of American States], and, most recently, the UN [United Nations]. TI is now working to ensure that these conventions become law in the signatory states and subsequently monitoring effective implementation. . . .

TRANSPARENCY PRINCIPLE FOR THE UN GLOBAL COMPACT

The voluntary agreement to comply with the ten principles of the UN Global Compact has now been signed by more than 1,700 companies and civil society organizations. The tenth principle, on anti-corruption, was added in June after receiving overwhelming support from the Compact's corporate members. The extension of the Compact to cover corruption was strongly supported by TI.

A separate effort, the Global Reporting Initiative (GRI), aims to codify reporting by businesses on non-financial performance. Areas covered include environmental, human rights, employment issues, and business ethics, including compliance with the OECD Anti-Bribery Convention and a description of a company's anticorruption policies. Use of the GRI is voluntary but growing, and civil society is scrutinizing its application by the corporate world.

TAKING A PRINCIPLED STAND AGAINST BRIBERY

TI and Social Accountability International worked with leading companies to develop the Business Principles for Countering Bribery as a guide to establishing and implementing corporate no-bribes policies. Since completion in 2002, the Business Principles have become recognized as a no-bribes standard for industry. They are seen as valuable "content" for the anti-corruption principle of the UN Global Compact, as a valuable starting point for the implementation of a no-bribes policy by industry sectors and as a potential pre-qualification requirement for bidders on internationally funded projects. TI and industry representatives are holding discussions to this end with the World Bank and other development banks. . . .

CLEANING UP PUBLIC PROCUREMENT

The Business Principles are complemented by the TI Integrity Pact; an agreement between a procuring agency and all bidders to a contract to comply with transparent and non-corrupt practices throughout the tendering process. Both represent voluntary agreements and both commit the private-sector players to no-bribes policies. But while the Business Principles cover the totality of a company's ongoing transactions and behavior, the Integrity Pact is ideally suited to large procurement cases, such as major infrastructure projects in developing countries, where the danger of bribes and kickbacks is often high. Just as the industry-sector approach to no-bribes policies attempts to draw potential competitors together, so the Integrity Pact joins all bidders together on a level playing field, where price and quality of bid alone can decide the outcome.

——— ———

CASE 10: WHAT IS A WHISTLE-BLOWER TO DO?

You recently retired from the U.S. Air Force and go to work for a nonprofit agency that works with the city's low-income housing program, which is funded by a federal grant. On four separate occasions over the next few months you are told by the city program administrator to use money from one federal grant to pay for a project that wasn't covered by the grant. At first you follow orders and then begin to realize that if anyone objected you would be vulnerable to charges of misusing federal funds. So what do you do?

You put your objections into writing and call the regional headquarters of the U.S. Department of Housing & Urban Development identifying yourself as a whistle-blower. In the meantime, you are asked to approve the expenditure of $87,150 on a private residence that would sell for $70,000. You resist, asserting that federal guidelines prohibit the city from spending that much money on any low-income housing. The program administrator complains to your boss that you are not attentive, productive, or responsive to city staff. Your boss removes you from the project. Frustrated but convinced that you did the right thing, you quit your job and write a letter to the mayor detailing your concerns about the misuse of federal funds. The mayor never responds. A few months later, HUD officials admonish city officials about using low-income housing funds to help residents who did not qualify.

Fast forward two more years. The city's internal auditing staff reports to the mayor that the housing administrator has issued questionable loans, kept poor

Source: Donald Menzel, "Ethics Minute: What Is a Whistle-blower to Do?" *PA Times*, April 2004. Based on a story reported in *St. Petersburg Times*, March 8, 2004, p. B1. Reprinted with permission from the American Society for Public Administration.

records, and awarded noncompetitive bids. HUD officials also warn the mayor that the administrator may have misused $1.4 million in federal funds. The mayor dismisses the criticism by HUD officials, saying that he has made changes in response to the internal audit report. Federal auditors are still not satisfied and warn that the city may have to repay the $1.4 million. The administrator claims that the feds are applying ridiculous rules. The mayor backs him. The administrator appears before the city council and asserts that "we do not intend to follow HUD's direction at this point." All but one member of the city council praises the administrator.

Fast forward two more years . . . a federal indictment charges that the city housing administrator used government jobs to reap thousands of dollars in gratuities for seven years. The city is required to wire transfer the U.S. Treasury a total of $1,402,650.

What's a whistle-blower to do?

CHAPTER DISCUSSION QUESTIONS

1. What circumstances and principles would lead you to "blow the whistle" on wrongdoing within your administrative organization? Conversely, what would lead you to remain silent even if you knew of wrongdoing within the organization? Why might you simply leave ("exit") an organization quietly rather than blowing the whistle?

2. Loverd argues that organizations can be, in effect, immunized against whistle-blowing by providing more active "listening" mechanisms for the communication of dissent and grievances. What would you consider to be the most effective such mechanisms?

3. Even with whistle-blower–protection legislation in place in many governments, dissenters can encounter serious difficulties. Should their protection be strengthened? If so, how?

FOR FURTHER EXPLORATION

Dobel, J. Patrick. *Public Integrity*. Baltimore: Johns Hopkins University Press, 1999.

Johnson, Roberta Ann. *Whistleblowing: When It Works—and Why*. Boulder: Lynne Rienner Publishers, 2003.

OECD, *Public Sector Transparency and Accountability: Making It Happen*. Paris: Organization for Economic Cooperation and Development, 2002.

Pagano, Barbara, and Elizabeth Pagano, *The Transparency Edge: How Credibility Can Make or Break You in Business*. New York: McGraw-Hill, 2004.

Perry, James L., "Whistleblowing, Organizational Performance, and Organizational Control," in *Ethics and Public Administration*, ed. H. George Frederickson (Armonk, NY: M. E. Sharpe, 1993), pp. 79–99.

Truelson, Judith A., "Whistleblower Protection and the Judiciary," in *Handbook of Administrative Ethics*, second ed., ed. Terry Cooper (New York and Basel: Marcel Dekker, 2001), pp. 407–27.

Weisband, Edward, and Thomas M. Franck, *Resignation in Protest: Political and Ethical Choices Between Loyalty to Team and Loyalty to Conscience in American Public Life*. New York: Grossman Publishers, 1975.

WEBSITES

Center for Public Integrity, www.publicintegrity.org/default.aspx
Government Accountability Project, www.whistleblower.org
Transparency International, www.transparency.org

Chapter 11

COMPLIANCE, OVERSIGHT,
AND SANCTIONS

GOVERNMENT ACCOUNTABILITY
GAO

*The Government Accountability Office (GAO) performs major oversight functions in
the U.S. federal government. The following selection from the GAO website, describes
the work of the office, how it has evolved, and some specific mechanisms for reporting
fraud, waste, abuse, or mismanagement of federal funds.*

WHAT IS GAO?

Under recently passed legislation, we have changed our name from the General Accounting Office to the Government Accountability Office. The Government Accountability Office (GAO) is an agency that works for Congress and the American people.
Congress asks GAO to study the programs and expenditures of the federal government.
GAO, commonly called the investigative arm of Congress or the congressional watchdog, is independent and nonpartisan. It studies how the federal government spends taxpayer dollars. GAO advises Congress and the heads of executive agencies (such as Environmental Protection Agency, EPA; Department of Defense, DOD; and Health and
Human Services, HHS) about ways to make government more effective and responsive.
GAO evaluates federal programs, audits federal expenditures, and issues legal opinions.
When GAO reports its findings to Congress, it recommends actions. Its work leads to
laws and acts that improve government operations, and save billions of dollars. . . .

THE BACKGROUND OF GAO

The U.S. Government Accountability Office (GAO) is an independent, nonpartisan agency that works for Congress. GAO is often called the "congressional

Source: Government Accountability Office website, www.gao.gov, retrieved July 7, 2006.

watchdog" because it investigates how the federal government spends taxpayer dollars. GAO gathers information to help Congress determine how well executive branch agencies are doing their jobs. GAO evaluating how well government policies and programs are working; auditing agency operations to determine whether federal funds are being spent efficiently, effectively, and appropriately; investigating allegations of illegal and improper activities; and issuing legal decisions and opinions.

With virtually the entire federal government subject to its review, GAO issues a steady stream of products—more than 1,000 reports and hundreds of testimonies by GAO officials each year. GAO's familiar "blue book" reports meet short-term immediate needs for information on a wide range of government operations. These reports also help Congress better understand issues that are newly emerging, long-term in nature, and with more far-reaching impacts. GAO's work translates into a wide variety of legislative actions, improvements in government operations, and billions of dollars in financial benefits for the American people.

HOW IS GAO STRUCTURED?

Headquartered in Washington, D.C., GAO has offices in several major cities across the country. The agency is headed by the Comptroller General, who is appointed to a 15-year term. The long tenure of the Comptroller General gives GAO a continuity of leadership that is rare within government. GAO's independence is further safeguarded by the fact that its workforce is comprised almost exclusively of career employees who have been hired on the basis of skill and experience. Its 3,300 employees include experts in program evaluation, accounting, law, economics, and other fields.

HOW GAO HAS CHANGED THROUGH THE YEARS

GAO has focused on governmental accountability from the time it began operations on July 1, 1921. While the agency always has worked for good government, its mission and organization have changed a great deal since 1921 in order to keep up with Congressional and national needs. The General Accounting Office was created by the Budget and Accounting Act (42 Stat. 20) in 1921. The law was aimed at improving federal financial management after World War I. Wartime spending had increased the national debt and legislators saw that they needed better information and control over expenditures. Congress passed the Budget and Accounting Act to require preparation by the president of an annual budget for the federal government and to improve accountability. The statute transferred to GAO auditing, accounting, and claims functions previously carried out by the Department of the Treasury. The act made GAO independent of the executive branch and gave it a broad mandate to investigate how federal funds are spent. Later legislation clarified or expanded GAO's powers, but the Budget and Accounting Act continues to serve as the basis for its activities.

During the 1920s and 1930s, GAO took a control-oriented view of its charter. It focused on whether government spending had been handled legally and properly. Much of the agency's work centered on reviewing vouchers, which were forms used by executive branch administrative officials and disbursing officers to record information on spending. Government disbursing agents made payments based on the vouchers, then sent the forms to GAO for checking. This early period of GAO's history often is called the voucher checking era. As government programs expanded during the 1930s and 1940s, GAO's audit clerks had to examine an increasing number of expenditure vouchers. An explosion in defense spending during World War II added to GAO's paperwork burden, creating a huge backlog of unaudited vouchers. After World War II, the Office shifted from checking individual vouchers to doing more comprehensive audits of federal spending. This change to examining the economy and efficiency of government operations in the postwar era marked the first major evolutionary change for GAO.

In the late 1950s and early 1960s, GAO focused on hiring accountants, professionalizing its staff, and expanding its offices during the Cold War. The late 1960s and early 1970s brought another major shift, as GAO broadened its work and moved into program evaluation.

During the 1980s and early 1990s, GAO examined high risk areas in government operations, paid close attention to budget issues and worked to improve federal financial management. Today the modern GAO serves the nation by carrying out a broad range of financial and performance audits and program evaluations. . . .

FRAUDNET MISSION

GAO FraudNET is a vital part of the Office of the General Counsel (OGC). Its objectives are to

- operate an automated means that anyone may use to report allegations of fraud, waste, abuse, or mismanagement of federal funds;
- refer those allegations to the Inspector General (IG) of the cognizant federal agency;
- expedite responses to congressional requests;
- review IG responses to allegations referred by GAO;
- advise GAO divisions and agency IGs of audit leads; and
- provide information to federal, state, and local organizations about establishing their own hotlines.

SEC AND OVERSIGHT
William H. Donaldson

Donaldson, former Chair of the Securities and Exchange Commission, discussed in 2004 the ways in which the SEC protects the public interest by overseeing the operation of the stock exchanges and other securities markets. What are the ethical implications of the SEC programs he describes? Do those programs appear to be more reactive than proactive? Is it possible for agencies like the SEC to play a more proactive role in combating corruption and encouraging ethics?

The stock market collapse, with three consecutive years of decline in the Dow, coupled with the corporate misbehavior, has led to a prolonged decline in investor confidence. As a principal regulator here in the U.S., we at the Commission have been well aware of the need for action to calm these fears. But this is much easier said than done. The malfeasance has continued, and our work to raise standards has presented a conundrum that Alexis de Tocqueville wrote of nearly 150 years ago: "Every abuse that is . . . eliminated seems to highlight those that remain, and makes them feel more biting." He added that, "the evil has decreased, it is true, but the sensitivity to it is greater."

While Congress and the president enacted Sarbanes-Oxley to improve financial reporting and prohibit a number of business practices that some had come to abuse, the Commission has pursued a sweeping reform agenda. Let me mention a few of our actions.

By mid-2003 we completed—under an extremely tight deadline—the extensive rulemaking related to Sarbanes-Oxley. Critically important has been nurturing the growth of the Public Company Accounting Oversight Board, mandated by the new law to restore integrity to the auditing and accounting profession.

Over the past two fiscal years, our enforcement division has intensified its aggressive pursuit of those who have violated our securities laws and the public trust. During this period, the division has filed more than 1300 enforcement actions and obtained orders for penalties and disgorgements totaling nearly $5 billion.

We have also made real progress on the vital issue of self-regulatory organizations [SROs], most particularly SRO governance. The Commission has fostered and approved a proposal by the New York Stock Exchange to implement reforms, such as its own organizational structure, aimed at insulating the regulatory functions from conflict with the business functions.

Source: Former SEC Chairman's Speech: Remarks Before the Caux Round Table (William H. Donaldson), www.sec.gov/news/speech/spchl13004whd.htm.

We also believe that SROs play a critical role as standard setters for issuing companies, operators of trading markets, and frontline regulators of securities firms. We must insist on holding them to higher corporate governance standards as well. The Commission recently voted to propose new rules, and amend existing rules, to improve the governance and financial transparency of all U.S. self-regulatory organizations.

We are also reviewing the structure of our national market system, and the Commission has put forward ideas on how to modernize our markets. Proposed regulation NMS encompasses a broad set of initiatives designed to improve the regulatory structure of U.S. equity markets. . . .

Another area we have focused on is the problems facing the mutual fund industry. The complicity of elements within the industry to condone certain unethical practices and to collude to engage in outright illegal behavior has been an unwelcome shock to the system.

In addition to unprecedented enforcement activity targeted at mutual funds, the Commission has approved 9 of 12 major new mutual fund reform initiatives. Taken together these initiatives seek to strengthen the governance structure of mutual funds, address conflicts of interest, enhance disclosure and transparency, and foster an atmosphere of high ethical standards and compliance.

In an attempt to reduce the incidence of ethical breakdowns at mutual funds, the Commission has approved a rule that requires them to maintain compliance policies and procedures, as well as a chief compliance officer. A critical new Commission rule requires funds relying on certain exemptive rules to have an independent chairman and 75 percent independent board members, creating a structure for implementation of both the letter and the spirit of our new regulations. A third significant initiative that will help to foster an ethical, compliance-oriented atmosphere is the new requirement that all registered investment advisors, including advisors to mutual funds, adopt a code of ethics. The code of ethics must set forth standards of conduct for advisory personnel and address conflicts such as those that arise from personal trading by advisory personnel. . . .

As important as these initiatives are, perhaps the most important—and most lasting—may be the internal reforms we have instituted at the SEC itself. For starters, we have brought in more people—1,100 additional accountants, lawyers, economists since December 2002. As we have brought in new people, we have worked to improve communications across the lines of our operating divisions and offices, to protect against any "silo" mentality from infecting the agency.

We have also created an infrastructure at the Commission around the concept of risk assessment. We are seeking to create an enhanced oversight regime that will equip the Commission to better anticipate, find, and mitigate financial risk, potential fraud, and malfeasance. The effort is designed around a new Office of Risk Assessment, which brings together professionals experienced in seeking out potential areas of concern, and helps us to concentrate our resources and investigations to the areas that pose the biggest potential threats to our markets. We want our efforts and oversight to be more anticipatory and preventative in nature—to look over the hills and around the corners of the securities markets in ways that will help us deter and detect fraud, and ameliorate damage when it occurs. Each of these initiatives represents progress, and together they are helping to restore faith in the fairness of our markets. But there is, of course, still more work to be done.

FUNDING GASB AFTER SARBANES-OXLEY
William Voorhees

Following a rash of accounting scandals, Congress passed the Sarbanes-Oxley Act (SOX, or SARBOX), requiring greater executive responsibility and more assurance that accurate and ethical accounting procedures were being followed. Voorhees discusses the operation of the program. How should the public sector be responsible for transparent and accurate accounting in private-sector enterprises?

The fallout from Enron, Tyco, and WorldCom has had far-reaching effects, often in unintended places. The financial scandals of 2002 and the passage of the Sarbanes-Oxley Act has not only resulted in significant changes to the way public firms and public accounting firms do business, but has also had an unintended impact on governmental financial reporting by eliminating substantial portions of the funding for the Governmental Accounting Standards Board.

Responsibility for establishing accounting rules for governments resides with the Governmental Accounting Standards Board (GASB). This organization along with its sister organization the Financial Accounting Standards Board (FASB), which sets accounting rules for the private sector, operates as an entity of the Financial Accounting Foundation (FAF). As the parent body of GASB and FASB, FAF is responsible for overseeing the boards, their advisory councils—the Governmental Accounting Standards Advisory Council (GASAC) and the Financial Accounting Standards Advisory Council (FASAC)—oversight of the standard setting process, selection of members, and raising operational funding for these organizations. Historically the operating funds for these organizations have come from voluntary contributions from accounting firms, state government, and local governments.

Source: William Voorhees, "Commentary: Funding GASB after Sarbanes-Oxley," *PA Times*, June 2004, pp. 7–8.

SARBANES-OXLEY THREATENS INDEPENDENCE

With the passage of the Sarbanes-Oxley Act, a new funding model was implemented for the private sector mandating that the FASB no longer receive voluntary funding from corporations or public accounting firms. Instead, all publicly traded firms are assessed a fee based on their market capitalization. Prior to the passage of Sarbanes-Oxley, the FAF received voluntary contributions and allocated these to both FASB and GASB. Sarbanes-Oxley has had two major impacts on GASB finances. First, overhead cost allocations between GASB and FASB must now follow stricter guidelines increasing GASB costs. Second, with the mandatory fee assessment, accounting firms and corporations are no longer contributing to the FAF resulting in reduced incomes for the GASB. The net result is that GASB has been forced into a deficit position.

Although the GASB had the option of accepting funding from the mandatory assessment, the Board decided that it would impair its independence to rely on federally controlled funding. It has been a longstanding principle of the GASB to maintain strict independence from the federal government because of the substantial amount of funds that the federal government contributes to state and local government operations. Receiving funding from the federally controlled fee assessment could result in undue influence by the federal government over the format and substance of financial reporting for state and local government. In the spirit of federalism and the U.S. Constitution's reservation to states of unspecified rights, the GASB Board has historically rejected federally linked funding. . . .

OF WHAT USE IS THE GASB ANYWAY?

The GASB is an organization that is known to very few people. Even those who are familiar with the name may often wonder what they do. Specifically, the GASB is responsible for setting Generally Accepted Accounting [Principles] (GAAP) for all state and local governments and public hospitals. These standards affect citizens in several ways.

First, the standards provide for a consistent means of reporting government financial activity. They allow citizens and other users of financial statements to compare the financial activities of one community to those of another. Without consistent and accurate measures between communities, citizens would be unable to assess the performance of local communities. If one ascribes to Charles Tiebout's model of local communities, where citizens look to the costs and services provided by a community in deciding where to locate, then consistent, standardized reporting is needed to prevent information asymmetry problems.

Secondly, when governments are audited they must be in conformance with GASB standards in order to receive an unqualified or "clean" audit. Failure to obtain an unqualified audit can raise accountability issues in the reporting government for financial intermediaries such as bond raters, potentially lowering the bond rating and increasing the cost of capital. The GAAP specifies both the format of the financial reports and the data requirements for those reports. Without consistent application of accounting principles, information asymmetries will arise resulting in decreased efficiency in the bond markets. When investors are unable to accurately determine investment quality, they will demand greater returns resulting in an increase in the price of capital to governments.

Finally, and probably most important, accounting standards are the unseen foundation of public confidence in government. Without accounting standards, governments are free to make their own reporting, a practice that could quickly lead to misrepresented fact and numbers. Only through audited resource reporting standards, can citizens feel confident that their tax dollars are being utilized in appropriate ways and their trust maintained by government.

GOVERNMENTAL NONPROFIT OVERSIGHT
PANEL ON THE NONPROFIT SECTOR

Part of the strength of charitable and other nonprofit organizations is their status as voluntary and nongovernmental organizations. As recipients of public benefits, including special tax treatment, they also need to have some degree of accountability to the general public as well as to their members, boards, and benefactors. A special panel was convened in 2004 to grapple with these and other ethical issues facing nonprofit organizations. The following discussion of governmental oversight of nonprofit management is extracted from the panel's 2005 final report.

INTRODUCTION

Effective oversight of the charitable sector requires vigorous enforcement of the law at both the federal and state level. State attorneys general and other state charity officials have long held significant responsibility for establishing and enforcing regulations on the governance and management of charitable organizations and for overseeing solicitations of charitable contributions in their states. Federal officials as well as many state oversight officials also play a role in educating board and staff members of charitable organizations about legal responsibilities and requirements to the extent that resources will permit.

Source: Panel on the Nonprofit Sector (Convened by Independent Sector), *Final Report to Congress and the Nonprofit Sector on Strengthening Transparency, Governance, and Accountability of Charitable Organizations, June 2005* (Washington, DC: Independent Sector, 2005), pp. 24–25.

STATEMENT OF PROBLEM

Funding for federal and state oversight of tax-exempt organizations has become increasingly inadequate as the size and complexity of the exempt sector has grown. Federal laws only permit the Internal Revenue Service to share relevant information with state revenue officers. The inability to share information about ongoing investigations with attorneys general and other state officials charged with overseeing charitable organizations increases the cost of oversight and enforcement and impedes the efforts of state officials to weed out wrongdoing efficiently and effectively.

Recommendations for Congressional Action

1. Congress should increase the resources allocated to the IRS for oversight and enforcement of charitable organizations and also for overall tax enforcement.

2. Congress should authorize funding to be provided to all states to establish or increase oversight and education of charitable organizations. Congress should authorize additional supplemental funding for states willing to provide matching dollars for further improvements in oversight and education. State matching funds should be new funding for regulation of charitable organizations that is not derived from fees imposed on charitable organizations. To qualify for matching funds, states should be required to adopt uniform state filing requirements and meet minimum standards for oversight and enforcement of regulations governing charitable organizations.

3. Congress should amend federal tax laws to allow state attorneys general, and any other state officials charged by law with overseeing charitable organizations, the same access to IRS information currently available by law to state revenue officers, under the same terms and restrictions.

Recommendation for Charitable Organization Action

Charitable organizations should encourage state legislatures to incorporate federal tax standards for charitable organizations—including prohibitions on excess benefit transactions—into state law.

BACKGROUND

Over the past twenty years, funding for Internal Revenue Service oversight of exempt organizations has remained essentially constant while the [nonprofit] sector has nearly doubled in size and become even more complex. Funding of oversight at the state level varies substantially among states, but all lack sufficient resources to provide adequate oversight of the charitable sector. The legislative history of the Tax Reform Act of 1969 indicates that the excise tax on the net investment income of private non-operating foundations was intended to fund the exempt organizations oversight function within the IRS. Those funds, to the disappointment of many, have never been designated for that purpose.

States currently have the authority to pursue federal tax violations if federal laws are incorporated into state law. Since 1975, 48 states and the District of Columbia have passed laws imposing the restrictions on private foundations in Chapter 42 of the Internal Revenue Code as a matter of state law.[1]

RATIONALE

The shortage of resources for oversight and enforcement extends beyond the charitable sector to many areas of tax enforcement. While the Panel believes it is critical to increase the resources allocated to exempt organization oversight, any such increase should not be at the expense of other vital areas of tax enforcement.

Revenues collected annually from the excise tax on private foundations—nearly $500 million in fiscal year 2002—now greatly exceed the current budget of the IRS exempt organizations division. The Panel recognizes the fiscal challenges facing Congress today, but believes that, without adequate resources for oversight and enforcement, those who willfully violate the law will continue to do so with impunity. The Panel would be strongly supportive of efforts by Congress to earmark funds derived from a variety of sources including excise taxes and penalties imposed on charitable organizations for improved oversight and education activities of the exempt organization division of the IRS.

The proposed new revenue sharing program must take into account that regulation of charities at the state level is quite diverse, and many states and territories do not currently regulate charitable activities and organizations beyond charitable solicitations. The program should be designed to encourage states that do not regulate, as well as states with insufficient state regulation, to adopt uniform state filing requirements for charitable organizations operating within the state. Each state should be required to have sufficient review and/or audit procedures and enforcement programs in place to ensure compliance with applicable laws and regulations.

Education of charitable organizations about changes in federal and state laws and reporting requirements will be critical to increased compliance and should be incorporated into the new funding program requirements.

Responsible sharing of relevant information between federal and state officials will enable these officials to perform their duties more effectively. It also will assist charitable organizations by reducing the burden they often face in responding to duplicative federal and state inquiries for information.

The Panel has some concern about the potential for improper disclosure of shared information by state officials but assumes that there will be sufficient protection if current legal safeguards against such disclosure by state revenue officers are applied to state officials charged with oversight of charitable organizations.

If states incorporate federal tax standards into state law, enforcement of federal standards will likely increase, and opportunity for collaboration between federal and state enforcement efforts will likely improve, resulting in more uniform federal and state standards. The Panel believes this approach is preferable to granting the states authority to enforce federal tax laws with the approval of the IRS.[2] Incorporating federal tax standards into state law grants greater flexibility to the states, while at the same time not burdening the already-stretched IRS with another task.

NOTES

1. Marion R. Fremont-Smith, *Governing Nonprofit Organizations: Federal and State Law and Regulation* (Cambridge, MA: Belknap Press of Harvard University Press, 2004), p. 267.
2. This approach offered in the Senate Finance Committee staff discussion draft, 108th Congress, June 2004.

HURRICANE RELIEF OVERSIGHT
PCIE/ECIE

The President's Council on Integrity and Efficiency (PCIE) is made up of presidentially appointed federal Inspectors General (IGs). The Executive Council on Integrity and Efficiency (ECIE) comprises IGs appointed by agency heads. Following the Hurricane Katrina disaster, the PCIE/ECIE issued a report, intended to be the first of a series of semi-annual reports, on Gulf Coast hurricane recovery. This selection from that report illustrates the oversight roles of IGs and various agencies.

INVESTIGATIONS

Each of the federal Inspectors General (IGs) investigates potential violations of law related to hurricane recovery efforts in the Gulf Coast region. Where concerns arise, criminal investigators are assigned to determine whether there has been a violation

Source: President's Council on Integrity and Efficiency/Executive Council on Integrity and Efficiency, *Oversight of Gulf Coast Hurricane Recovery: A Semiannual Report to Congress, April 30, 2006*, pp. 109–12, available online at www.ignet.gov.

of law, statute, or regulation. Members of the President's Council on Integrity and Efficiency (PCIE) and Executive Council on Integrity and Efficiency (ECIE) submit monthly reports listing the key details about their investigations.

Since the hurricane relief and recovery process was initiated, through March 31, 2006, 174 indictments, 152 arrests, and 48 convictions have been reported by the IG investigative community.

Investigative teams have been deployed to each of the IG Joint Field Offices in Alabama, Mississippi, Louisiana, Texas, and Florida to provide technical assistance to Federal Emergency Management Agency (FEMA), state, and local officials. The investigators are coordinating with their respective federal, state, and local law enforcement agencies and prosecutors as part of their "fraud awareness" initiatives. They have also initiated a series of investigations of allegations received through the Katrina Fraud Hotline and other sources.

"Due to our efforts, along with the highly publicized work of the U.S. Attorney's Office, approximately 2,484 individuals have returned checks to FEMA for a total of $6.3 million," said Richard L. Skinner, Inspector General for the Department of Homeland Security (DHS), when he testified before the Senate Committee on Homeland Security and Government Affairs on February 13, 2006.

THE HURRICANE KATRINA FRAUD TASK FORCE

The task force, established on September 8, 2005, by the U.S. Attorney General, works to deter, investigate, and prosecute hurricane-related fraud. The Department of Justice's (DOJ) Criminal Division heads the task force, whose members include the U.S. Attorney's Offices, the Federal Bureau of Investigation (FBI), the federal IGs, the U.S. Secret Service, and the U.S. Postal Inspection Service, among others. It works closely with other federal and state partners. The task force focuses on specific areas of fraud common in post-disaster environments, including the following:

- Fraudulent charities—cases in which individuals falsely present themselves as agents of a legitimate charity or create a "charity" that is in fact a sham
- Identity theft—cases in which the identities of innocent victims are stolen and assumed by criminals who convert the funds of, or otherwise defraud, the victims
- Disaster relief benefit fraud—cases in which persons misrepresent their status as hurricane victims to receive private or public disaster relief benefits
- Government-contract and procurement fraud and public corruption—cases in which individuals and companies engage in fraud and public corruption relating to federal funds provided for the repair and restoration of infrastructure, businesses, and government agencies in the affected region
- Insurance fraud—cases in which false or inflated insurance claims are filed

CRIME TRENDS AND ENFORCEMENT ACTIONS

To identify criminal trends in the hurricane recovery process, the federal IGs have collected agency-level statistics. As of March 31, 2006, members of the PCIE/ECIE have reported 785 open cases of potential criminal activity.

. . . [M]ost of the cases were reported through the DHS, with 466 cases opened. In general, most of these cases involved fraudulently seeking or receiving disaster relief funds.

The Department of Labor (DOL) reported the second highest number of cases, with 206 opened. Most of its investigations involve potential unemployment insurance and/or disaster unemployment insurance fraud.

The number of open cases reported by other contributing departments and agencies include 6 by the Department of Defense (DOD), 1 by the Department of the Interior (DOI), 17 by the Department of Health and Human Services (HHS), 18 by the Department of Housing and Urban Development (HUD), 6 by the Department of Justice (DOJ), 10 by the Department of Transportation (DOT), 6 by the Environmental Protection Agency (EPA), 2 by the General Services Administration (GSA), 11 by the National Aeronautics and Space Administration (NASA), 3 by the Small Business Administration (SBA), 17 by the Social Security Administration (SSA), 2 by the Treasury Inspector General for Tax Administration (TIGTA), 11 by the U.S. Department of Agriculture (USDA), and 3 by the United States Postal Service (USPS).

Compared to the number of investigations reported in the first 90 days following the storms, after 180 days, there are more than three times the numbers of cases opened, more than four times the numbers of arrests made, nearly four times the numbers of indictments, and more than 14 times the numbers of convictions handed down.

PCIE/ECIE KATRINA FRAUD HOTLINE

Between October 5, 2005, and March 19, 2006, the Hotline operated as the PCIE/ECIE Katrina Fraud Hotline. The Department of Defense Office of Inspector General (DOD OIG) managed the hotline on behalf of the federal IGs involved in hurricane recovery oversight. Each of the Inspectors General also has a separate hotline for receiving complaints.

On March 20, 2006, control of the Katrina Fraud Hotline passed from DOD OIG to the Hurricane Katrina Fraud Task Force Joint Command Center in Baton Rouge, Louisiana. This office manages the hotline on behalf of the federal IGs involved in hurricane recovery oversight. The consolidated hotline facilitates reporting, logging, relaying, and tracking of calls about fraud, waste, and abuse by contractors, government employees, and the public in Gulf Coast recovery activities.

CASE 11: IGNORANCE OR INSIDER TRADING?

A young policy analyst is in his second month of work for a federal law enforcement agency. He received no ethics orientation, and stuck the ethics booklet he was handed into his desk drawer unread. His basic job is to analyze agency operations to make them more effective and efficient. To do this, it is necessary for him to read the case reports of the agency's field agents. These reports are classified confidential or secret as the case may be. The analyst has been granted an interim Secret clearance, pending completion of a background investigation, which will take a year.

As a related duty, he sits on a grant and contract review board that evaluates proposals from outside contractors for studies with the same general purpose. Over the few weeks he has sat on the board, he has been quite disappointed by the low quality of the bids. Few proposers seem to have carefully read the RFPs, and many are at best only nominally qualified to do the work.

One day an acquaintance of his who is affiliated with a very prestigious think tank calls and explains that the think tank is thinking about filing a proposal. His friend says that he has several questions about the RFP, and what the agency is really looking for. The analyst eagerly fills him in. "Finally," he thinks, "we'll get a good proposal, and the government will get some solid research for all the dollars they're granting."

A few days later the analyst comes across the ethics manual in his desk drawer, and, it being a slow day, reads it. He is both surprised and a little apprehensive to learn that no one but the contact person named in the RFP is to reveal any information about a Request for Proposals. Upon reflection, the analyst realizes that what he has done could be considered a form of "insider trading"—that is, providing information which could be advantageous to only a few persons.

He discusses the problem with his office-mate, a 30-year veteran government employee who has been in this agency for more than 10 years. "If you tell Max (the division chief) you divulged confidential material, you'll never see another confidential file," she says. This is very plausible. "Max" cut his teeth as a Security Investigator protecting nuclear weapons secrets at the height of the Cold War.

What should our analyst do?

CHAPTER DISCUSSION QUESTIONS

1. What role should government play in regulating the economy? During the last two decades of the twentieth century the "reinvention of government" included

Source: Donald Menzel, "Ethics Minute: Ignorance or Insider Trading—What's an Analyst to Do?" *PA Times*, December 2001. Original author's name/organizational affiliation withheld per request. Reprinted with permission from the American Society for Public Administration.

deregulation of private enterprises and privatization of governmental services. What challenges does this entail for protecting the public interest (or the public's interests)?

2. What ethical issues are faced by public managers who deal with contractors and with regulation of private-sector activities?

⸻

FOR FURTHER EXPLORATION

Caiden, Gerald E. "Enron, Accountancy, and Professional Ethics," *Public Integrity*, 4:4 (Fall 2002), pp. 321–32.

Frederickson, H. George, and Richard K. Ghere, eds. *Ethics in Public Management* (Armonk, NY: M. E. Sharpe, 2005.

Light, Paul C. "Federal Ethics Controls: The Role of Inspectors General," in *Ethics and Public Administration*, ed. H. George Frederickson (Armonk, NY: M. E. Sharpe, 1993), pp. 79–99.

———. "Federal Inspectors General and the Paths to Accountability," in *Handbook of Administrative Ethics*, second ed., ed. Terry Cooper (New York and Basel: Marcel Dekker, 2001), pp. 387–405.

O'Brien, Justin. "Ethics, Probity, and the Changing Governance of Wall Street," *Public Integrity*, 7:1 (Winter 2004–2005), pp. 43–56.

WEBSITES

Association of Inspectors General, www.inspectorsgeneral.org

Inspectors General Page (IG Net), www.ignet.gov

Project on Government Oversight, http://pogo.org/p/x/aboutus.html

U.S. Government Accountability Office, www.gao.gov

Chapter 12

LEADERSHIP AND INDIVIDUAL RESPONSIBILITY: ENCOURAGING ETHICS

ETHICS ADVICE TO A NEW PUBLIC SERVANT
KENNETH ASHWORTH

Kenneth Ashworth draws upon his long experience in Texas state government to offer a series of letters of advice on surviving public service. The letters are addressed to a fictitious niece or nephew named Kim, who is about to embark on a career in public service. If you were Kim, how would you respond to "Uncle Ken" concerning the following advice on ethics?

> Mankind are very odd creatures: One half censure what they practice, the other half practice what they censure; the rest always say and do as they ought.
>
> —Benjamin Franklin

Dear Kim,

Now I come to a special topic I have been putting off talking with you about. It is perhaps the heaviest of the subjects I've written to you about. Very soon you will start thinking about ethical behavior in your career because it will inevitably confront you, as it does every public official. You will not escape it, that I guarantee you. In the hope that perhaps another bureaucrat's experience may get you started thinking on this question, I will give you some sense of my own personal search for guidance for my behavior in public jobs during my career.

John Steinbeck sums up the dilemma well in one of his novels. His plot is built on a decision made by the French to reinstate their monarchy after the collapse of yet another one of their republics. As I recall, they locate the heir to their throne in

---

Source: Kenneth Ashworth, *Caught Between the Dog and the Fireplug, or How to Survive Public Service* (Washington, DC: Georgetown University Press, 2001), pp. 152–53, 162–67. Reprinted with the permission of Georgetown University Press.

Petaluma, California, where he's running a chicken farm. When he comes to rule as Pippin IV, he begins to deal with public issues and immediately he faces questions of good versus bad, having to pick among the best of bad choices, and having to compromise what he wants to do or what he feels is right. In grappling with such moral and ethical questions, he asks a trusted advisor, "What is a person to do?" His advisor replies that one usually does what one is.

That, although a keen observation, is far too simple and simplistic advice to be of much help. So what can I give you from my experience and thinking about this topic that might help you as you have to confront such conundrums? I can only share with you some of my own odyssey in trying to find my way among rocky shoals.

All successful public executives spend a lot of time in apprenticeship as subordinates. It is there you will first be tested. As an ambitious person, you will experience two things that can or should result in disappointment in yourself or even self-disgust. One is to have to carry out orders you feel are wrong or unfair to those affected or improper in how they are being carried out. The other is to compromise your own integrity in order to further your career or not to hurt your advancement. It is from the choices you are forced to make in these kinds of situations that you will learn much about who you really are. How you handle difficult options that come to you in subordinate positions will begin to shape the kind of leader you will become. . . .

First, I believe there does exist what Maslow calls an "intrinsic conscience, a court of ultimate appeal for the determination of good and bad, of right and wrong." This is not the traditional conscience, the small voice that originates in childhood upbringings and helps you sense what is right or wrong. This "inner nature" is inborn in most of us to tell us when we are being stultified, misused, or compromised in our inner natures. Most people can feel when their needs for fulfillment are being denied, when they must represent mendacity or falseness as truth, when they are required to do something unprincipled or against their own self-concept. or self-defined sense of what is proper. Maslow says "every falling away from species-virtue, every crime against one's own nature, every evil act, *every one without exception records itself* in our unconscious and makes us despise ourselves" (Maslow's emphasis). He is quick, however, to acknowledge that when a person feels uncomfortable with a situation, we cannot tell automatically whether that is good or bad. But at least it is an alarm, a starting place.

If your very being, your sense of personal destiny and capacity, and your psychological center are touched in certain circumstances in some way that causes you to feel violated or at least uncomfortable, whether by external forces or by your own decisions, pay attention. Here is a chance for you to ask why you feel that way. Here is a chance for you to raise that inner feeling to the surface for more complete examination. . . .

Working inside organizations, you will feel pressures to carry out orders you feel uneasy about, and, to get ahead, there will be temptations to compromise yourself and your principles or instincts. If you have a weak "intrinsic conscience," you may never in the least be pricked or prodded by it. Therefore, reliance on the inner nature of each of us can be only marginally useful in searching for a touchstone for moral behavior in public office. Yet I do believe that most people possess that intrinsic conscience that can help to guide them to avoid improper behavior—if they will just pay attention to it.

Second, for all my apparent cynical rejection of religion, upbringing, loyalty, being true to oneself, and history and philosophy as guides to conduct, I do readily accept the judgment of humankind over time: All of these reference points I have examined make their contributions to rational and ethical comportment. From these sources come attitudes, frames of reference, a part of the "intrinsic conscience," and elements of social lubrication that will assist you in tough choices on public issues. Not one of them alone is adequate to serve as a universal basis for public decision-making and action. But they do, together, deliver valuable aids that promote humane responses and empathy and understanding. Consequently, they will be helpful as part of your guide to proper conduct. So don't give up on them.

. . . [W]e have to apply what we know and what we can discover in order to act responsibly to improve the lot of humanity. Or more simply, we must choose either to let the events shape us or we undertake to shape the events. To fail to do this is to relegate the improvement of ourselves to some kind of "natural law" by which some "hidden hand" will mete out blessings and burdens among those from the most privileged at the top to the lowest of the underclass. And we know from long experience that that "hidden hand" will not do this equally or reasonably or fairly. Because favoritism and partiality and bias exercised by the privileged classes will always influence the natural law and its so-called hidden hand. "Property will purchase power, or power will take over property," as one of our founding fathers put it. But as Shaw (along with the pragmatists) says, leaving the "natural law" to deal with mankind's problems is neither organized *nor* civilization. It is abdication. Rather than be master of our destiny, we would be content to drift rudderless into our future. That is not why you and I chose the public service as a career.

And if we pursue a rational civilization, it can be organized only through legislative, judicial, and administrative actions. In the modern world no government can sit on the sidelines and permit some mindless social mechanism to define how we all relate to one another. Government must be the major organized intelligence in a society for pursuing the interests and progress of all the people. No other institution can do it. No hidden hand will do it equitably. So I reject any "natural law" and I take my public service totem from pragmatism: We can maintain continual progress and improve the condition of humankind through the application of intelligence to our problems and conditions. We will always have adequate injustice and problems to work with.

Now, lastly, I finally come to what I can give you as one universal guide. I will label it simply the Democratic and Constitutional Imperative. Let us start by accepting this premise: "Presume not God to scan; the proper study of mankind is man." The subject I believe we must examine is the truly democratic person.

People live together most productively and harmoniously if four conditions are met. First, if they have the opportunity and freedom to participate and be heard in setting the goals and purposes of their society. Second, if they have the opportunity to share in the country's productive capacity and to participate in the actions and work of their society. Third, if they may share reasonably equitably in the benefits of their society. And fourth, if they are free from oppression and unnecessary constraints on their mobility, thoughts, and other liberties. . . .

So we come back to that question we began with, Pippin IV's query, "What is a person to do?" For your moral decisions in your personal life consult your religious beliefs and upbringing, your conscience, your loyalty to our nation and your boss, your idea of being true to yourself, history, and biography, and philosophy. For your decisions in your public role consider the same sources. But in your public role pay special attention to your "intrinsic conscience" and devote yourself to promoting the Democratic and Constitutional Imperative. Short of attracting attention to yourself or appearing stuffy, you should not be reluctant to see yourself as a model of ethical behavior, someone whose conduct could ideally serve as a guide to all members of society. This will at least make *you* more responsible *for* your own behavior even if you never become a model worthy of a pedestal. We might make this goal a subpart of the Democratic and Constitutional Imperative and call it the Bureaucratic Code of Comportment: Conduct yourself so that your behavior may serve as the pattern for the behavior of every bureaucrat. . . .

So now we return to the one question I left hanging. Is it enough to declare, "My country, right or wrong?" No. We need to remember the rest of Carl Schurz's quotation engraved on the wall in the old Philadelphia Customhouse: "Our country, right or wrong. When right, to be kept right; when wrong, to be set right." So if all else fails, remember in performing your public duties that disobedience and insubordination in a democratic government do, on occasion, have their place.

What you have here is an intimate and true tracing of my own prolonged trek through the public service in search of a code or discipline for personal behavior in acting for public good. We all have to undertake our own search and find our own answers. . . .

Your absolving,
Uncle Ken

THE MORAL RESPONSIBILITY OF INDIVIDUALS
IN PUBLIC SECTOR ORGANIZATIONS
DEBRA STEWART

Debra Stewart argues that individuals in public organizations remain responsible for their actions and decisions regardless of whatever other administrative roles and obligations they might have. What are the practical implications of this position?

In public administration much . . . reflection focuses on developing or enhancing existing jurisdictional codes of ethics and conflict-of-interest statutes; some explore organizational protection for whistle-blowers; still other discussions consider enhancing the power of oversight committees and other monitoring groups to ensure that missteps will be exposed or discouraged. In these discussions across professions, one concern is common: To what extent should the individual be cast as a "moral actor" in a work setting? The extent to which this particular question dominates the debate about professional ethics correlates strongly with the extent to which the profession must be practiced as part of a collective. Where the sole professional is able to deliver a service to a client directly, issues of individual responsibility pale in comparison to issues of the morality of the interaction. Should a physician lie to a dying patient about prospects for recovery? Should a lawyer maintain client confidentiality if it puts another person at risk? But in public sector organizations where large numbers of professionals are working through complex organizations to achieve broad public policy objectives, the traditional basis for "moral accountability," i.e., the relationship between the individual professional and his/her client, evaporates (Anderson et al., 1980). Hence, the first question for the public manager when faced with a moral quandary is often: "What right do I have to exercise moral judgment at all?" . . .

To say that people are morally responsible is to "[evaluate] their behavior relative to some principle or standard" (Flores and Johnson, 1983: 538). Evaluative responsibility doesn't imply legal responsibility. But moral responsibility does mean the ability to hold an individual blameworthy for an act carried out even though that act is carried out as part of a collective. . . .

Three formidable arguments are marshaled against assigning significant moral responsibility to individuals in organizations: the argument from role, the argument from systems theory, and the argument from executive accountability. Each of these arguments will be presented and assessed with the objective of bringing sufficient closure to the question to permit further development in the management ethics field.

Source: Debra Stewart. "Ethics and the Profession of Public Administration: The Moral Responsibility of Individuals in Public Sector Organizations" *Public Administration Quarterly* 8, no. 4 (Winter 1985), pp. 487–95.

THE ARGUMENT FROM ROLE

Roles are sets of sanctioned, expected behaviors in an organizational setting (Stewart and Garson, 1983). The argument from the role suggests that when one acts in an organizational role, "pursuing objectives and employing methods designated by it," one doesn't satisfy the necessary conditions for being held morally responsible. An individual can be morally responsible for actions only if "the action is free and the individual is himself at the time of the action" (Flores and Johnson, 1983: 541). Individuals bound by organizational roles are not free in this sense. This absence of freedom stems from the fact that they are acting as the representatives of the organizations and, as such, are obligated to carry through on past commitments and decisions as well as those dictated by their current roles. They are acting in a public rather than a private capacity. Acts taken by individuals in organizational roles as distinct from private roles are, in other words, acts taken by individuals within roles they themselves did not define (Flores and Johnson, 1983: 541). Hence conditions of moral responsibility cannot be met, not even in the sense of apportioning to individuals part of the collective responsibility of the group.

The counterargument here can be summarized in four points. The first three points address role-governed behavior in any organization and the fourth point focuses on special characteristics of the public administration role. First, unless one is coerced to play a role, the fact that behavior is role-governed doesn't relieve one of the moral responsibility for actions and their consequences. While some work might provide more opportunity for individuals to change, rather than escape from, an objectionable state of affairs, no organization compels individuals to stay. In A. O. Hirschman's (1970) terms, both "Exit" and "Voice" remain viable options. Admittedly, the lack of another organization in which to practice one's profession might hold exit at bay. But the nature of modern work organizations is that the prohibition of the exit option doesn't exist.

Second, the distinction between public and private acts which relieve individuals of responsibility for acts undertaken in their public role fails because individuals generally gain some personal benefit from performance of their public or organizational role. While advancing organizational objectives, personal goals are also served—at the minimum by compensation for time and effort. In other words, the role is one means of securing personal ends (Flores and Johnson, 1983).

The third point is that, notwithstanding constraints implied by roles, individuals bring their own moral qualities to any position. All that is required for behavior is never totally spelled out by a role definition. Even role-constrained decisions permit individual judgments, reflecting the unique moral makeup of the decision-maker (Flores and Johnson, 1983).

All of the counterarguments presented thus far portray a scenario where there is tension between the demands of a morally neutral role and individual judgments of right or wrong. However, this discussion of moral judgment in public sector organizational roles introduces a new factor because the very setting of the role implies a moral dimension. The historic debate in public administration over the proper mix of politics and administration highlights the central place of values in interpreting the public administrator's role. One might attribute this emphasis to historical circumstances, since the founders of our field were deeply involved with political reform movements, before, during, and after the progressive era (Waldo, 1980: 93). Or the source of the moral emphasis in the public administrator's role may simply be in the nature of the work to be done. Ralph Chandler (1983: 37) notes, "Most public policy has as its declared aim some public good" and Dwight Waldo (1980: 110) has identified more than a dozen sources of obligation relevant to the conduct of the public administrator's role. Whatever the reason, the role of a public administrator carries a kind of moral weight not found in private sector counterparts' roles.

THE ARGUMENT FROM SYSTEMS THEORY

The second argument against assigning significant moral responsibility to individuals in organizations relates to the nature of complex organizations. Complex organizations are systems composed of several components that interact with one another to create a whole. Component parts include people, processes, structures, and cultures. Organizations have boundaries that differentiate them from their environment, but they interact with their environment regularly. Organizations, driven by systemic imperatives, convert inputs from the environment into outputs impacting the environment. Organizations are constantly interacting with the environment, changing and adapting to develop congruence between people, processes, structures, and sectors in the external environment (Katz and Kahn, 1966: 14–29).

Thus, behavior in the organization can be understood less as the deliberate choice of specific people and more as outputs of large systems functioning according to standard patterns of behavior (Allison, 1971). In order for large organizations to function, the behavior of large numbers of individuals must be coordinated. Coordination is achieved through organizational routines—a fixed set of standard operating procedures. "The behavior of these organizations . . . relevant to an issue in any particular instance is determined primarily by routines established in that organization prior to a particular event" (Allison, 1971: 68). These routines change incrementally in response to changes in the environment. . . .

The counterargument to the systems analysis rationale against holding individuals accountable has two parts. First, the systems approach to analyzing organizations is a descriptive and not a prescriptive enterprise. Systems theory is advanced to help us understand how organizations *do* behave, not how individuals *should* behave. For example, a major insight from systems theory as applied to organizations is that organizations like all systems are impelled toward survival and will adapt toward that objective. While survival makes perfect sense as a goal (i.e., we can better understand organizations by seeing them as systems striving to survive), survival is not the right objective in every situation. Some organizations should cease functioning from a public interest viewpoint. Any argument that individuals can't be held accountable because they are just part of the organizational system makes the error of confusing "system," as a description, with "system" as a prescription. System is a metaphor to describe how organizations function; it can't be used to address the question of normative judgment in organizations.

Second, even as a metaphor of organizational life, systems theory is deficient when it ignores the political process that unfolds in an organization. Organizational power holders in "dominant coalitions" decide on courses of strategic action, which both establishes structural forms and manipulates environmental factors. In doing so, these collections of individuals make significant value choices that advance some goals and inhibit others. Thus, even in a descriptive sense, the dominant coalition in an organization is not at the mercy of the organization as a system (Child, 1972). Significant "outputs" are intentional. In deciding on courses of action, individuals are engaging in behavior that will help or hurt specific interests. For their contribution to such action, they are individually accountable.

THE ARGUMENT FROM EXECUTIVE ACCOUNTABILITY

The third argument against assigning moral responsibility to organizational members is that it places emphasis on "good people" rather than on executive accountability where it belongs. The ultimate objective of the focus on management ethics is to reduce unethical behavior in organizations. In reality, unethical behavior is reduced only by strategies which place individuals in fewer compromising situations (rotation, clear guidelines, etc.) and by increasing sanctions for illegal action (Doig, 1983). Since the objective is actually to change unethical behavior, that is where the focus should remain. To ensure that strategies for reducing opportunities for unethical action are adopted, responsibility should be placed on the top of the organization, the office of the CEO.

The response to this assertion is not so much that the analysis is wrong; it is not. Whatever steps can be taken to buffer public servants from "occasions of sin" should be taken. Efforts to induce CEOs to adopt preventative measures to ensure that their subordinates avoid unethical action are worth considering. That is particularly so where the focus is on unethical actions which constitute a violation of the law.

However, at some level we also want to "get better people." The moral quality of our public servants is important because the alternative approach, if relied on exclusively, means to tighten control in a way that makes the exercise of moral judgment on the part of individuals unnecessary or impossible. We know that "the capacity to make moral judgment is strengthened by enabling members of organizations to respond to situations, to project alternative ends-in-view to solve those problems, devise means to reach ends, and test their self-generated moral judgments in use" (Spence, 1980: 146). The experience in lack of opportunity to make moral judgments increases the moral degeneration of organizational life. In other words, it might be advisable to put substantial energy into reducing the occasions of sin for public administrators particularly in those areas where sin translates into violation of civil and criminal law. But this strategy, if used exclusively, will produce the undesirable consequence of a trained incapacity for moral judgment in the large majority of public managers not occupying CEO slots.

CONCLUSION

Is it appropriate to consider the public administrator an ethical agent in his or her work setting? In this author's opinion, the answer is yes. The preceding analysis of arguments to the contrary compels the conclusion that public administrators find no easy escape from the uncomfortable task of making moral judgments. Inevitably moral quandaries arise because not all claimants can be equally served, not all goods are equally compatible, and not all outcomes are equally desirable. There is no simple moral equation which political executives use to generate the "right" solution to moral quandaries. In their work lives, public administrators will be confronted by choices weighed with ethical implications.

Helping to develop the "art of voice" (Hirschman, 1970: 43) is part of the task of public administration scholars. The first step is to clear the decks with respect to the question of exercising moral judgment at all. This article is an attempt to achieve that goal.

REFERENCES

Allison, Graham T. 1971. *The Essence of Decision*. Boston: Little, Brown.

Anderson, Robert A., Robert Petrucci, Dan E. Schendel, and Leon E. Trachtrnase. 1980. *Divided Loyalties: Whistle-Blowing at BART*. West Lafayette: Purdue University.

Chandler, Ralph Clark. 1983. "The Problem of Moral Reasoning in American Public Administration: The Case for a Code of Ethics." *Public Administration Review* 43 (January/February): 32–39.

Child, J. 1972. "Organizational Structure, Environment and Performance: The Role of Strategic Choice." *Sociology* 6, 1–22.

Doig, Jameson W. 1983. "Placing the Burden Where It Belongs: The Role of Senior Executives in Preventing Illegal Behavior in Complex Organizations." Paper prepared for the panel on "Anti-Corruption Strategies in Public Agencies" at the National Conference on the American Society for Public Administration, New York, April 16–19.

Flores, Albert, and Deborah C. Johnson. 1983. "Collective Responsibility and Professional Roles." *Ethics* 93 (April): 537–545.

Hirschman, Albert O. 1970. *Exit, Voice, and Loyalty*. Cambridge, MA: Harvard University Press.

Katz, Daniel, and Robert Kahn. 1966. *The Social Psychology of Organizations*. New York: John Wiley and Sons.

Spence, Larry D. 1980. "Moral Judgment and Bureaucracy," in *Moral Development and Politics*, ed. Richard W. Wilson and Gordon J. Schochet. New York: Praeger.

Stewart, Debra W., and G. David Garson. 1983. *Organizational Behavior and Public Management*. New York: Marcel Dekker.

Waldo, Dwight. 1980. *The Enterprise of Public Administration*. Novato, CA: Chandler and Sharp.

ELIOT SPITZER AS A MORAL EXEMPLAR
WILLIAM B. EIMICKE

New York State Attorney General Eliot Spitzer has gained national attention for his prosecution of prominent public-interest lawsuits. William Eimicke argues that Spitzer can be viewed as a moral exemplar and explores the implications of that characterization. Does Spitzer display the virtues—described earlier by Bailey—of "optimism, courage, and fairness tempered by justice" or are there other virtues here that Eimicke is suggesting we emulate?

Eliot Spitzer became New York State's sixty-third attorney general on January 1, 1999. . . . The attorney general is the state's chief legal officer, supported by a staff of more than 1,800, including 500 attorneys. The office handles criminal prosecutions, engages in public advocacy, enforces anti-trust laws, ensures the integrity of charities, enforces civil rights laws, investigates consumer fraud, enforces environmental laws, and represents state agencies and officials in litigation proceedings. It is a very broad mandate. . . .

During his time in public office, Spitzer has faced at least one key moral crisis (prosecuting organized crime), several significant moral confrontations (reforming Wall Street and seeking to curtail acid rain) and has embarked on one moral project (gun control). It could be argued that Spitzer chose these confrontations (NYS Attorney General, 2004). At the same time, it could also be said that when faced with these obvious wrongs, it was his obligation as a moral exemplar to seek to right them. In every situation, Spitzer applied the same methodology—pursue the offender relentlessly with every available resource, and engage the media to pressure the offender to enter into a settlement. The settlements routinely include a public apology, a new code of conduct, and reformed standard operating procedures, instead of jail sentences for individuals. . . .

Source: William B. Eimicke, "Eliot Spitzer: 'The People's Lawyer,'" *Public Integrity* 7:4 (Fall 2005), pp. 353–72. Reprinted with permission from the American Society for Public Administration.

ELIOT SPITZER AS AN EXEMPLAR

Terry Cooper writes of those "who have exemplified virtue understood as specific character traits and as the quest for a life of integrity in the practice of public administration" (Cooper, 1992a; 7). For Cooper, virtues are acquired traits of character that integrate thought and feeling and are cultivated and refined throughout life. For traditional Christian philosophers, the cardinal, or pivotal values are prudence, temperance, justice, and fortitude (Lewis, 1996, 74–78). Optimism, courage, fairness, honesty, consistency, humility, sympathy, self control, a willingness to compromise, reciprocity and duty are often suggested as characteristics of effective and ethical public officials (Bailey, 1965; Van Wart, 1998; Wilson, 1993).

Duty is especially appropriate in considering public officials, such as Eliot Spitzer, who take an oath of office. Indeed, a major focus of the field of ethics and the public administrator comes from the constitutional-legal perspective (Frederickson, 1997). Rohr's assessment of public service and ethics makes a direct connection to the U.S. Constitution, which "holds us together as a people" (Rohr, 1998, 148). Practitioners appear to view ethical behavior as part of their professional duty. A major finding of a survey of managers who were members of the American Society for Public Administration (ASPA) was "the key role of leadership—both by its presence and absence—in encouraging honorable public service" (Bowman and Williams, 1997, 525).

This concept of duty as a key aspect of the exemplary public administration dovetails very nicely with the benefits and responsibilities of citizenship and Cooper's view of the public administrator as a fiduciary professional citizen (Cooper, 1991). Self-government, if it is to be good government, requires an enlightened public opinion. As Madison said, "Knowledge will forever govern ignorance. And a people who mean to be their own governors, must arm themselves with the power knowledge gives them" (Wiggins, 1956, vii). In a complex, global society, a major responsibility of democratic public officials must be to enlighten and educate the people about the important issues of the day (Eimicke, 1974). Frederickson goes even further. In addition to being fair, just and equitable, the exemplary public official requires benevolence, a genuine caring for and love of the citizen. Benevolence also involves serving the greater good while also attending to the needs of the individual citizen (Frederickson, 1997).

In a time when elected executives and legislatures leave the great issues of the day—educational aid formulas, environmental protection, gun control, equal rights—to the courts, Spitzer has been an exemplary "moral activist" (Frederickson, 1997). In the cases of acid rain, gun control, and corrupt practices on Wall Street, Spitzer, as an elected official and head of a large administrative agency, has forced industries to act in the public interest through investigation, public information, and, when necessary, legal action. Rather than wait for the courts to act, he forced us all to pay attention to important but neglected issues of public interest and pursued those issues until reforms were initiated, no matter how long it took.

Acting in the general interest may be suspect as a criterion for judging exemplars because of its broad scope and various interpretations (Cooper, 2004). Nevertheless, serving the public is included as a major theme in the extremely useful set of rules constructed by Carol Lewis to guide administrators seeking to behave ethically (1990). Moreover, the first of five themes in the major revision of the Code of Ethics of the American Society for Public Administration in 1994 is "Serve the Public Interest. Serve the public, beyond serving oneself" (Van Wart, 2003, 338). In assessing the ethics of public entrepreneurship, "serving the public interest" can be an extremely useful criterion for assessing controversial projects (Cohen and Eimicke, 1995, 1996, 1999; Cohen, Eimicke, and Perez Salazar, 2000). Cooper suggests using the public interest in the form of a question before making important decisions: "Are you acting on behalf of broad shared interests or limited particular ones?" (Cooper, 2004, 399). Acting in the public interest can be a very useful evaluation tool if defined, following Walter Lippmann, as "what men would choose if they saw clearly, thought rationally, and acted disinterestedly and benevolently" (1955, 46). Viewed this way, Lippmann's framework ties together the aforementioned constructs of Cooper, Frederickson, Lewis, and Wilson. How does Spitzer measure up to the public interest test?

Spitzer has pursued cases that were either obscure (acid rain), seldom successful (gun control), high risk (Wall Street), or dangerous (organized crime). There was little outside pressure to pursue any of his high profile cases. Indeed, as we have discussed, he was urged to "be careful" for reasons legitimate and not so legitimate. In each of the moral episodes and moral processes, Spitzer pursued the case to protect the interests of the average citizen, often when others had refused to act or acted ineffectively.

Administrators work in the structure of their employing agency, which is their primary obligation, and the focus of loyalty and effort. Systems of staffing often reflect the values and ethics of the organization and, to the extent that there is discretion, of the leader as well (Van Wart and Denhardt, 2001). Spitzer's first act as attorney general was to prohibit his employees from contributing to his political campaigns.

At the same time, effective and efficient management frequently dictates cooperation among agencies, collaboration, and even formal partnerships. As Terry Cooper suggests, "Responsible administrators should also bear a larger obligation to encourage collaboration rather than competition with other units, organizations, elected officials, and the public" (Cooper, 1998, 257). Eliot Spitzer is not known for "playing well with others." His critics frequently cite his propensity to unreasonably stretch his jurisdiction to pursue issues and cases that are the province of other agencies. In the case of acid rain, the EPA under Clinton was pursuing the case before Spitzer stepped in. The Securities and Exchange Commission also claimed that it was pursuing conflicts of interest on Wall Street. Spitzer responds that they may or may not have been pursuing the same cases but they were proceeding at a snail's pace and were not getting results. Spitzer is also criticized for trying his cases in the media. Certainly he is very effective in getting the message out about his cases. Critics argue that Spitzer is primarily publicizing himself in his quest for higher office. Spitzer argues that publicity serves the public interest by forcing reluctant industries and individuals to reform and do a better job of serving the public.

Spitzer does not deny his political ambitions. In late 2004, he held a $1,000-a-seat fund-raising luncheon, only halfway through his second term as attorney general. The event added $2 million to a campaign war chest that exceeds $10 million (Dicker, 2004a, 2004b). Spitzer announced his candidacy for governor nearly two years in advance of the election in November 2006.

Despite these flaws, in his work and public life Spitzer exhibits many of the characteristics used to describe exemplars—courage, fortitude, honesty, consistency, self-control, and willingness to compromise. His integrity is seldom questioned. The only ethical questions raised to date concern his lack of candor about his father's financial support in his first run for Attorney General. Public officials need not be perfect to serve as exemplars. The senators portrayed in John F. Kennedy's *Profiles in Courage* acted bravely in the public interest despite some significant personal failings or weaknesses (Carson, 2004).

Judging character is a difficult and dangerous endeavor (Cooper, 1992b). It is particularly risky when the public official being evaluated is in the middle of what might be a long and very political career. At the same time, the public, the media, and many academics are concerned that public service ethics are becoming a "lost world" (Menzel, 1999). Eliot Spitzer's ubiquitous presence in the news and his parade of moral crusades can be overwhelming. His political ambition leads some to question his motives. However, if you examine what he has tried to do, his results and the changes that have been made, Eliot Spitzer is clearly a moral exemplar of the first order. He tilts at windmills, and wins.

REFERENCES

Bailey, Stephen K. 1965. "Ethics and the Public Service." In *Public Administration and Democracy: Essays in Honor of Paul H. Appleby*, ed. Roscoe C. Martin, pp. 283–98. Syracuse, NY: Syracuse University Press.

Bowman, J. S. and R. L. Williams. 1997. "Ethics in Government: From a Winter of Despair to a Spring of Hope." *Public Administration Review* 57, no. 6: 517–26.

Carson, Carol. 2004. "Profiles in Courage for Our Time," *Public Integrity* 6, no. 1: 83–86.

Cohen, Steven and William B. Eimicke. 1995. "Ethics and the Public Administrator." *The Annals of the American Academy of Political and Social Sciences* 537, no. 1: 96–108.

———. 1996. "Is Public Entrepreneurship Ethical?" *Public Integrity Annual*. Lexington, KY: Council of State Governments.

———. 1999. "Is Public Entrepreneurship Ethical? A Second Look at Theory and Practice." *Public Integrity* (Winter 1999): 54–74.

Cohen, Steven, William B. Eimicke, and M. Perez Salazar. 2000. "Ethical Public Entrepreneurship: Common Dilemmas from North and South America." *Public Integrity* (Summer 2000): 229–45.

Cooper, Terry. 1991. *An Ethic of Citizenship for Public Administration*. Englewood Cliffs, NJ: Prentice Hall.

———. 1992a. "On Virtue." In *Exemplary Public Administrators*, ed. Cooper and Wright, pp. 1–8. San Francisco: Jossey-Bass.

————. 1992b. "Reflecting on Exemplars of Virtue." In *Exemplary Public Administrators*, ed. Cooper and Wright, p. 338. San Francisco: Jossey-Bass.

————. 1998. "Big Questions in Administrative Ethics: A Need for Focused, Collaborative Effort." *Public Administration Review* 64, no. 4: 395–407.

————. 2004. "Big Questions in Administrative Ethics: A Need for Focused, Collaborative Effort." *Public Administration Review* 64, no. 4: 395–407.

Dicker, Fred. 2004a. "Dems Avert Disaster as Path Is Cleared for Eliot," *New York Post*, November 16, p. 7.

————. 2004b. "Dec. Date for 'Gov.' Spitzer," *New York Post*, November 22, p. 12.

Einicke, William B. 1974. *Public Administration in a Democratic Context: Theory and Practice*. Beverly Hills, CA: Sage.

Frederickson, H. George. 1997. *The Spirit of Public Administration*. San Francisco: Jossey-Bass.

Lewis, Carol. 1990. *The Ethics Challenge in Public Service*. San Francisco: Jossey-Bass.

————. 1996. *Mere Christianity*. New York: Simon & Schuster.

Lippmann, Walter. 1955. *Essays in the Public Philosophy*. Boston: Little, Brown.

Menzel, Donald C. 1999. "Rediscovering the Lost World of Public Service Ethics: Do We Need New Ethics for Public Administrators?" *Public Administration Review* 59, no. 5: 443–47.

New York State Office of Attorney General. 2004. "Biography of Eliot Spitzer." Available at www.oag.state.ny.us/bio/html.

Rohr, John A. 1998. *Public Service, Ethics, and Constitutional Practice*. Lawrence: University Press of Kansas.

Van Wart, Montgomery. 1998. *Changing Public Sector Values*. New York: Garland.

————. 2003. "Codes of Ethics as Living Documents." *Public Integrity* (Fall 2003): 331–46.

Van Wart, Montgomery, and Kathryn Denhardt. 2001. "Organizational Structure: A Reflection of Society's Values and a Context for Individual Ethics." In *Handbook of Administrative Ethics*, second ed., ed. Terry Cooper, pp. 227–42. New York: Marcel Dekker.

Wiggins. J. 1956. *Freedom or Secrecy*. New York: Oxford University Press.

Wilson, James Q. 1993. *The Moral Sense*. New York: The Free Press.

AS A CITY UPON A HILL
JOHN F. KENNEDY

As he prepared to assume the presidency, Senator John F. Kennedy identified several criteria by which he thought his administration should be judged. Do his four questions provide a standard for evaluation that can be applied to government leaders and their aides? This speech was delivered in the Massachusetts State House to Kennedy's friends, colleagues, and "cronies." What message do you think he was delivering to them?

During the last sixty days, I have been engaged in the task of constructing an administration. It has been a long and deliberate process. Some have counseled greater speed. Others have counseled more expedient tests. But I have been guided by the

Source: Address by John F. Kennedy before the Massachusetts Legislature, January 9, 1961.

standard John Winthrop set before his shipmates on the flagship *Arabella* 331 years ago, as they, too, faced the task of building a new government on a perilous frontier. "We must always consider," he said, "that we shall be as a city upon a hill—the eyes of all people are upon us."

Today, the eyes of all people are truly upon us—and our governments, in every branch, at every level, national, state and local, must be as a City upon a hill—constructed and inhabited by men aware of their grave trust and their great responsibilities.

For we are setting out upon a voyage . . . no less hazardous than that undertaken by the *Arabella* in 1630. We are committing ourselves to tasks of statecraft no less awesome than that of governing the Massachusetts Bay Colony, beset as it was then by terror without and disorder within.

History will not judge our endeavors—and a government cannot be selected merely on the basis of color or creed or even party affiliation. Neither will competence and loyalty and stature, while essential to the utmost, suffice in times such as these.

For of those to whom much is given, much is required. And when at some future date the high court of history sits in judgment on each one of us—recording whether in our brief span of service we fulfilled our responsibilities to the states— our success or failure, in whatever office we may hold, will be measured by the answers to four questions:

First, were we truly men of courage—with the courage to stand up to one's enemies—and the courage to stand up, when necessary, to one's associates—the Courage to resist public pressure as well as private greed?

Secondly, were we truly men of judgment—with perceptive judgment of the future as well as the past—of our own mistakes as well as the mistakes of others—with enough wisdom to know what we did ill not know, and enough candor to admit it?

Third, were we truly men of integrity—men who never ran out on either the principles in which they believed or the people who believed in them—men whom neither financial gain nor political ambition could ever divert from the fulfillment of our sacred trust?

Finally, were we truly men of dedication—with an honor mortgaged to no single individual or group, and compromised by no private obligation or aim, but devoted solely to serving the public good and the national interest?

CASE 12: MAYORS AS EXEMPLARS?

Elected officeholders can be, but too often are not, exemplary leaders. Suppose you were the mayor of a city, population 31,580, and ran successfully for office on a platform of

Source: Donald Menzel, "Ethics Minute: Mayors as Exemplars—Fact or Fiction?" *PA Times*, August 2005. Based on information in "Managing Municipal Ethics," November 5, 2002, www.gmanet.com. Reprinted with permission from the American Society for Public Administration.

bringing ethical government to the community. You are a genuinely committed mayor and you are also a devoted father. You find yourself in a situation in which you need to get your daughter to summer camp and at the same time, negotiate an agreement for a local option sales tax. What would you do? Your assistant speaks up: "Oh, I can get your daughter to summer camp. No big deal!" Done deal.

Forty-five minutes later you realize that you have violated the city's ethics code by allowing your assistant to transport your daughter to camp while on duty. You are embarrassed by this ethical lapse. What do you do? Should you (a) take out your pen and file an ethics complaint against yourself; (b) talk the matter over later with the assistant and resolve not to allow this sort of situation to happen again; or (c) shrug it off as an innocent mistake and just avoid doing it again?

This is a real case of Mayor Steven Brown of Peachtree City, Georgia. Mayor Brown filed the ethics complaint against himself. After due deliberation, the Ethics Board found that no formal reprimand was necessary but that Mayor Brown should reimburse the city for the employee's time. Mayor Brown readily complied and reimbursed the city $8.94.

In retrospect, do you think that this was the best way to handle this situation? Why?

CHAPTER DISCUSSION QUESTIONS

1. Do you know people in public service whose ethical behavior you would like to emulate? If so, what would you describe as their outstanding characteristics?

2. If you were asked to write a personal code of ethics for your own professional life, what would be the most important things you would want to include?

3. Is there a "gap" between what you know to be ethical and what you practice in your everyday professional or personal life? If so, how can this gap be narrowed? How can what we know to be right be better translated into daily practice?

FOR FURTHER EXPLORATION

Cooper, Terry L., and N. Dale Wright, eds. *Exemplary Public Administrators: Character and Leadership in Government.* San Francisco: Jossey-Bass Publishers, 1992.

Dobel, J. Patrick, "Managerial Leadership and the Ethical Importance of Legacy," *International Public Management Journal* 8, no. 2 (2005), pp. 225–46.

Haught, Robert L., ed. *Giants in Management.* Washington, DC: National Academy of Public Administration, 1985.

Keohane, Nannerl O. *Higher Ground: Ethics and Leadership in the Modern University.* Durham, NC: Duke University Press, 2006.

Moore, Mark H., and Malcolm K. Sparrow. *Ethics in Government: The Moral Challenge of Public Leadership.* Englewood Cliffs, NJ: Prentice-Hall, 1990.

Richardson, Elliot. *Reflections of a Radical Moderate.* New York: Pantheon Books, 1996.

WEBSITES

Ethics and Public Policy Center, lecture by George Weigel, "Moral Clarity in a Time of War," (William E. Simon Lecture, published Washington, DC, October 24, 2002), www.eppc .org/publications/pubID.1554/pub_detail.asp

Heritage Foundation, Statements by Matthew Spalding, Don Eberly, Samuel Gregg, and Joseph Loconte on "Building a Culture of Character," August 6, 2002, www.heritage.org/Research/ PoliticalPhilosophy/HL755.cfm

Leadership Development Resources for Public Managers, website designed to promote "better leadership and management in the public service," with numerous links to resources, www.govleaders.org/index.html

Online Ethics Center for Engineering and Science, brief profiles of scientists and engineers as moral exemplars, including Roger Biosjoly, who blew the whistle in the *Challenger* shuttle disaster, onlineethics.org/moral/

INDEX

ABOUT THE EDITORS

Frances Burke, professor emerita of Suffolk University, is president of Integrity International and executive vice president to goredbeard.com, a promotion/protection company. She trains executives globally in Management Ethics and Anti-Corruption Practices. Her research focuses on Ethical Decision Making and Government/Business Ethical Accountability. Dr. Burke is a recipient of the Charles Levin Award for Excellence in Teaching, Research, and Service from the American Society for Public Administration (ASPA).

William L. Richter is professor of political science at Kansas State University. He has served for more than two decades as an academic administrator, most recently as K-State's associate provost for International Programs and founding director of the Office of International Programs. He has written widely on public and international affairs in South Asia. He has served as president of the Kansas Chapter of ASPA and on several national ASPA committees.